Democracy and Regulation

D0395638

Democracy and Regulation

How the Public Can Govern
Essential Services

Greg Palast, Jerrold Oppenheim and Theo MacGregor

Pluto  Press

LONDON • STERLING, VIRGINIA

First published 2003 by Pluto Press
345 Archway Road, London N6 5AA
and 22883 Quicksilver Drive,
Sterling, VA 20166–2012, USA

www.plutobooks.com

British Library Cataloguing in Publication Data
A catalogue record for this book is available from the British Library

ISBN 0 7453 1943 2 hardback
ISBN 0 7453 1942 4 paperback

Library of Congress Cataloging in Publication Data
Applied for

10   9   8   7   6   5   4   3   2   1

Designed and produced for Pluto Press by
Chase Publishing Services, Fortescue, Sidmouth EX10 9QG, England
Typeset from disk by Stanford DTP Services, Towcester
Printed and bound in the European Union by
Antony Rowe, Chippenham and Eastbourne, England

We are grateful for the support of the United Nations International Labour Office, Sectoral Activities Programme, Geneva, which published our Working Paper, "Democratic regulation: A guide to the control of privatized public services through social dialogue". This book is an update and expansion of our original ILO Working Paper.

Updates, additional information, research documents and an opportunity for readers to speak to the authors can be found at **www.DemocracyAndRegulation.com**

Dedicated to the memory of Lois Rosen

To Bill, Ken, Leah, and Sonia

Contents

List of Tables and Figures

Acknowledgments

A work like this is a cooperative one, building on the efforts of others, and we have acknowledged in the notes the many specific works we relied on. Here we want to give particular thanks to those who provided one or another of us with inspiration, provocation, advice and a sounding board, not always even knowing it would wind up in this book (which it sometimes did not): Daniel Berman, David Boys, Nancy Brockway, Joel Eisenberg, Susan Geller, Jan Willem Goudriaan, David Hall, Charlie Harak, Ogmundur Jonasson, D. Neil Levy, Meg Power, Harvey Salgo, Rob Sargent and Steve Thomas. Carl Wood not only wrote the Foreword, but also provided us with his insight and wisdom as we wrote.

We are particularly thankful to Bert Essenberg and Valentine Klotz, of the United Nations International Labour Office, Sectoral Activities Programme, Geneva, for publishing our Working Paper on this subject. That publication provoked a series of conversations from which we continue to benefit.

We apologize in advance for the misinterpretations that no doubt remain, despite all the efforts of these people, and others, to set us straight.

Roger van Zwanenberg, of Pluto Press, has extended to us more patience than we deserved, for which we are grateful.

Foreword

Hon. Carl Wood

We Americans are notoriously immodest about the virtues of our political system, and others may be properly skeptical of claims for the universal applicability of institutions that developed in particular historical and national contexts. Nonetheless, there is broad agreement in labor and progressive circles that the interests of working people are best served by open and democratic processes that are accessible to participation by people's organizations.

Palast, Oppenheim and MacGregor have drawn on a vast pool of practical experience, wide international contacts and profoundly democratic motivation to examine and explain the US utility regulatory system as a model for an epoch which is characterized worldwide by the sudden and often unconsidered privatization of essential utility services previously owned and operated (however well or poorly) for the public good.

The problem of oversight of this process of protection for the people and the economies of both developing and highly developed countries is exacerbated by the capital-intensive nature of these industries and a world economy in which massive capital flows are virtually unconstrained by national policies.

Today's situation has remarkable parallels to that which obtained in the United States in the early part of the twentieth century, and out of which our present regulatory regime emerged. In large part, it is the product of a broad popular movement for people's control over the privately owned utility monopolies. It is part of the democratic legacy of President Franklin D. Roosevelt's New Deal, and has served us well – though not perfectly – for nearly 70 years. Hence, its relevance as a model to other countries.

The most characteristic feature of today's world economy is the ease with which private investment capital travels across national boundaries. For industries in which regulation is necessary to protect the public, this reality has far-reaching implications. Just as in manufacturing, where corporations routinely move operations across borders to escape environmental and labor standards, so do the newly internationalized telecommunications, energy and water companies seek the lowest common denominator of regulatory oversight in deciding where to move their dollars, yen and euros.

This process has led to economic disruption and social misery in both highly developed and less developed countries. But its consequences are particularly dangerous for industries like utilities in which societal goals and standards are inextricably tied up with the provision of the service itself. The questions raised by the unfettered reign of investment capital over utility service are as old as the industry itself. How can a modern industrial society function if security of supply, that is, reliability, is dependent on a free market subject to economic cycles and shortages? Can the provision of telephone, water and electric service to rural and poor communities be trusted to a market notorious for pursuing only the most profitable opportunities?

These are the questions that regulation addressed in the United States. The results, as described by the authors of this book, are striking. Despite its continental geographical scope, by the 1950s electrification and telephone service had reached virtually every home, business and farm in the United States. Service was unsurpassed in the world for its quality and reliability. North American utility prices were the lowest in the world.

Many states enacted additional protections for poor customers, including subsidized rates and moratoriums on shut-offs during months in which extreme temperatures make power for heating or cooling a necessity of life.

But the benefits of regulation have not flowed to small customers alone. Whole regions of the country owe their economic development and viability in no small part to massive federal investments in giant hydro-electric projects as well as subsidies to cooperative and municipal electric utilities in areas where private investment had failed to provide service. While rates vary from place to place, for half a century businesses have been free to locate their operations anywhere in the United States, knowing that a highly reliable supply of electricity will always be available at a reasonable cost.

The US regulatory system is not without its problems. Because of the tension between private utility ownership and public policy, between the interests of different classes of customers, even "independent" regulation is a highly politicized process. Utility companies exploit their superior understanding of their own operations to attempt to skew the information they provide to regulators. Large industrial and commercial users contend with residential and small business customers over allocation of the costs of running the utility systems. But despite outcomes that are always less than perfect, open, democratic utility regulation has generally served the people of the United States very well.

In light of this record, it may seem strange that, in the 1990s, a clamor arose to abandon this regulatory model for electricity and to move toward "competitive markets" and "customer choice." The call for change, however, came exclusively from big business and its academic and political spear carriers. While small customers often grumbled about prices, it was difficult to find a single residential ratepayer who wanted to get rid of regulation.

The big business demand for deregulation had several drivers. With barriers to capital investment across the world being battered down in the push for unrestricted free trade, government franchised utility monopolies seemed anachronistic. Many utility companies had accumulated vast reserves of cash, which they sought to invest outside of their franchise territories. Both they and their would-be competitors hungered for the higher profits they believed would flow in an environment freed from regulation by the appearance of "competition."

At the same time, corporate customers had learned from the deregulation of long-distance telephone service that they could achieve a more favorable apportionment of prices vis-à-vis small customers in a market environment, and they demanded deregulation so they could stay "competitive." Also, a new group of marketing companies such as Enron had proved from experience in deregulated natural gas markets that enormous profits could be extracted from arbitrage and manipulation of markets for essential utility services, and they were eager to commoditize electricity as well.

Changes in federal law in 1978 and 1992 opened the door for the emergence of an electrical generation industry not tied to the local regulated distribution monopolies. The forces backing deregulation reached critical mass in California when, on March 20, 1994, the state's Public Utilities Commission released a proposal to largely deregulate the state's electric utilities. The proposal would radically alter the six-decade-old system of public oversight of this vital component of the economic and social infrastructure of the nation's wealthiest and most populous state.

As the Business Agent of a Southern California local of the Utility Workers Union of America, I knew that this development did not bode well for the 2,000 workers my union represented. Several years earlier, our employer, Southern California Edison Company, had set up a holding company to take advantage of a new federal law permitting partial deregulation of the electric generation industry. New non-union generating plants and massive new costs for consumers were the outcome. But sufficient regulatory authority remained that the union and consumer groups were able to publicly expose the abuse and force Edison to refund tens of millions of dollars to consumers.

The company's foreign investments brought me into contact with trade unionists in Australia and the United Kingdom, who were in the throes of coping with the fallout from privatization of their electric utilities: massive job reductions, loss of trade union rights and higher prices for consumers. I was surprised to learn from my foreign colleagues that their countries had nothing like our public utilities commissions and open rate-making processes to use as venues for intervening in the management of their industry.

When the California deregulation proposal was published, the state's utility unions immediately formed a coalition, of which I was elected secretary, to participate in the Commission's regulatory process. We retained counsel and an economist to offer expert testimony and analysis, challenge the testimony and views of other parties, and help direct the process itself so that the final decision, originally scheduled to be jammed through in three months, was not issued for nearly two years.

When the decision did emerge, a public record had been established revealing many of the flaws of the scheme. Even though the corporate interests supporting deregulation were politically powerful enough to force it through the Commission and the state legislature, skeptics in the labor, environmental and consumer movements were able to salvage some important components of public regulation. When the deregulation project famously turned to disaster scarcely two years after its implementation, this previously ignored public record helped to guide decision-makers as they tried to rebuild from the rubble.

In March, 1997, I went onto the national staff of my union as national deregulation coordinator, using the experience gained in California to help colleagues in other states develop strategies to protect workers and consumers from the accelerating free market juggernaut. The new job also gave me exposure to utility regulation in different states as well as new international contacts.

On June 19 of that year, I presented testimony on behalf of the union to a congressional committee considering federal deregulation legislation. As the only witness who was willing to challenge the free market orthodoxy, I warned that "Business and residential users could face sky-rocketing prices and brownouts." (Reading that testimony today makes me feel eerily like Cassandra; would that I had been wrong.) Predictably, my words were dismissed by industry experts as ignorant panic-mongering by self-centered workers who just didn't understand the imperatives of the new economy.

And the seemingly inexorable march toward deregulation continued. By the end of 1998, more than half the states, encompassing more than three-quarters of the nation's economy and population, had begun deregulating their electrical utilities.

Meanwhile, in California, Gray Davis had just been elected Governor with strong support from the labor movement. Recognizing the importance of utility policy both to workers in the industry and to working-class consumers, the state's unions urged Governor Davis to appoint me to the powerful five-member Public Utilities Commission. And in May, 1999, I was appointed to a six-year term on the Commission.

As I took office, the transition to a liberalized market was well underway. The state's regulated utilities had sold their fossil-fueled generating plants to new unregulated owners, who had not yet begun their assault on the unions on their property. The Power Exchange (PX), the new wholesale electrical commodity exchange, was up and running, and was producing prices a little lower than before deregulation. Maybe this new system could work.

On May 22, 2000, prices on the PX spiked upward, then came down for a few days. But in early June, wholesale prices rocketed to 5, 15 and at some points even 50 times the pre-deregulation price of electricity, and did not begin to subside until the Federal Energy Regulatory Commission reluctantly and temporarily re-imposed partial regulation a year later.

The California events are still the subject of legal, legislative and academic investigations, but the reasons for the crisis are now quite clear. Generators and marketers figured out how to game the market through strategic bidding on the PX and, especially after that entity's collapse and bankruptcy in early 2001, through actual physical withholding of electrical generation to drive up prices. It is a shocking fact that California's rolling blackouts, supposedly caused by supply shortages, generally occurred when demand was less than two-thirds of the state's generation capacity!

If any good at all came out of the crisis, it is that this spectacular breakdown in California, a virtual nation-state with 37 million people and the world's fifth largest economy, has moved the issue of utility deregulation to the international center stage. And for this reason, the message of *Democracy and Regulation* is urgent and timely.

Arguments against democratic oversight of any aspect of the economy, exalting commercial secrecy over regulatory openness, supposed private efficiency and vigor over governmental bureaucracy and torpor, ultimately boil down to the justification used by Mussolini's defenders: "He made the trains run on time." But, as this book so persuasively demonstrates, it is democratic processes that make the utilities run better, cheaper, more efficiently and more reliably.

In a world which has largely moved away from public ownership, it is naive and dangerous to leave control of these crucial elements of society's infrastructure in the hands of profit-maximizing corporations with no public oversight. The US utility regulatory model, a product of over a century of democratic popular struggle to lower prices, universalize service and rein in corporate abuses, is worthy of study and consideration throughout a world increasingly linked by a transnational economy, multinational companies and, hopefully, local and international movements to put the interests of people before corporate profits.

Carl Wood
San Francisco

Democracy and Regulation: An Introduction

British residents pay 44 per cent more for electricity than do American consumers, 85 per cent more for local telephone service and 26 per cent more for natural gas – and by European standards, British prices are low. In the developing world, where costs for labor and other inputs are lower than in the US, prices are typically far higher. Domestic electricity customers in Sao Paulo, Brazil, pay nearly US$0.13 per kilowatt-hour, 58 per cent more than the US average of $0.08.[1]

Except in a few places (such as California, where price regulation was temporarily replaced by markets), Americans pay astonishingly little for high-quality public services, yet low charges do not suppress wages: American utility workers are the nation's industrial elite, with a higher concentration of union membership than in any other private industry.[2]

In our travels throughout Europe, Latin America and Asia, we have been asked for the secret to America's low prices. Experts expect us to answer with a technical discussion of pricing formulae or a description of the energy futures trading market. Most are surprised by our response: low-cost, high-quality service rests on a simple, two-part formula we call Democratic Regulation:

1. Complete open public access to information; and
2. Full public participation in setting prices and standards of service.

Despite its relative success in practice, America's democratic process of regulating privately owned systems is virtually unknown outside its borders. What little is written of US regulation concentrates on recent experiments with so-called "market pricing mechanisms" and "deregulation." While market-driven utility pricing (first introduced in Britain in 1990 when utilities there were privatized) is currently in vogue worldwide, in most states, the US holds fast to its core system of highly elaborate regulation involving an extraordinary level of public involvement and control.

Unique in the world (with the exception of Canada), every aspect of US regulation is wide open to the public. There are no secret meetings, no secret documents. Any and all citizens and groups are invited to take part:

individuals, industrial customers, government agencies, consumer groups, trade unions, the utility itself, even its competitors. Everyone affected by the outcome has a right to make their case openly, to ask questions of government and utilities, to read all financial and operating records in detail. In public forums, with all information open to all citizens, the principles of social dialogue and transparency come to life. It is an extra-ordinary exercise in democracy – and it works.

Over the past 20 years, a wave of privatization of public services worldwide has forced governments to scramble to create new laws and agencies to regulate these new enterprises. Expert consultants, mostly American and British, have been hired at enormous fees to design rules and regulations to insure that the new private owners of water, electricity, gas, telephone and electricity systems provide quality services at reasonable prices and treat consumers and employees fairly. For the most part, the result has been disastrous. In Rio de Janeiro, prices following privatization shot up 400 per cent, 40 per cent of the electricity workers lost their jobs – and the lights went out. In Britain, water prices since privatization rose 58 per cent in real terms. In one case, the new Yorkshire water company, having drained its distribution system physically and financially, suggested abandoning part of the city of Leeds in response to a water shortage. In Peru, some telephone prices jumped by 3,000 per cent. Neither regulators nor market forces have reined in overcharges by the new monopoly enterprises.

The International Labour Office (ILO) held a Tripartite Meeting on Managing the Privatization and Restructuring of Public Utilities in Geneva, April 12–16, 1999. Among the unanimous conclusions adopted at that Meeting, the following statements summarize what has been learned from the international wave of privatization:

- The provision of water, gas and electricity supplies for all – regardless of the type of ownership of the provider – must be in the public interest.
- [T]he participation of workers' representatives [footnote omitted] in such processes, as well as transparency in information and procedures, should be taken into consideration so that there can be positive results for all.
- Also, public accountability is necessary for restructuring or privatiza-tion, to strengthen public utility services and prevent deterioration in quality of and in access to services.

- Lessons about the effectiveness of benefits and problems arising from different approaches can also be learned from countries that have carried out extensive restructuring or privatization.
- Social dialogue should take place at all appropriate stages of the decision-making process, including within the regulatory framework.
- A fundamental requirement of restructuring and privatization is that it is carried out in an open and transparent process involving all parties concerned without damaging commercial confidentiality.
- The replacement of the public monopoly by a private monopoly should be avoided or if a monopoly continues it should be strongly regulated.
- Utility and government information and methods must be open for review by industry, workers' representatives and the public. When utilities are privatized, the state should still retain a responsibility in ensuring universal access to water, electricity and gas services at affordable prices.

The issue we address here is not whether privatization is wise or foolish. We leave the quarrel over privatization to others. The questions we will answer are, once privatization occurred, *why did regulation fail?* And, more importantly, *how can these systems be fixed?*

This is why we turn for a cure to the American experience where we find that it is not the *rules* of regulation but the *method* by which the rules are designed which makes all the difference. America's relatively successful control of privately owned utilities is the direct result of its democratic process, with decisions made by public debate in a public forum with all information available freely to all parties. Until now, no book has been written to give an explanation of the day-to-day workings of this system of wide-open regulation. Our goal is to provide that initial guide. This monograph includes a step-by-step explanation, based on the authors' 75 years' combined non-academic practical experience in utility regulation, of how to conduct a democratic review of prices and services.

Is the American experience useful to Brazil or Germany? Unequivocally, yes. What we find astonishing is that nations from Australia to Peru have adopted the US system of private ownership of utilities while ignoring the US system of strictly regulating their operations. It is not lost on us that so many of the new owners of utility corporations are the very US firms that submit to stringent, democratic regulatory regimes at home. By 1999, US public utility companies had already invested more than $13 billion in overseas companies.[3] There is no reason to believe these American companies cannot abide by similar rules of democratic governance when operating outside the United States.

Another little known fact is that, despite the recent experiments with markets in electricity, the US holds to the strictest, most elaborate and detailed system of regulation anywhere: private utilities' profits are capped, investments directed or vetoed by public agencies. Privately owned utilities are directed to reduce prices for the poor, fund environmentally friendly investments, protect community employment and open themselves to physical and financial inspection. This is a natural consequence of democratic rule-making. Public control of the procedure tends to lead to more rules, seldom fewer. For example, after the Three Mile Island nuclear accident in 1979, the code for safe operation of nuclear plants, designed in public, expanded to several thousand detailed pages. This goes against the grain of current economic fashion, which is to disparage regulation. But Americans, while strongly attached to private property and ownership, demand stern and exacting government control over vital utility services.

The US system is no regulatory Garden of Eden. It has many snakes and traps, many failings; and the theory of the American system often promises more than reality delivers. That makes this book especially helpful. The authors, workers in the field, can warn readers away from America's mistakes and muddles, as well as mark its real achievements.

We recognize that, today, the US system of democratic regulation is under attack by the promoters of market pricing in America itself. Led by industrial customers seeking to corner the lowest-priced resources, market advocates seek to exempt the generation portion of the electricity infra-structure from price regulation and open it to what they assert is competition. Thus America itself is engaged in a struggle between setting electricity prices by democratic regulation – as it has done for about a century – and setting prices in a marketplace.

But even these market experiments, conducted in a few of the 50 states, have been developed and are monitored with full democratic public par-ticipation. The widely publicized debacle in California is instructive. Prices tripled in parts of the state; one utility approached bankruptcy while another filed for bankruptcy court protection; blackouts rolled across the state; and deregulated generation suppliers made extraordinary profits. The details of profiteering became known almost immediately, partly as a result of government-required public financial filings by the price-gougers. The democratic political process, led by the state's Governor and Legislature, quickly called for correction (albeit in part because of the financial threat to politically powerful utilities). And the democratic result across the country is that, of the 25 states that have taken steps toward their own market experiments, at least a third are already backing away. The half that have taken no steps to abandon their full regulatory structures are now confirmed in their opinions. Only a handful of states are plunging full speed ahead in the face of California's experience (including Pennsylvania, Massachusetts, Texas, and Ohio). None of the American market experiments has yielded much in the way of positive results for large numbers of consumers when compared to the system of democratic regulation.

Chapter 1 illustrates the consequences of privatization with and without democratic regulation through case studies of three nations: the US, Britain and Brazil. This is followed, in Chapter 2, by a fuller description of what it means to use the democratic process in regulation. Chapter 3 discusses the creation and dissolution of a power pool and so-called "competition" in the electricity market in California, while Chapter 4 shows how the current regulatory trends in the US do not abandon the democratic principles of regulation.

Chapter 5 provides a step-by-step description of the US utility regulatory system and Chapter 6 describes how social pricing is done in the US to provide price protections to the poorest customers. Chapter 7 describes several other issues that are publicly decided in the US. Chapter 8 provides examples of how key issues of importance to domestic and industrial customers, as well as to labor unions, environmentalists and low-income advocates, are resolved in the US by democratic participation in negotiations.

Chapter 9 provides some guidelines for democratic participation in the regulatory process. This is followed, in Chapter 10, by a short history of the development of democratic regulation in the US over the 100 years of the twentieth century. Chapter 11 discusses the issues of transparency and open dialogue and their implications for society's regulation of the multinational corporation. Chapter 12 describes the specific failures of undemocratic experiments in deregulation in the US and privatization in the UK, while Chapter 13 provides more detail about the debacle in California and the rise and fall of Enron. Chapter 14 reviews similar failures in the rest of the world. The book concludes, in Chapter 15, with an analysis of secrecy versus democracy and answers the question: Why regulate at all?

1 Secrecy, Democracy and Regulation

The average price of a measured domestic local telephone call in the US is 2.7 cents per minute, although nearly all US households pay a flat rate for all their local calls, making their effective rate even less. In every utility service – gas, telephone, electricity and water – the US provides the average citizen with high-quality services at prices lower than in almost any other nation served by privately owned utility corporations.[1] Variations in costs cannot account for the price differentials. Argentina charges 74 per cent more than the US price for electricity, yet the US lacks Argentina's bountiful hydroelectric resources.

Table 1.1 Residential Prices for Telephone and Electricity

Residential Prices Country	Telephone per minute* August 1997	Electricity per kWh 1999
Argentina		$0.141
Australia***	$0.046	$0.080
Brazil**		$0.128
Chile		$0.090
Denmark	$0.041	$0.207
France**	$0.031	$0.129
Germany	$0.039	$0.152
Greece	$0.017	$0.090
Ireland	$0.049	$0.117
Japan	$0.019	$0.212
Netherlands	$0.043	$0.132
UK	$0.050	$0.117
US	$0.027	$0.081

* 4-minute call, adjusted for cost of living
** Electricity price, 1998
*** Electricity price, 1997
Sources: OECD; International Energy Agency; Eurodata; US DOE EIA; *Wall Street Journal*.

What America has is the toughest, strictest, most elaborate system for regulating private utility corporations found anywhere in the world (with the possible exception of Canada). This may come as a surprise. America, after all, has sent out an army of consultants to every corner of the Earth to extol the virtues of deregulation, free markets and less government. But this is an export-only philosophy, not applied within the US itself, and for good reason. In the land of free enterprise, a century of practical experience has led Americans to adopt as faith the idea that public services – especially those owned by stockholder corporations – are unique monopolies which the government and public, not markets, must tightly control.

But strict regulation alone is not the secret behind low prices. Rules themselves, however stringent, do not make the difference. The US and Britain share a formula for calculating the price for distributing electricity and water, yet Britain's prices are far higher than America's. Britain's relatively compact geography should result in lower prices for water distribution. Therefore, based on the common formula alone, prices for water in England should be lower than in the US, because of lower costs. But the opposite is true.

While regulators in the two nations use formulae for setting prices that are mathematically identical[2] (e.g., both measure investments, fair profits and expenses), the *process* for reviewing the data is radically different. In Britain, as in almost every country, prices are set in secret meetings between the government's regulatory experts and utility executives. Under the guise of "commercial confidentiality," the public is denied a view of all but a few bits of summary information. Public participation is limited to ineffective commentary on the small scraps of information not deemed confidential. The US system is the opposite.

For those who have never participated in a US price review, the documentation available is unimaginable. To justify its prices, a company typically files 300–3,000 pages of explanation, calculations and documentation. If requested by the regulator or by any customer, the utility company must provide all documents which back up its initial filing and answer in writing all questions relating to costs and operation (and provide documentation to back these). A typical price review can easily exceed 100,000 pages of information, all of it available for public inspection. In most cases, if requested by a customer or union, the documents are copied at the company's expense. By law, there are no secrets, no hidden documents. Crucially, the law bars regulators from issuing decisions on price or service unless every calculation and finding of fact is based on documentary evidence in the public record.

In this example from Texas, three aspects of the case of *Pace and Williams* v. *Houston Power & Light* deserve note.

First, citizens have the right to initiate and participate in price reviews. There is no value to open information without the authority to use it. Consumer organizations, labor unions, industrial groups and local government agencies all had legal authority to participate in negotiations over the Houston price reductions. The regulator was barred from reaching a private

The Case of the Houston Power & Light Refund

In 1992, two utility workers, Charles Pace and Kenneth Williams, were sacked by Houston Power & Light, one of Texas's privately owned electricity companies. Although they knew nothing about the technical details of utility finance or accounting, the two men suspected the company was earning excess profits by pocketing dismissed workers' wages rather than passing the savings on to customers. Pace and Williams filed a demand for a public investigation of the utility corporation's alleged profiteering under Section 42 of the Texas Public Utilities Regulatory Act. This law permits any citizen to force the government to investigate a utility's prices. (Similar rights apply in all 50 US states.)

To back their demand for an investigation, the two union members took advantage of their right as citizens to obtain the account books and records of the privately owned electricity company. Based on the internal company records ferreted out by Pace and Williams, the government, several consumer organizations and large industrial customers began their own examination of the company records. It is important to note that all the information was shared by the parties: neither the electricity company nor the government could keep financial documents out of public view.

What information did the two workers have available to them? In theory, all documents: every record, account book, memorandum, report, computer tape, file, photograph – even the hand-scrawled notes in the executive's desk or home which might reflect on the costs, income or operating decisions of the company.

The utility, faced with further public scrutiny of its account books, agreed to reduce its prices and refund a total of $1.5 billion to its Texas utility customers.[3]

agreement with the utility; nor could the regulator conduct negotiations without the participation of consumer groups.

Second, prices are based on cost. While this is true in every regulatory regime worldwide, in the US, the link between cost and price is explicit. If a utility cuts costs, it must pass savings to the public in the form of lower prices. But the link to cost is far more explicit – and enforced – than in other nations where the price–cost connection is often lost in a fog of "efficiency incentives" from which consumers rarely benefit.

Third, utility employees greatly benefit from the open system designed for protecting the consumer. All information available to consumers, including investment plans, employment projections and service quality measures, are also tools for unions and employees.

Rio Light Goes Dark

Compare the open US method to the alternative. In 1997, Brazil's federal government sold the Rio de Janeiro electric company, Rio Light, to foreign operators who promised to improve service. The new owners swiftly slashed the number of employees. Unfortunately, Rio's electricity system is not fully mapped. Electricity workers kept track of the location of wires and transformers in their heads. When they were sacked, the workers took their mental maps with them. Nearly every day, a new neighborhood would suffer a blackout, which earned the company the sobriquet "Rio Dark."

Despite the cost savings from wages avoided by eliminating workers, the company increased prices. The windfall from cutting the workforce while raising prices helped the foreign owners increase dividends to stockholders by over 1,000 per cent. Rio Light's share price jumped from £194 to £259 in one year.[4]

What went wrong? First, set aside the issue of whether Brazil should have privatized Rio's electricity grid. The practical question is, once the utility was put in private hands, how could the regulator have prevented this community disaster? It has been argued that Brazil's new regulators lacked both experience and authority. (In fact, Brazil's regulatory agency began operations only *after* Rio Light was sold.) But the real problem is a lack of democracy in Brazil's system of services oversight. Unlike consumer groups in the Houston case, Brazil's consumer organizations, such as Instituto Brasileiro de Defesa do Consumidor (IDEC), were denied complete access to company financial records. This made it impossible to calculate how much the foreign investors profited by reducing workforce and investment. Union workers, seen by government and investors as impediments to "restructuring" the market for private ownership, were also locked out of the process of determining the terms of operation. Yet, by the nature of their work, line employees are the ultimate experts on how to maintain standards on the electricity grid.

Perfunctory public hearings in Rio led to a penalty for the company, but at a level so low as to barely dent the profits to be made from reducing service quality. The result was that, despite the lower costs of operating in Brazil, electricity prices in Rio are about 87 per cent higher than in Houston, while quality is far lower and employment less secure. The irony is that Rio Light is partly owned by the same US corporation, Reliant of Texas, that owns the Houston electricity company.

In 1998, the Brazilian government sought to reform the system by establishing a new regulatory agency, ANEEL (Agencia Nacional de Energia Eletrica). The improved system of regulation would control the new privatizations planned for the rest of Brazil's electricity system.

Nevertheless, the new proposals for Brazil are as certain to fail as did the old regime: overcharges, job losses and service curtailments are effectively written into the guidelines for the new regulators' operation. The new rules are the product of the same undemocratic processes that led to the Rio Light failure. That process began with an American consulting firm, Coopers & Lybrand, which, in coordination with a select group of civil servants, drafted proposals based on evidence that was kept hidden from the public. For example, the Ministry of Mines, in the plans issued in 1998, concluded that prices should be set to reflect real post-tax rates of return on equity of 11–13 per cent, which it states is four percentage points higher than returns sought in the US and UK.[5] The Ministry says that it reached this conclusion "based on [the Regulator's] analysis" and on "interviews with investors." The Ministry fails to provide information on who provided the data that went into the analysis or to list the investors interviewed – investors who might have had good reason to inflate the numbers. In any case, we can state this: US electric utility real returns for 1999 averaged only 3.7 per cent.[6] Even assuming a "risk premium" of 4 per cent (an assertion also without visible evidence), the excess earnings built into Brazilian electric bills will cost the nation billions of dollars over the coming years.

Again, the issue is not whether the ministry is capable or ill informed. This costly error is the result of keeping the system closed, exclusive and secretive. In the US, returns are relatively low because the returns are discussed openly, before the public. Investor-owned utilities and their consultants as well as the regulators present their justification for returns, typically in hundreds of pages of calculations and discussion in open meetings. *Any* member of the public can question them in public and present alternative proposals for profits. The lower US returns (and thus, lower prices) are not the result of more consultants but more democracy.

Regulatory failure is not limited to Brazil and the developing world. In the decade since privatization of utility services, as noted above, Britain's regulators have made a string of erroneous financial projections which cost the public billions of pounds in excess water and electricity charges. A close study of regulation in the UK is especially important because the British model, not the American, is the template worldwide for the new post-privatization regimes.

Collapse of Investment in British Water

Figure 1 shows the UK government's projection for investment in system quality by the water industry for 1989 through today. When privatized in 1989, the government ministry projected that the new companies would increase investments to over £3 billion per annum by 1992 to repair a badly leaking pipe system. On that basis, the regulator permitted the companies a so-called "K" factor, a multibillion pound surcharge to cover this rising expenditure. Once the water companies received the authority to collect the extra money from customers, they barely increased their spending to fix the system. The companies kept most of the surcharge collected from customers to pay out in embarrassingly huge dividends.

In 1994, the regulator re-set prices. This time, to avoid being misled by the companies, the regulator projected (as Figure 1 shows), virtually no increase at all in investment. But the companies stayed a step ahead of the government watchdog. This time the water companies *decreased* their investments in the system. Again, utility shareholders pocketed the difference.

At the end of 1999, the beleaguered regulator tried a third time, publishing a new set of permitted prices. Within weeks of publication, it became clear that government projections of expenditures were, once again, off the mark, allowing the companies to collect charges for phantom spending.[7]

By the regulator's permitting British water companies to under-spend on investments in the system, these utilities have garnered breathtaking returns on equity. In the first five years following privatization, profits averaged 25–32 per cent return on equity after inflation and taxes, several times the regulator's projections. The companies paid out huge dividends – while the water infrastructure deteriorated.[8]

£ billions

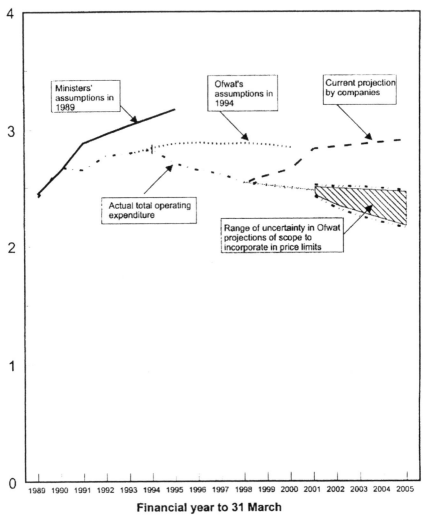

Figure 1   Comparison of Total Operating Costs (1997–98 prices) (Source: Ofwat, *Prospects for Prices* (1999 Periodic Review, Consultation Paper on Strategic Issues Affecting Future Water Bills), p. 51

Had US rules been applied to the case of British Water, no application for a price increase based on new investment would even have been entertained until after the investment had been made and a detailed accounting of it been filed. Even where permission to make the investment is given in advance, prices cannot be based on the investment until the project is completed and its finances publicly reviewed. It is thus impossible to base charges on phantom investment. For very large projects, an exception can be made to allow prices to be based on a portion of an investment not yet completed, usually called "construction work in progress" (CWIP). But this too requires a detailed accounting of investments already made.

We must not lay the failure in projecting UK utility investment to the shortcomings of the water regulator. The same under-investment occurred in Britain's electricity system, with utilities pocketing £453 million for the three-year period ending in 1997.[9] The huge profits of utilities in gas, telephone and electricity as well as water suggest the problem is systemic. It applies to transactions besides infrastructure investments.

Overcharges by Britain's National Grid

In November 1997, the National Grid, Britain's electricity transmission system, floated its telecommunications subsidiary Energis for £846 million. Only months earlier, the electricity regulator projected the flotation would not exceed £250 million. Because the profit from the sale of telephone assets is subtracted from the value of assets charged to the Grid's electricity customers when setting electricity prices, the regulator's error ultimately cost British electricity consumers £596 million.[10]

How could the electricity regulator have made such a disastrously wrong projection? The answer is not to look for a more qualified regulator: in this case, the government appointed an internationally acclaimed regulatory economist. The problem is the process. The Grid company's price review was conducted in secrecy befitting a military operation. Only the staff of the Office of Electricity Regulation (OFFER) could review documentation of the proposed flotation proffered by the Grid's management. The public was barred from reviewing the financial records on the grounds of "commercial confidentiality." As in most nations, the utility's executives and the regulator met in secret, away from the public view, to discuss the flotation.

In those meetings, the Grid executives told OFFER that the subsidiary they were about to float had a *negative* value. The regulator did not demand that the company produce projections of flotation proceeds, which the company must have received from its investment advisors. In fact, OFFER did not believe it had the legal authority to seek those financial documents. With no hard information to rely on, the regulator, acting in isolation and in secret, arbitrarily guessed at a sales prices for the telecommunications subsidiary well above the company's assertion of zero value but still grievously below the correct sum.[11]

What went wrong? First, the electricity regulator was operating blind. He was denied crucial documents by the Grid which, in the US, the utility would have been forced to place on the public record. Second, the whole process was doomed to failure by its secrecy and exclusiveness. No outside party could challenge the utility's assertions – indeed, no formal record was made of the company's evidence. Had OFFER opened up the process to public debate, the regulator could then have enlisted all the nation's financial talents to assist in the review. Commercial confidentiality sabotaged a proper and expert examination of the facts.

In the US, the value of the sold property would not have been set until after the sale was concluded. Had such a gross under-valuation been adopted, consumers would have had the right to appeal to the courts for redress.

There is another, more subtle problem when regulators exclude the public from meetings. The clubby atmosphere of a dark-paneled room can impart an air of reason to utility claims, which, in a public meeting, could not withstand a single skeptical question. The US rule regarding such secret meetings between regulators and the companies they regulate to discuss pending price proposals: they are prohibited by law.

2   Regulating in Public

Open information versus secrecy

If not in secret, how then do American state regulators determine the prices charged by private companies? After the utility has opened its file cabinets to public view, the corporation's executives must answer in writing questions raised by regulators and members of the public. The questions and answers are open for public review. Then the executives must stand for questioning in public tribunals, first by government experts and attorneys, then by customers, their experts or their attorneys. The daily questioning can continue for a period of one to three months. (Details of the US price review process are discussed in Chapter 5.)

Do not assume the public's questions are ill informed. Poorer consumers are aided by experts and attorneys funded by the government and well-funded consumer organizations. "Consumer" is a term that also encompasses giant industrial customers and other parties who may outspend the regulatory agency itself in investigating prices. Even non-expert citizens, armed with documents and imagination, can, as we saw in the Houston Power example, successfully challenge financial projections.

While American regulators make their share of mistakes and are liable to errors in judgment just as are any other human beings, it is inconceivable that the UK regulator's £596 million error in setting electricity grid prices could have withstood the type of open inquiry that takes place in the US. For not only are the utility's records open, but government-funded consumer advocates also present evidence and financial data. These calculations, estimates and "guesstimates" are placed on the public record, and must withstand questioning by the public in public. In many states, the experts who conduct the technical reviews for the regulators must also stand for questioning. In any event, the regulators' written decision must be based solely on public evidence and must provide all reasoning and calculations – all of which are subject to judicial review. Three-hundred-page decisions are not unusual. The failure of the UK regulator to review the Grid's investment bankers' projections would have been exposed. OFFER's arbitrary and unjustified estimate of the Energis flotation value would not have survived direct questioning by consumers.

Table 2.1 is one page taken from a several-hundred-page calculation by a US regulatory agency to determine the allowed profit for the US electricity company serving New Orleans. Note the detail. Every calculation must be supported and estimates clearly marked as such. In this case, the government's economist (one of the authors of this monograph) had to withstand 40 hours of detailed questioning by the public – and by the utility.

Note that the democratic process, unquestionably better for consumers, provides benefits to the privatized utility company as well – because the corporation and its stockholders gain the same rights as consumers and workers to question the regulator's calculations and judgments.

Compare Table 2.1 to the British regulator's calculation of the cost of capital for the National Grid, in Table 2.2. The entire calculation made public in Britain consisted of this single page. It tells us virtually nothing. We know only that the regulator concluded the utility's cost of capital lies somewhere between 5.9 per cent and 7.5 per cent based on an equity risk factor ("beta") of 0.59 to 0.75. Neither the public nor the utility has a clue how the regulator calculated the "beta" factor: there are no back-up documents. Doubtless, these calculations are partly based on data provided by the company – which remain sealed from public view. No one – neither consumers nor employees nor the company itself – may question the regulator or his expert advisors to find out their reasoning behind this calculation.

The first problem with wrapping calculations in mystery and secrecy is that there is no method for preventing errors. It is no wonder that the official projections are consistently wrong. Second, the errors are almost always biased against the public – favoring the utility over customers. The same utility company that was the subject of the US price review cited in Table 2.1 also owned London Electricity. British regulators permitted the company to charge 80 per cent more per unit of electricity than American regulators permitted the company to charge in New Orleans. The price differential is accounted for totally by differences in regulatory regime, not costs. (In fact, costs of the US operation per unit were substantially higher than those in the UK.) In effect, British customers pay a huge price premium for their system's democratic deficit.

Who is "the public"?

When we say that US law requires participation in regulation by "the public," who does that include? Any person, business or organization that pays for utility service, as well as others affected by utility practices, is invited to every public hearing and every meeting between the regulator

Table 2.1 Cost of Capital for New Orleans Public Service

CASH FLOW SUMMARY

Item	Basis	Note	1986	1987	1988	1989	1990	1991	1992	1993	1994	1995
Sources:												
Reduce common dividends		(1)	0.0	0.0	0.0	0.0	(2.9)	(3.3)	(1.1)	(0.4)	0.6	3.1
Reduce preferred dividends		(1)	3.8	2.9	2.7	2.4	(11.8)	0.0	0.0	0.0	0.0	0.0
Reduce preferred sinking fund		(1)	0.0	1.5	1.5	1.5	(4.5)	0.0	0.0	0.0	0.0	0.0
Subtotal			3.8	4.4	4.2	3.9	(19.2)	(3.3)	(1.1)	(0.4)	0.6	3.1
Pension amortized		(2)	0.0	29.3	(1.5)	(1.5)	(1.5)	(1.5)	(1.5)	(1.5)	(1.5)	(1.5)
Correction to gas income		(3)	0.0	2.0	0.0	0.0	0.0	0.0	0.0	0.0	0.0	0.0
Interest, reduction from NOPSI		(4)										
Interest, compounded savings		(5)										
Hold United Gas refund		(6)										
Added internal funds		(7)	3.8	35.7	2.7	2.4	(20.7)	(4.8)	(2.6)	(1.9)	(0.9)	1.6
Fund A/R			25.0	5.0	0.0	0.0	4.0	0.0	0.0	0.0	0.0	0.0
Extra short-term funds		(8)	13.0	15.7	12.2	14.1	10.8	12.2	0.0	0.0	(22.0)	0.0
Sale lease-backs, cap. leases		(9)	10.1	20.7	12.2	14.1	14.8	12.2	0.0	0.0	(22.0)	0.0
Added external funds			48.1	56.3	14.9	16.5	(5.9)	7.4	(2.6)	(1.9)	(22.9)	1.6
Added sources, total			51.9	56.3	14.9	16.5	(5.9)	7.4	(2.6)	(1.9)	(22.9)	1.6
Capital Needs:												
Added sources, total			51.9	56.3	14.9	16.5	(5.9)	7.4	(2.6)	(1.9)	(22.9)	1.6
Write-off, less cash tax benefit		(10)	(10.6)	5.5	11.1	11.4	(7.2)	22.3	(7.0)	(6.8)	(6.8)	(6.8)
Net added cash flow			41.3	61.8	26.0	27.9	(13.1)	29.7	(9.5)	(8.7)	(29.6)	(5.2)
Bond borrowing, NOPSI plan		(11)	25.0	19.0	30.0	15.0	0.0	0.0	8.0	0.0	30.0	0.0
Adjusted funds required (surplus)			(16.3)	(42.8)	4.0	(12.9)	13.1	(29.7)	1.5	8.7	(0.4)	5.2
Added equity, per NOPSI		(12a)	25.0	35.0	20.0	10.0	0.0	20.0	(20.0)	(10.0)	(5.0)	0.0
Added equity, per UA		(12b)					13.1	20.0	20.0	5.0	5.0	5.2
Adj new bond sales (retrmts)		(13)	(41.3)	(77.8)	(16.0)	(22.9)	27.9	(34.7)	21.5	18.7	(0.4)	5.2
Total new debt		(14)	6.8	(57.1)	(3.7)	(8.8)	0.0	(22.5)	21.5	18.7	(22.4)	5.2
Cum added equity, per UA		(12b)	0.0	0.0	0.0	0.0	0.0	20.0	20.0	20.0	25.0	25.0
Interest saved 11.0%		(15)	0.0	0.0	0.0	0.0	0.0	2.2	2.2	2.2	2.8	2.8
Surplus less New External funds			(6.8)	57.1	3.7	8.8	(27.9)	22.5	(21.5)	(18.7)	22.4	(5.2)
Cum surplus			(6.8)	50.4	54.1	62.9	35.0	57.5	36.0	17.3	39.7	34.5
Reduce total LT debt, per UA												
Cum redux LT debt			0.0	0.0	0.0	0.0	0.0	0.0	0.0	0.0	0.0	0.0
LT Debt Redux, Int.saved		(16)	0.0	0.0	0.0	0.0	0.0	0.0	0.0	0.0	0.0	0.0

(1) from UA "Reduction of Dividends."
(2) see Pension Amortized, note (2), (UA-MMI)
(3) from "Corrections to Gas Income," note (4).
(4) from "Interest Reductions from NOPSI," note (1); interest savings reduced from rate after rate freeze ends, in 1989–90
Carry forward as reduction of tax savings in "Adjustments to NOPSI"

Source: Gregory A. Palast, "Financial consequences of a Write-off of Grand Gulf 1 Expenses" (Testimony and Exhibits to the City Council of the City of New Orleans in *New Orleans Public Service Inc.*, Imprudence Inquiry, Docket CO-85-1.

Table 2.2   Cost of Capital for National Grid

Component	OFFER on NGC August 1996		MMC on NIE May 1997	
	Low %	high %	Low %	High %
Cost of debt				
Risk free rate	3.5	3.8	3.5	3.8
Risk premium for debt	*0.4*	*0.4*	*0.3*	*0.8*
Cost of debt	3.9	4.2	3.8	4.6
Cost of equity				
Risk free rate	3.5	3.8	3.5	3.8
Risk premium for equity	3.5	4.5	3.5	5.0
Equity beta[1]	0.55	0.75	0.6	0.75
Post-tax cost of equity*	5.4	7.2	5.6	7.55
Taxation adjustment[1]	1.194	1.194	1.194	1.194
Pre-tax cost of equity**	6.5	8.6	6.69	9.01
Weighted average cost of capital				
Percentage of debt finance[2]	24	24	8	8
Pre-tax WACC***	5.9	7.5	6.46	8.66

Notes:
(1)   Absolute number not a percentage figure.
(2)   The percentage of equity finance is (100-percentage of debt finance).
*   The post-tax cost of equity is calculated by multiplying the equity premium by the equity beta and adding to the risk free rate. For example, in the MMC low case (3.5 × 0.6) + 3.5 = 5.6.
**   The pre-tax cost of equity is calculated by multiplying the post-tax cost of equity by the taxation adjustment. For example in the MMC low case (5.6 × 1.194) = 6.69.
***   The pre-tax WACC is calculated as a weighted average (according to the level of gearing) of the cost of debt and equity finance. For example, in the MMC low case (6.69 × 92/100) + (3.8 × 8/100) = 6.46.

and the utility. Figure 2, "Intervenor List," is a list of participants from a recent case in the state of Oregon to determine if a foreign company, Scottish Power, could purchase PacifiCorp, an American electricity utility. The list includes dozens of organizations and individuals, including:

- the regulator's staff;
- private consumer advocacy groups;
- local government agencies;
- official consumer watchdog agencies;
- labor union coalitions;
- environmental organizations;
- poor people's organizations;
- large industrial and commercial enterprises (customers);
- a group representing utility stockholders;
- competitor electricity firms;
- suppliers to the utility;

- several interested individuals;
- independent power producers (competitors);
- government-owned utility companies (wholesale providers);
- and, of course, the American and foreign utilities themselves.

Who is excluded? No one. The whole point of democracy is that it is open.

Among the most influential groups in any price review or regulatory decision are the large industrial and commercial customers. With their enormous financial resources, they can field large teams of lawyers, accountants and economists to investigate the utilities' claims. Much of

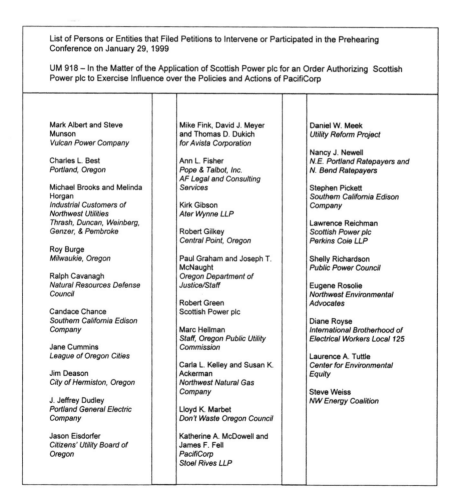

List of Persons or Entities that Filed Petitions to Intervene or Participated in the Prehearing Conference on January 29, 1999

UM 918 – In the Matter of the Application of Scottish Power plc for an Order Authorizing Scottish Power plc to Exercise Influence over the Policies and Actions of PacifiCorp

Mark Albert and Steve Munson *Vulcan Power Company*	Mike Fink, David J. Meyer and Thomas D. Dukich *for Avista Corporation*	Daniel W. Meek *Utility Reform Project*
Charles L. Best *Portland, Oregon*	Ann L. Fisher *Pope & Talbot, Inc.* *AF Legal and Consulting*	Nancy J. Newell *N.E. Portland Ratepayers and* *N. Bend Ratepayers*
Michael Brooks and Melinda Horgan *Industrial Customers of* *Northwest Utilities* *Thrash, Duncan, Weinberg,* *Genzer, & Pembroke*	*Services* Kirk Gibson *Ater Wynne LLP* Robert Gilkey *Central Point, Oregon*	Stephen Pickett *Southern California Edison* *Company* Lawrence Reichman *Scottish Power plc* *Perkins Coie LLP*
Roy Burge *Milwaukie, Oregon*	Paul Graham and Joseph T. McNaught	Shelly Richardson *Public Power Council*
Ralph Cavanagh *Natural Resources Defense* *Council*	*Oregon Department of* *Justice/Staff* Robert Green	Eugene Rosolie *Northwest Environmental* *Advocates*
Candace Chance *Southern California Edison* *Company*	Scottish Power plc Marc Hellman *Staff, Oregon Public Utility*	Diane Royse *International Brotherhood of* *Electrical Workers Local 125*
Jane Cummins *League of Oregon Cities*	*Commission* Carla L. Kelley and Susan K.	Laurence A. Tuttle *Center for Environmental*
Jim Deason *City of Hermiston, Oregon*	Ackerman *Northwest Natural Gas* *Company*	*Equity* Steve Weiss
J. Jeffrey Dudley *Portland General Electric* *Company*	Lloyd K. Marbet *Don't Waste Oregon Council*	*NW Energy Coalition*
Jason Eisdorfer *Citizens' Utility Board of* *Oregon*	Katherine A. McDowell and James F. Fell *PacifiCorp* *Stoel Rives LLP*	

Figure 2   Intervenor List

the effort of industrial customers in US price reviews is spent trying to insure that large customers get large price discounts; but much of their work, such as questioning the allowed return on investment, greatly benefits all consumers.

Note also that labor unions have a role, if they choose to make use of the opportunity.

Of all the participants, the most extraordinary are the utility's competitors: in this case, government-owned electric systems, independent power producers and other utility corporations. This participation allows companies access to their competitors' internal documents and cost analyses, items which in other nations are sealed away as "commercially confidential." But confidentiality and secrecy are enemies of well-functioning markets. There is a great value to consumers in having utility competitors investigating each other's data. Competitors are well positioned to argue against a utility's abuse of its monopoly status. In the case of the Scottish Power/PacifiCorp review, competitors were concerned that the Oregon company, PacifiCorp, not use its control of the transmission and grid system to disadvantage competitors in sales to large customers.

Finally, the utility itself is a party to the decision-making process. This may seem obvious, but in fact, in most nations, while utilities have control of the input in the decision-making process, they are often kept in the dark about other information relied on by the regulator in making a decision. Utility companies are routinely denied the opportunity to analyze the details of criticism of the utility, which the regulator has received from third parties. Under US law, democratic rights apply to the utility as well as to its adversaries.

"Consultation" is not participation

Britain, like most governments, does not prohibit public comment on the setting of prices or terms of utility service. Officially sanctioned consumer bodies are "consulted" and "comments" are requested from interested members of the public. *But consultation is not participation.* Neither the public nor even the official consumer advocates are allowed to sit in a meeting of company and regulator.

Consider the case of the failed valuation of the UK National Grid's subsidiary. What was the value of the public's right to comment on the regulator's decision to value the Energis subsidiary at £250 million? The regulator, in an attempt to "open" the review process, invited the opinions of three experts. But the public was kept in the dark about what each of the three advised and the evidence on which they advised the regulator (or, in this case, the lack of evidence). None of these alleged experts had to withstand questioning by the public (nor by the utility which, after all, had much at stake in the decision). Therefore, there was no basis for informed comment by the public. Why were these experts chosen and others excluded? Why were the affected customers (and that would include industry and local government) barred from having their own experts review the evidence? The right to "comment" on proposed decisions, without the ability to directly participate in all discussions with full access to information, is an empty and useless privilege. Truly democratic methods – open dialogue and transparency of information – instead of hollow "opportunities to comment" – would have spared Britain the £596 million error.

India, like most nations, is under intense pressure from the International Monetary Fund and World Bank to privatize power, water and telephone systems. State-owned electricity systems, for example, are to be broken up and privatized with the objective that privately owned generation suppliers will compete to sell to privately owned distribution companies, who will sell electricity to the public.

Indian observers point out that the regulatory oversight of this new structure that is being developed lacks accountability both because its decisions cannot be appealed except in very limited circumstances and because such potentially high-cost decisions as generation contract terms can be taken in secret with no public participation. Although there are rights to public participation on paper, in reality these rights may be set aside; necessary information is not available to the public; and deadlines for participation are unrealistically short. This lack of accountability, the commentators predict, will lead only to "a new lobby of regulators and utilities" that serves vested interests. Indian experience is their teacher.[1]

The Indian case of the Dabhol power plant project is a good example of economic and social disaster following from autocratic, secretive regulatory regime. In that instance, Maharashtra State officials, in confidential negotiations, contracted with American Corporation Enron of Houston, Texas, to build a gas-fired plant. Because the negotiations were conducted in secret, the government officials could not obtain outside advice or public input. The result was a contract that forced the state's electricity board, and therefore the state's consumers, to pay unit prices wildly above the world market price. Terms of the agreement with the foreign investor were poor, in part because there was no open public discussion of price, the environment or ownership. Opposition parties charged that bribery was involved; local citizens demonstrated in the streets; and police response resulted in injuries and imprisonments.

A new government renegotiated the contract with Enron, this time after much more public discussion, and the terms of the contract improved. Nevertheless, the contract never received a full public review. Expert economists believe, for example, that the state made a US$145 million arithmetic error in Enron's favor – but there is no way to know, because none of the calculations behind the contract was published and neither Enron nor state officials would answer all questions on the project. The government counters that it permitted public comment on the project – and 30 parties made dissenting representations. But all these public comments lacked the authority of information, so they were ignored. Indeed, the right to *comment*, as opposed to *participate* with full information, is often worse than nothing at all because opportunities to comment lend a false legitimacy to autocratically made decisions.[2]

Goaded by advice and pressure from the World Bank, Brazil's government effectively turned over the design of its regulatory system to foreign consultants, such as Hunton & Williams of Washington, DC and Coopers & Lybrand, who work principally for potential foreign buyers. Consumer organizations, labor unions, poor people's organizations and the nation's academic experts were limited to symbolic opportunities for "comment;" that is, they could review the details and evidence on which the foreign consultants based their proposals. The results for Brazil's electricity system were predictable: high prices, poor service, industry job losses and hardship for the poor.[3]

One grave mistake of newly developed regulatory regimes is to choose the members of the public who will be watchdogs. This approach is a formula for failure. In Britain, during the 1990 privatization process, the government established "Consumer Councils" to watch over the public interest in setting electricity prices. The "Consumer Council" members were not chosen by consumer organizations, but by the regulator himself. It is no surprise that the Councils issued several statements praising the regulator and never once mounted a serious challenge to the regulator's decision. It undermines the process to have government choose its own watchdog.

Recently, the British government announced a "reform" of utility regulation to make it more "participatory." The regulator would no longer choose the consumers' representatives; rather, the central government would select consumers who would, as representatives of the public, see otherwise confidential documents. This "reform" is no improvement at all, even though the new Council is expected to include respected consumer organizations such as Consumers' Association. The problem is that government retains the right to *exclude* groups it does not like – and those are usually the groups most militant in the cause of public protection. A government's choosing "responsible" consumers to participate in regulation is no more democratic than a government's selecting which newspapers may publish stories about it.

The US does have official consumer protection agencies that participate in the process. These are well funded and provide a high level of expertise. But in no instance do these official organizations replace consumers or individuals who also want to participate. The US rule is: *the government can exclude no one affected by the outcome.*

Employees, service quality and democracy

Who pays the price for failed regulation? Poor service and high prices hurt consumers, burden governments and hobble industry. But no group has felt the sting of regulatory malfeasance more than the employees of the utility industry who, in most nations, are helpless to stop wholesale reductions in workforce which have followed the sale of state industries.

In Britain, the gas, water and electricity industries cut 90,000 jobs in the first seven years following privatization – and service has declined to the point of crisis. Job losses and deteriorating service go hand in hand. Consider the case described above of the water regulator's overestimating, year after year, the amount of spending for system upgrade. By 1996, the system reached a crisis point, with water use restricted and water rationing planned. The newly privatized Yorkshire water company considered evacuating part of the city of Leeds. But there was no water shortage. The problem was that one-third of Britain's water was lost into the ground through leaking pipes. Rather than hire more workers to fix the leaks, the water companies *reduced* employment by 3,700, despite the special surcharge levied on the public for repairs.[4]

One would assume that the UK water regulator would have been angered by the reduction in workforce just when system repairs were needed most. Instead, the regulator applauded the water companies' increased "efficiencies."[5] Unfortunately, inexperienced regulators falsely equate job losses with efficiency, by using the simplistic yardstick of "output per worker" as a measure of productivity. This practice is naive, even dangerous. Britain has shown that it is very easy to improve "productivity" – by allowing the infrastructure to fall apart. There is no such thing as a free lunch or free repairs without paying workers to accomplish the job.

No one has a greater stake in the outcome of the regulatory process than the utility worker. When the UK regulator permitted water companies to under-spend on repairs to their pipe networks, that caused inconvenience for the public but personal devastation for the workers who lost their livelihood. The same shortsightedness occurred in the case of Rio Light, where the government did nothing to stop massive reduction in electricity employment – until the lights went out.

The problem, however, is not regulators' misjudgments or privatization per se. The real threat to the utility employee is lack of democracy, the exclusion of workers and their union representatives from true participation in the regulation of the companies. Most regulatory agencies are hostile to union participation; but excluding the workers and their representatives costs the public the expertise and concern of those ultimately entrusted to keep the lights on and the water pumping. In the US, unions have the same legal authority as the utility itself to intervene in the public hearings that determine prices and levels of service, as in the following examples.

Peoples Gas, Chicago, System Repair

Between 1970 and 1990, gas pipes in the city of Chicago, Illinois, exploded on six occasions, killing more than a dozen residents. Peoples Gas Company, a private corporation, hired experts who concluded that miles of gas pipe under Chicago's streets were made from inferior steel and clay. The company attempted to conceal these reports, but a coalition of 26 labor unions used their right to review company documents to discover and disclose these internal company reports. The unions demanded that the utility commission hold a public inquest. Joined by several community groups concerned about the danger of future explosions, the unions' lawyers and experts conducted an inquisition of the utility executives lasting three years. Ultimately, the regulator ordered an elaborate, detailed and expensive plan for replacing most of the city's gas pipes.[6]

In this Chicago case, the unions' self-interest was clear: an expansive repair program meant more jobs. But self-interest of the unions should not bar their participation in regulatory reviews any more than self-interest of a utility in profits should bar company participation. In Chicago, the union's concern for jobs led to a great improvement in public safety.

No one would suggest that regulators should order utility companies to maintain bloated payrolls of unneeded employees. But the regulator can and must make certain that monopoly utilities maintain quality service available to all citizens. By that rule, there is no utility that has too many workers so long as there are citizens without electricity, water or gas connections. It is not possible for a utility to have an excess number of workers so long as water leaks into the ground or sewerage into rivers, or phone connections fail.

It is nearly always the case that inexperienced regulators leave to utility management decisions to spend or not spend, invest or not invest, hire or not hire. New regulatory regimes merely set the maximum price that can be charged, as in the latest incarnation of Brazil's electric regulatory scheme previously described.[7] But for monopoly utilities (especially natural gas, electricity distribution, water services and local phone networks) there is an enormous incentive to slash the workforce well beyond any justification of efficiency. If prices remain unchanged as utilities cut cost, the result is unjust enrichment for the company, system deterioration and unemployment.

In 1998, the Brazilian Ministry of Mines changed a single word in its privatization and regulation proposal which eliminates any reduction in prices to consumers between price reviews to reflect "benefits of efficiency improvements," i.e., workforce reductions.[8] Unfortunately, this provision will provide an incentive to remove not just excess workers, but needed workers, and service will suffer as a result. The question is, who proposed this change? What is the rationale? The Ministry concedes that investors were consulted, but why not unions? The government's proposal may have a justification. If so, why not open the matter to full, open social dialogue?

Failings of the American system

The American system of regulation, in this swift summary, sounds magical: lower prices guaranteed by democratic rights. But the system has its serious failings. In Chapter 1, we cited the case of two utility workers who, using their right to information and authority to challenge utility prices, forced a Texas electricity company to refund $1.5 billion in overcharges. What was left out of the story is that it took the workers three years to overcome the government's resisting and obstructing the exercise of their legal rights.

Americans have extraordinary political rights in the regulation process, but these rights are under constant attack. Immediately after the refund to consumers in Houston (described above), the electricity company nearly succeeded, through its influence on the Texas state legislature, in changing the law that allowed the workers to bring their case.

US workers and customers may have the right to challenge private utilities in public hearings, but as a practical matter they never match the ability of a multi-billion-dollar corporation to field teams of expensive lawyers and experts. While the law states that the public and utilities have equal authority before the regulator, it is never a battle of equals: the American system merely allows David to fling rocks at Goliath. It is only by comparison to the virtual absence of citizen rights in other nations that the American system appears at all fair.

The law says regulators may not make secret deals with utilities, but there is evidence that some do. Companies may not conceal documents, but some have been caught doing so. In the case of the Southern Company of Atlanta, for example, the government discovered that the company kept two conflicting sets of account books. The concealed set of books indicated that the information presented to the public, the regulator and tax authorities included tens of millions of dollars in charges for equipment parts which had not, in fact, been used.[9] In other words, America has exceptional rules making all documents public – but that assumes all utilities follow the rules.

Also we have said that in these cases there are "no secret documents" withheld from consumer groups and other parties. But we must note there are a few permissible exceptions to rules against secrecy which government and corporations may abuse. While a very few commercially sensitive documents may be kept from public view, consumers, labor unions and other participants in the price review who sign a confidentiality agreement may have access to this material.

Every nation's regulatory system is, ultimately, a human endeavor. Therefore, regulation is only as good as the regulators. America is no exception. While many of our regulators are thoughtful and public-spirited, too many others use their office as a stepping-stone to lucrative work consulting for utilities they regulated. And regulation is political. What private corporations cannot win before regulators they can sometimes obtain through financial control of the election of state legislators or influence in the US Congress.

Some American states take their democracy to the extraordinary extent of making regulators stand for election. But this practice opens the door to seizure of the electoral process by heavy funding from the utilities, although direct campaign contributions to candidates from utilities are generally prohibited by law.

The biggest failing of the American system is that the rights given the American consumer and worker are more admirable in theory than practice. Rights are, in most states, extremely difficult to assert. The reality is a long way from ideal. Sometimes laws and rights are simply ignored. We told the inspiring story of the Chicago unions that obtained an order forcing the private gas company to replace the city's deteriorating pipes. However, the regulator resisted the unions' complaint for five years until a gas explosion killed four people and caused an uproar in the community.

Today, the biggest threat to the 100-year-old US system of regulation is the push by private power companies and the telephone industry to "deregulate" the industry, eliminate public hearings and replace the entire system with market structures. Right now, American states are in a political war over the question of whether market competition (through power pool bidding systems and individual choice for telephone services) can replace democratic regulation. (Water is not an issue in America – 85 per cent of the public is served by community water systems, according to the American Waterworks Association, and that number has been growing.) So far in the US, deregulation and market experiments have eroded consumer rights without providing offsetting benefits. Indeed, the experiment in deregulation of the California electricity market has led to disastrous increases in prices. We will take on this issue in Chapters 3, 12 and 13.

Finally, it should be understood that the United States is a federated system: most utility regulation is in the hands of distinct public regulatory commissions in each of the 50 states and territories, including separate commissions for the cities of New Orleans and Washington, DC. Although every state must operate under the same national democratic constitution, democracy means one thing in New York, another in Alaska. Therefore, all the figures we give for low prices are a national average. New York residents pay several times the cost per local telephone call that residents in Alaska are charged, and residents in Arkansas pay much less per kilowatt-hour of electricity than do residents in New Hampshire.

Nonetheless, we can conclude that America, for all its failings, provides a practical model to nations newly privatizing industry. The US experience proves that democracy and openness – social dialogue and transparency – produce lower prices, better service and more secure employment than the autocratic, secretive systems that predominate in Europe, Asia and Latin America.

3 Competition as Substitute for Regulation? Britain to California

The overwhelming majority of academic writers, theoreticians and regulators new to the field hope that they can avoid the complex and difficult work of setting prices by relying on market forces to put a reasonable lid on the prices of electricity, water and local network telephone services. In the real world, this has proven a costly fantasy. Britain was the first nation to attempt to control the price of power generation through an unregulated market, the Power Pool. The nation's new electricity regulator now concludes that, after a decade of attempting to leave pricing to the market:

> There is strong evidence that manipulation of Pool prices has in fact been occurring; that participants in the Pool have been operating within the existing Pool Rules to take advantage of those rules for their commercial interests – the 'gaming' of complex rules; that prices have been manipulated; and that higher wholesale prices have been established which will result in higher prices for customers.[1]

Indeed, Alfred E. Kahn, an economist at Cornell University and Chair of the New York State Public Service Commission in the mid-1970s, who helped oversee the creation of free markets in the rail, trucking and airline industries as well as the electricity industry, now says: "I am worried about the uniqueness of the electricity markets. I've always been uncertain about eliminating vertical integration . . . It may be one industry in which it works reasonably well."[2] He also said that although free markets do a better job managing rail, phone and airline prices, they have yet to match regulators' ability to juggle the complexities of electricity.[3]

From the first days of electricity privatization in 1991, oligopolists cornered and controlled bids in the England–Wales Power Pool. England's market is worth a closer look because, despite its rueful history, it has become the worldwide model for competition in the electricity generating market.

The theory behind the Power Pool, originally conceived by Professor Stephen Littlechild of Leeds University, is simple: every day, generating companies bid to supply power to the nation's grid system for each half hour of the following day. The lowest bidders supply the system. Dr.

Littlechild theorized that fierce competition between generating companies would slash the price of power; the only worry would be that generators would bid so low that they would not earn enough to stay in business. Markets, not the regulator, would set prices.

Monopoly in the England–Wales Power Pool

In 1991, Britain privatized its non-nuclear generating plant, floating two companies. Professor Littlechild, appointed Director-General of the Office of Electricity Regulation, instituted his Power Pool bidding system and soon found his market theories skewered by reality. The promise of low prices evaporated. Although world oil and gas prices plummeted, UK generating prices remained so far above the cost of production that the power companies literally did not know what to do with all their profits. In a single year, National Power paid dividends to stockholders that exceeded the entire initial flotation price of the company at privatization. Rather than compete against each other, the two biggest producers bid in lock-step and ended up winning an astronomical 85 per cent of all bids to supply the system.[4] His market competition method in tatters, the regulator did what he never dreamed he would do as an academic: he issued an order setting the average top price (at 2.4p per kilowatt-hour). The so-called "competitors" were adept at manipulating the bidding. While they stayed within their price cap agreement, the two companies created prices so volatile that buyers needing stable prices were forced to buy from the duopoly outside the Pool at premium prices.

The benefits of the windfall reaped by the duopoly were not shared with the workers. As power prices increased, employment at the plants fell drastically.

The professor-regulator, still hunting for a market solution to a market failure, forced the two biggest operators to divest half their power plants. Yet prices remain stubbornly high above cost. In the past year, according to OFFER's own investigation, "There is strong evidence that manipulation of Pool prices has in fact been occurring; that participants in the Pool have been operating within the existing rules to take advantage of those rules for their commercial interests – the 'gaming' of complex rules; that prices have been manipulated; and that higher wholesale prices have been established which will result in higher prices for customers. The occurrence of this manipulation has been accelerating."[5]

What went wrong in the England–Wales Power Pool system? Pious devotion to theories about market forces at first blinded the government to its obvious failings. There is nothing wrong with the concept of bidding or the use of price signals to help the process of regulation. Trouble comes when regulators are enticed into believing that competitive markets, where none exists in reality, can substitute for public control.

But the main error was not wrong theory but, once again, a deficit of democracy in the regulatory process. England's regulator ultimately came to realize that the large generating companies had far too much control of the market – but the regulator admitted that he was trapped into continuing the system by the peculiarities of British regulatory law. Under UK rules, *only the utility* could appeal the decision of the regulator to higher government authority, *Consumers and unions* had no right of appeal – they were locked out of the negotiations over market share.

Regulator Littlechild stated in January 1997 that he preferred to cut the oligopolists' share of the generating market to under 40 per cent.[6] The utility's threat to appeal, with no balance from the consumer or labor side, fed the regulator's fear of taking corrective action. This contrasts to the US, where any participant may appeal (although a utility generally initiates the action), and attorneys representing consumers may argue the opposite side – that the regulator is too lenient.

Crisis in California: electricity competition comes to America

In 1999, a revolution occurred in the American utility industry. That year, San Diego become the first major city in America whose retail electricity prices and supply would be controlled principally by market forces rather than be determined by the state's utility commission. A year later, retail prices in San Diego tripled.

When we began this book in 1999, America was one of the world's last hold-outs against "deregulation" of the utility marketplace. While there were many experiments and proposals to take apart the century-old system of American regulation, most US states continued to regulate electricity by the methods we have described here in which prices are set by the government after open and public meetings and debate.

But America is not immune from the forces of economic fashion sweeping the rest of the planet. Big industrial customers, multinational power companies and even some consumer and environmental organizations, pushed to replace the US system of cost-based regulation of electricity with variations of the market-pricing systems conceived in the

1980s which quickly became dominant worldwide, from Brazil to Britain. Several states participated in the debate over ending regulation of electricity and putting the system in the invisible hands of the marketplace. San Diego's citizens and industries became the laboratory rats in this market experiment.

When the California legislature passed the law to deregulate the electricity system in 1996, several claims were made for the superiority of markets over government and citizen control, principally:

- Prices would fall. Indeed, the California legislature wrote directly into the law its prediction that average electricity prices would fall by at least 20 per cent.
- The electricity industry would become more "efficient," and therefore provide lower cost, better service with more protection for the environment than the old regulatory system.

The results of the experiment were quickly known. In the second year of deregulation, electricity prices to San Diego residents and businesses *tripled* – at a time when prices in the rest of the US remained relatively unchanged. The price of power purchased by San Diego's electricity distribution company from unregulated power plant companies was, in the summer of 2000, 380 per cent higher than the year earlier, although demand was lower.

The advocates of deregulation claimed the San Diego disaster was just a one-time breakdown created by unexpected events during transition. Following this debacle in San Diego, California's government, power industry, some consumer advocates and their academic advisors devised several reforms, which they assured the public would prevent similar problems. Despite these elaborate preparations, the wholesale system collapsed, economically and physically. For the first time in decades, California suffered rolling blackouts, electricity shortages and voltage fluctuations. Prices did not fall by 20 per cent as predicted. Rather, prices paid to generating companies rose, in December 2000 and January 2001, by over 1,000 per cent compared to the prior year, causing the two biggest power distributors in the state to default on payments and face bankruptcy. One of them is in bankruptcy proceedings as we write.

Prior to the collapse of the system at the beginning of 2001, summer peak prices signaled impending problems. On average, wholesale prices (power sold by generators to distributors) were *seven times* the price at peak summer hours in 2000 compared to 1999 on equally hot days.[7] At some peak use hours, the deregulated price rose to *$1.40* per kilowatt-hour versus less than *4 cents* the year before. That is equivalent to the wholesale price of Coca-Cola rising from 25 cents a bottle to about $10 a bottle. Manufacturers shut down and what was the world's strongest economy faced ruin.

If there ever was a clear result of an economic experiment, this was it. Compared to the old, stable, low-cost regulated industry, markets had failed, disastrously. The Governor of California said: "California's deregulation scheme is a colossal and dangerous failure . . . It has resulted in skyrocketing prices, price gouging, and unreliable supply of electricity. In short, an energy nightmare."[8] Yet despite the results, the advocates of deregulation have continued to defend the marketization of electricity. And so powerful is the international acceptance of the superiority of markets over deregulation that even this governor of California has said that he prefers markets to regulation.

Once again, deregulation advocates claim that the high prices and blackouts in California were caused by unique, one-time conditions and failures in the transition program, which can be corrected. That is a claim they make after each disaster. After the pricing system in San Diego went wild in 2000, the industry and government claimed they had solved the problem. The fixes themselves added to the catastrophe of 2001. This is not surprising. The deregulated California electricity market is a variation of the British power pool model, which had already proven itself an incorrigible failure subject to seller manipulation.

Manipulation and monopoly abuse are impossible to prevent

For the last 20 years, it has become unpopular and unfashionable to say that regulation produces better results than market pricing. In part, this is because market advocates have had the advantage of comparing tempting but untested theoretical models of market electricity pricing to the awkward reality of regulation. Now as market pricing moves from theory to reality, the unrelieved disasters of price increases and supply problems can no longer be excused as transitional growing pains.

Consider some of the specific problems that produced the California debacle. California, like Britain, established a "power pool," an auction house for electricity. As in Britain, generating companies bid to supply power for a specific hour of the next day. The price for all bidders was determined by the price paid to the highest bidder whose power was taken. This was an attempt to replicate the market concept of setting prices at "marginal cost."

Almost immediately, the California Pool was "gamed" – the term used by traders to indicate the various types of manipulations and maneuvers used to distort a competitive marketplace. For example, in California, some of the big generating companies held back power from the next-day auction, causing panic and high prices the next day when utilities had to scour the spot market for supply.

Before California deregulated, the market advocates and their experts assured the public that California's power pool was designed to avoid problems encountered in Britain's power pool. Yet in operation, California's problems were worse than in the UK. The complex "fixes" to the market structure only created new opportunities for gaming by sophisticated power traders.

Never conceding the virtual impossibility of preventing manipulation of power markets, the systems operators are trying yet more technical reforms to trading procedures. The proposals are contradictory, frantic and do not succeed. At various times, the market experts have proposed barring hedging contracts, then encouraging hedging contracts; barring long-term contracts, then encouraging long-term contracts; banning bilateral sales agreements, then encouraging bilateral sales agreements; having one major bidding auction, then fragmenting the auction into several market segments.

So far, every fix has failed. Ultimately, all technical proposals to prevent monopoly abuse of power trading will fail because no change to trading systems can alter the fact that, at certain peak hours, on very hot or very cold days, or when a big power plant unexpectedly goes off-line, there simply may not be enough capacity to fulfill demand. In a free market, the sky's the limit on price: sellers know that the system *must* have electricity and therefore can charge what they wish. And they do. In California on a day in 1999 in which demand outstripped capacity, sellers raised their prices to $9,999.99 per megawatt-hour ($9.99 per kilowatt-hour). It could have been worse. California power buyers would have been bankrupted in a day, except that sellers wrongly believed the power pool computers could not read bids with more than six digits.

The only means left to California to stop prices from rising 100,000 per cent in a shortage hour has been the blunt instrument of a bid price cap. California imposed price caps of $1.00 per kilowatt-hour, later reduced to $0.25. But price caps in any market (unlike a regulated system) lead automatically to shortage. When caps were imposed, power sellers took their wares elsewhere, or withheld their product. As a result, California experienced both massive price hikes and power blackouts, combined.

Utility services are different

In trying to fix the problems of the electricity markets in California, as in Britain, failure is certain – because electricity services are fundamentally different from other products. In the real world, as opposed to a world of academic models, power markets are too easy to control, monopolize and manipulate. No set of rules has yet prevented wild price increases (and sometimes price collapse).

There are unique aspects of electricity, which tend toward monopoly. There are no good substitutes. Only one provider can efficiently distribute the service (i.e., there is only one electricity wire to most customers). Market entry barriers are high: capital investments in power plant require millions of dollars; a competitive distribution or transmission system would require billions of dollars to rewire a city and may, in fact, be physically impossible. Electricity is economically infeasible to store. Demand is notoriously unresponsive to price. Finally, given the limited number of sellers in any market segment, signaling for the purposes of price collusion is ludicrously easy.

Most of these factors tending toward monopoly are inherent in other utility services as well. Therefore water, sewerage, local phone services and natural gas distribution cannot be deregulated without the price hikes, service deterioration and destructive price volatility we have seen in electricity deregulation.

Even more importantly, electricity, water, sewerage, heating and basic communications are not like other goods. They have become essential to life and production. If the price of a bottle of Coca-Cola rose from $1 to $250, no one would buy it. But when the price of power rose in like manner in California, power use dropped by only a tiny fraction. Human beings and industry can do without a Coca-Cola, but cannot practically survive without electricity. We *need* this product.

In debates over creating markets in utility services, this basic element of economic theory has been forgotten: there is a difference between *need* and *demand*. Shortsighted economists tend to define an "efficient" price solely as one that "clears the market," where demand meets supply. However, what is "optimal" for theorists is not necessarily optimal for society. Society's goal is to provide water and electricity services *at a low cost* with *uniformly high quality* to *every person*, no matter their financial circumstance or physical location. What some economists call the "efficient" price may be much higher than society can tolerate, certainly more than every citizen can pay, and unnecessary to insure supply.

To illustrate: we write this in the midst of the latest California crisis. Market advocates claim that, to prevent further blackouts, the state should remove the last shreds of price controls on sales of electricity to homes and small businesses. That is, the state should let retail prices reflect the full price distributors pay to power speculators so industrial and residential customers will have the correct "price signals" and thereby radically reduce use. In theory, that may sound reasonable. In practice, that could mean electricity bills for homeowners of $1,000 a month (instead of less than $100), factory closings, economic depression and, for some of California's population, homelessness and starvation. That strikes us as too high a price to pay to save a market experiment.

"Deregulation" creates new rules and bureaucracies

One of the great ironies of "deregulation" is that it has caused an astonishing explosion of regulations and a massive expansion of government and corporate bureaucracies. Within a short few years, the number of rules and the number of rule-makers have hugely *expanded* in California as power pricing and supply is supposedly left to the markets.

This is not surprising – the same has occurred in Britain over the ten years of power market deregulation. Every new "game" created by the traders and power sellers requires government and purchasers to come up with new countermeasures to prevent price-fixing and system collapse. In the olden days of bureaucratic regulation, California had only a Public Utilities Commission (PUC). The "deregulated" system had the PUC plus an ISO (Independent System Operator), a PX (Power Pool), a Market Surveillance Committee and an alphabet soup of new agencies, committees and a whole new army of market police. Bureaucracy is bigger than ever.

While the free-market advocates once derided the rule-books and accounting requirements of the old regulatory regime, the new Power Pool spewed out hundreds of pages of technical specifications which changed radically month to month. Go to the web-site of the California Independent System Operator and watch the rules grow and mutate day by day. One randomly chosen page announces that the DMA (a new agency) will attempt to address "market power, gaming and market efficiency issues," by establishing new rules to prevent "Uninstructed Deviations . . . Intra-zonal Congestion," and myriad other market failures. We are assured that "[t]he DMA is also implementing provisions in the design of its FTR Market Monitoring System (MMS) to facilitate tracking of FTR concentration by affiliate groups as well as by Owner and SC, along with other

FTR market indices."[9] To translate: several committees are busy writing rules to prevent new games conceived by generating companies selling power to their own affiliated companies. These will replace old market rules, which failed to protect the public.

So, the "deregulated" market has more rules than the regulated system, but most disturbing, the rules are set in an anti-democratic manner, often in closed committees with information sealed away as "commercially confidential." The results, as in any undemocratic economic process, are predictable: arbitrary decisions and high prices.

The problem of volatility and new inefficiencies

As market pricing of electricity moves from academic journals to the real world, new and intractable problems arise, which theoreticians failed to predict.

There is the damaging new volatility in the marketplace. The huge increase in prices in California has tended to mask the fact that, while prices are often wildly high, sometimes prices plunge to ludicrously low levels. The problem with wild swings in prices, hour-to-hour, day-to-day and year-to-year, is threefold.

First, society – residents and businesses – cannot tolerate unpredictable and incoherent changes in prices. Price volatility hampers industrial production as much as high prices do. And families living paycheck-to-paycheck cannot budget for unpredictable swings in the price of essentials.

Second, extreme price volatility scares away new entrants into the generation market. What bank will lend money to a plant project which may earn huge profits but which stands some chance of selling its output for far less than cost?

Third, volatility increases risk and therefore raises utilities' financing costs. Under the old "regulatory bargain" in the US, utilities were virtually guaranteed recovery of their costs and in return could accept relatively low returns on capital. In California's "free" market, risk and the cost of capital for electricity companies have skyrocketed. Ultimately, the public will pay as investors demand higher returns.

Increasing volatility should come as no surprise: the British power pool experienced a similar increase in price variation, suggesting that increasing price swings are inherent in the change from regulated (or state-owned) systems to market pricing.

Attempting to let markets determine price and supply for electricity and other easily monopolized utility services such as water and sewerage also leads to investment inefficiencies. In an easily monopolized market, the incentives are towards strangling the market, not supplying the market. Generating power shortages becomes far more lucrative than generating more electricity.

In economic theory, such shortages will encourage others to build supply, leading to *surplus* capacity and falling prices. Thus, the theory *demands* the price volatility that consumers cannot tolerate. Shortages and high prices reduce demand and encourage new supply, which leads to surplus and low prices, which encourage consumption until new shortages lead to high prices, and the price cycle begins anew. This investment and pricing scheme may look efficient to a theoretical economist, but it is not efficient for those who depend on a stable and reasonably priced supply of electricity.

Some environmentalists hope the high prices will reduce harmful waste of resources and eliminate unnecessary power plant construction. But in California, we see a push to eliminate environmental rules for the purpose of creating new excess plant to keep down prices. And deregulation has given a new lease on life to the nuclear industry – something most environmentalists did not want nor predict. Indeed, California environmentalists are coming around to the position that "there is a crucial portfolio management function associated with electricity resources, which has many features of a classic natural monopoly . . . Without designated portfolio managers operating under incentives to promote long-term public interests, deregulation of wholesale electric markets is unlikely to succeed."[10]

The union worker, service quality and deregulation

Other than the poorest consumers, the group in society most at risk from deregulation is the utility industry's employees. Here, both business and residential customers share common interest with the workforce because deregulation's threat to employment is deregulation's threat to service quality.

Under the old, cost-based system, with utility wages passed on to consumers dollar-for-dollar, no more nor less, companies had little incentive to reduce wages or workforce. If anything, some critics complained that utility operations in the United States were "gold-plated" – operating at quality way beyond the standard of reason.

In states moving toward deregulation, and especially in California, that is no longer true. Electricity power pool auctions set prices regardless of cost. Utilities, which previously had an incentive to slightly over-invest in repair and maintenance, under market conditions, have every incentive to slash workforce and investment in maintenance.

It was considered quite strange that California prices soared highest in December and January, because the peak period of electricity use in that sunny state is in July and August. However, several big plants were off-line because maintenance had been deferred. Prices doubled and doubled again, showing a grave fault in the market for generation: when a plant goes down suddenly, prices soar. The incentive, therefore, is to cut repair costs. Crisis breeds profitability, whereas keeping plants in good repair only increases supply and reduces profits. This condition assumes operators have more than one plant – and indeed, the industry trend is toward massive concentration.

In August 2000, for example, plants that could produce 3,391 megawatts of capacity were out of service in California: a 461 per cent increase from the previous August. This contributed to the quadrupling of power prices as sellers bid into a power pool with a known shortage (a rise to $28 billion in revenues from $7 billion over the year before).

Under US regulation, utilities were rewarded financially for hiring employees for safety, reliability or environmental work. When markets rule, these expenditures become a cost burden for utility companies. Society, as well as employees, suffer. Unfortunately, some government functionaries and academics in the field equate "productivity" with output-per-worker, a misleading indicator of efficiency. In the first chapter, we described how England's water industry invested far less in system repair and upgrade than it collected in repair charges from customers. Rather than punish the companies for reducing their spending on personnel, the regulator praised the companies for increasing "productivity," i.e., output per worker. He seemed unable to grasp the relationship between this false increase in productivity and the 1996 crisis in which almost the entire nation was placed under hose pipe restrictions and Yorkshire nearly ran out of drinking water.

Turning over electricity pricing and supply to market forces exacerbates these quality, reliability and supply problems. Because a few large firms control the market, neither the loss of a plant's operation, nor voltage fluctuations, nor transmission overloads, nor failure to connect new customers in a timely manner results in an economic penalty to power firms. There are none of the usual market incentives which cause firms in competitive industries to insure quality and reliability. For example, a baker that constantly sells moldy bread will lose customers, but utility customers remain captives of power distribution companies whose voltage fluctuates; and no generator loses the right to bid into a power pool even if it has failed to provide power when it is required.

For this reason, regulators in the US, after open hearings, once set quality standards, and authorized or commanded levels of investments – authority that has been lost in the process of deregulation. Consumers suffer blackouts or other problems; workers lose steady employment; and utility firms that do invest in system repair suffer because they must compete with low-cost firms which cut back on safety, environmental and trade union protections.

Price discrimination

A key rule of US regulation has been that price tariffs may not discriminate among customer groups. Differences in prices must relate to differences in cost so that captive domestic and small business customers do not subsidize big, economically and politically powerful customers.

With the introduction of markets, those protections go out the window. While California was a disaster for *all* customers – commercial, industrial and residential – not all shared the pain equally. Large industrial customers were able to bargain for preferential contracts directly with power merchants.

In a world of perfect competition, each customer group, industrial or domestic would, in the long run, pay prices equal to the costs they impose. But electricity markets are neither perfect nor very competitive. Unlike domestic customers whose demand is relatively inflexible, large industrial customers have the means to respond more easily to price signals – many can take power from more than one source, produce their own power, shift production to other facilities elsewhere, or even shut a factory. As a result, power suppliers would tend to grant major discounts to these players, while charging captive domestic and small business customers higher sums.

Under US regulation, utilities must justify charges to each class of customer on the basis of verifiable costs. In reality, big customers still receive preferential treatment but, because the prices charged can be challenged on the basis of illegal cross-subsidy, the variation under regulation is not so great as we see under "market" price setting.

While our example focuses on electricity, we would expect to see these same problems of volatility, inefficiency, reduced employment and service quality, and price discrimination arise as markets are deregulated for water, natural gas distribution, sewerage and, in most cases, local telephone services.

Democratic control of deregulation

The electricity industry restructuring and deregulation debacle in California is an excellent illustration of how democracy drives utility oversight decisions in the United States. For, although electricity deregulation was disastrous for California, it was a disaster of the state's own choosing, through democratic means. And now, deregulation will be partly reversed, and consumers protected, through democratic means.

In most other nations, the decision to shift from regulation to markets or from government ownership to markets has been imposed by outside forces – the International Monetary Fund, the European Commission or other national and super-national agencies – without a vote of the people and generally after only the most cursory public debate. Not so in California. In 1998, two years after the democratically elected California legislature passed the restructuring law, the state held a referendum in which every citizen had the opportunity to vote whether to proceed with deregulation of the electricity system. The public, lured by the promise of low prices, voted for markets over regulation. (This grand illustration of democracy is, admittedly, tarnished by the fact that utility companies spent nearly $40 million on advertising to promote a "Yes" vote.)

The particular plan put to the vote was devised by years of public hearings, involving over 100 active parties, from consumer groups to environmental organizations to industrial groups. This is radically different from privatization/deregulation decisions made in Brazil, for example, where terms are imposed from central governments and international agencies.

One problem of democracy is that voters often get it wrong. They voted for a system promising price reductions and instead received price increases. Nevertheless, to woo the public to grant deregulation, power companies had to grant concessions and protections to the public in the deregulation agreement. The local power companies Southern California Edison (SCE), San Diego Gas & Electric (SDG&E), and Pacific Gas & Electric (PG&E) had to turn over to their customers all the profits made from the sale of their power plants to outside vendors. There were protections for utility workers[11] such as guaranteed retraining programs, funds for making homes more energy efficient and financial assistance for low-income families. Each group won some protections in the bargaining.

In addition, these California distribution companies had to agree to a price limit, or cap, which would last for several years for SCE and PG & E.[12] This last provision proved exceptionally valuable to the public and ruinous for the companies. It is true that power prices charged by generators have shot up, but still the caps have kept the charges per kilowatt-hour for domestic customers to no more than typical prices charged in Europe and South America. Because the distributors had to buy power at prices rising 700 per cent at peak, they swiftly incurred losses of over $12 billion, putting them at the risk of bankruptcy.

Compare this to the case of Rio Light in which the foreign operators simply passed on all higher costs to customers and continued to earn high profits as prices soared.

As we write, California is in the midst of correcting the deregulation disaster, with active public and worker input into every detail of the correction. (Notably, one of the utility regulators, Commissioner Carl Wood, is a former officer of the Utility Workers Union of America.) Even though the new market system closed access to some information previously available, nevertheless, government-required public financial filings quickly exposed profiteering by power generators (including those with financial ties to the distributors).[13]

Political pressure required correction of the California disaster, albeit in part because the politically powerful distribution companies, not just domestic consumers, faced financial devastation. California Governor Gray Davis, while a supporter of markets, nevertheless has called for the maximum possible reversal of deregulation and proposes partial state ownership of the electricity generating system.[14]

As we stated earlier, democracy does not guarantee an ideal result. Democracy got California *into* the deregulation mess, and democracy may get the state *out* of the mess. Proposals which will go to a vote of the legislature will probably be a complex combination taking into account the interests of customers, the power industry (distribution grid owners) and groups with special concerns such as environmentalists and advocates for the poor. Some changes may prove quite positive: government purchase or re-regulation of generating capacity; a huge increase in conservation funding; changes in the design of rates to encourage conservation; and assistance for low-income families unable to pay their bills. For the utilities, the state will purchase contracts, borrow funds on their behalf and require the public to pay off a portion of their losses over several years.

It must be noted that if the market experiment survives in California, it is only because the old regulatory tools of "command and control" came to the rescue. When California power distribution companies could no longer afford to purchase power from out-of-state plants, the Secretary of the US Department of Energy (DOE) *ordered* power plant owners to sell their output to California even if the utilities could not pay.[15] Furthermore, the Federal Energy Regulatory Commission (FERC)[16] abolished the day-ahead power pool (the "PX") and effectively barred some of the large speculative electricity traders from the marketplace, at least temporarily.[17]

Because of political pressure arising from the debacle in California, at this writing at least eight US states are backing away from prior plans to deregulate their electricity industries. Twenty-five states (half of America) are likely to stiffen their already existing resistance to deregulation and "restructuring" in light of the California experience. And only a handful of states are plunging full speed ahead – including Massachusetts, Texas, Ohio and Pennsylvania.

4   Re-regulation is not Deregulation

Recent history

In Chapter 3, we discussed some of the impacts of electricity industry restructuring in California and how those impacts are affecting restructuring efforts elsewhere in the US. The move to market pricing in telephone, electricity and natural gas services (but not water) arose from a number of factors coming together by the mid-1990s. From the 1930s through the 1960s, increasing economies of scale in electricity generation led to a series of price decreases; by 1970, average domestic prices in the US were 2.2 cents per kilowatt-hour and industrial prices were around a penny. Thus there was little attention paid to price regulation. This changed in the 1970s, when those economies disappeared and prices started to rise, particularly as a result of costly nuclear construction and oil price spikes.

In 1978, the US government passed the Public Utility Regulatory Policies Act (PURPA) which fostered competition in the electricity generation market by requiring utilities to purchase power from non-utility generators who could beat the utility's projected price for generation. PURPA stimulated the growth and development of new, more efficient generating technologies.

Domestic consumer advocacy was very effective during this period at shifting the lion's share of the price increases to industrial customers – domestic consumer prices tripled but industrial prices quintupled. The pendulum started swinging the other way during and beyond the years Ronald Reagan was President of the US, beginning in 1982, as industrial customers regained some of the ground they had lost to consumers. Still, in real (inflation-adjusted) terms, consumer prices resumed their fall. This trend has continued into the 1990s, with industrial prices fairly flat and consumer prices rising at less than the rate of inflation.

The largest industrials were not satisfied with this state of affairs, as they spied on the horizon a new generation of relatively inexpensive generating plants: gas-fired combined cycle generators (essentially, modified and very efficient jet engines). Having paid a large share of the cost of the last new generation technology – nuclear power – industrials set out to compensate themselves with the lion's share of the benefits of the next: combined cycle gas plants. To do this, they proposed being allowed to directly purchase power from these plants through their local utilities, leaving the more costly older generation for everyone else to pay for.

This plan almost succeeded. Utilities developed what were called "economic development" prices giving discounts to their largest customers, or signed individual contracts with customers who threatened to leave the system through self-generation or to move out of the service territory if they were not given favorable treatment. At the same time, domestic consumers and environmental advocates saw an opportunity to further their own goals. Discussions were held around the country to lay out principles under which the electricity industry should be restructured – but not deregulated.

Principles

The argument for competitive markets is that full and fair competition will lead to greater efficiencies and lower prices, with more and better choices for consumers. However, most states recognized that "full and fair" were terms used to describe an ideal, but not necessarily real, marketplace. They also knew that continuing regulation of the monopoly segments of the business was critical, as were rules to guide the transition from total regulation to mixed regulation and competition. As the regulator in Massachusetts put it in an order of inquiry into opening the generation market to competition: "The . . . overall goal . . . is the development of an efficient industry structure and regulatory framework that minimize long-term costs to consumers while maintaining the safety and reliability of electric services with minimum impact on the environment."[1]

Also in that order, the regulator set out principles for restructuring the electric industry which were to be followed over the next few years as the laws and rules were written. Most other states and the National Association of Regulatory Utility Commissioners (NARUC) adopted a similar set of principles to guide the restructuring of an industry that had been regulated for over a hundred years. Several principles from the Massachusetts order follow:

- Provide the broadest possible choice.
- Provide all customers with an opportunity to share in the benefits of increased competition.
- Ensure full and fair competition in generation markets.
- Functionally separate generation, transmission and distribution services.

- Meet public service obligations, including affordable service.
- Support and further the goals of environmental regulation and maintain energy conservation programs.
- Rely on incentive regulation where a fully competitive market cannot or does not yet exist.
- Honor existing commitments.
- Seek near-term rate relief.
- Ensure that the transition is orderly and expeditious, and minimizes customer confusion.

Restructuring the industry

The industrial proposals to purchase cheap power through their utilities evolved into broader statutes and regulations that, in some states, actually spun off electricity generation altogether from distribution utilities. As part of these restructuring laws, however, protections were put in place to prevent the largest industrials from cornering all the cheap power. One state, Connecticut, even limited the difference between industrial and domestic prices that would be allowed in the deregulated market without triggering a response from the Legislature. In other states, these protections included regulated prices for those who do not choose a competitive generation supplier, discounts for poor people, energy conservation programs, mandated investments in renewable energy resources, strict anti-slamming (changing someone's power supplier without their authorization) and other anti-fraud rules, licensing of sellers and power brokers, price and pollutant disclosure requirements and strict service quality standards. Sellers and brokers who violate the consumer protection rules are subject to sanctions, including the revocation of their license to do business in the state.

US electricity regulation occurs within a federal system. A federal agency, the Federal Energy Regulatory Commission (FERC), regulates generation and transmission sales to utilities (considered to be wholesale sales) while states regulate prices to customers (retail sales). Federal statute requires FERC to assure that the prices under its authority are "just and reasonable." In April 1996, the FERC issued a rule, Order 888, that opened the transmission system to all generators on a regulated, non-discriminatory basis.[2] Since the issuance of Order 888 and the restructuring of some state electricity markets, the FERC determined that competition, rather than its regulation, is adequate to provide just and reasonable generation prices to utilities, although it retained traditional cost-of-service regulation of transmission. Under FERC theory, competition in the wholesale markets would lead to efficient pricing.

Events in California, described in Chapters 3 and 13, have led many to question FERC's determination – and to several law suits, pending as this is written.[3]

The federal regulator thus does not set prices to consumers and cannot even determine the generation that utilities choose to distribute. State regulators choose among generation prices – prices that are set by the state if the generation is owned by an integrated distribution-and-generation utility, set (or allowed) by FERC if not. Other generation prices are set, outside this structure, by government owners of generation (such as public power authorities, which California is considering establishing).

Thus, restructuring in the US is *not* deregulation. Transmission and distribution remain regulated monopolies. The federal government must approve mergers and acquisitions between holding companies. Federal law still requires "just and reasonable" prices for generation under federal jurisdiction; indeed, refunds of prices charged in the "competitive" California marketplace are pending.[4] In addition to prices for sales to end-use customers by distribution utilities, state governments regulate system reliability, service quality and energy conservation programs. By opening the electricity generation industry to competition and encouraging market forces, restructuring may actually *increase* the use of other forms of government intervention (e.g., antitrust and anti-fraud actions). Thus, regulatory staffs are not shrinking; indeed, many consumer protection staffs are growing (and with good reason).

Market power

As utilities sell off their generators, a major concern is that a small number of owners may come to control a state or region's generation supply, as happened in the UK. This concentration of ownership of an essential good like electricity generation could lead to an abuse of horizontal market power, or the ability of one or a few market participants to influence prices to their own benefit (as was seen in California). The federal regulator has set out market power guidelines for its merger reviews, and delegated to regional independent system operators (ISOs) the job of policing price gaming in regional energy markets. This is an important area of regulatory policy that is still developing in the US. While the overall principle of maintaining robust competition is clearly established, the means for implementing the principle in this new market are still being invented.

To prevent the abuse of vertical market power – as regulated utilities use the cash obtained from forced generator sales to enter new, unregulated businesses – the need has arisen to police the relationship between regulated and unregulated subsidiaries of a common holding company. The same company can now own, for example, regulated gas and electric utilities and unregulated appliance service companies, cable television companies, or even tugboats. The danger comes from the incentive to divert the resources of regulated utilities with guaranteed revenues to the benefit of unregulated businesses. Codes of conduct have been developed to restrict this tendency. (See Appendix 2.) These rules require regulated and unregulated entities within a holding company to maintain separate books and accounts (subject to inspection by the regulator); they prohibit the sharing of resources (e.g., office space, employees) or information (including customer lists); they prohibit the bundling (tying) of regulated and unregulated products, and favorably pricing regulated services to the unregulated subsidiary. Companies that break the rules or abuse their power are subject to penalties from the regulator (although, as we have seen, it is very difficult for understaffed regulators to monitor uncompetitive behavior by sophisticated players in the market).

Market segmentation

For small customers, one of the dangers of competition is that markets tend to segment the population into smaller groups that are easier (and more lucrative) to sell their products or services to. Prices are set on the basis of what customers will pay, rather than cost, and smaller customers (with less buying clout) are often required to pay higher prices.

Before restructuring, utility prices were set according to "cost causation" principles; that is, the customer class or group that was the reason for certain expenditures being made was responsible for paying prices that would cover those expenditures. These principles, however, were balanced against other principles such as fairness, price impacts, economic development and social equity. (See the discussion of utility price-setting in Chapter 5.)

There was some cost justification for a difference between industrial and domestic prices. For instance, there are some economies in billing one large customer instead of many small ones. And some large customers do not use the distribution portion of the utility system. But as costs rose sharply in the 1970s, regulators adjusted the difference between industrial and domestic prices to reflect what they determined to be a fair allocation of costs. As costs leveled off in more recent years, industrial customers have persuaded regulators to restore a portion of their lost discount and thus shift a growing share of the nuclear debacle back to the shoulders of domestic consumers. At the same time, as noted, industry worked to keep for itself the economies of the truly cheaper new technology for electricity production, the gas-fired combined cycle generators.

Indeed, early experience with restructuring of other US utility industries has brought better deals for large utility customers at the expense of others, mirroring the market segmentation that occurs in many industries where price is unregulated. One early example of market segmentation after restructuring is in the natural gas industry. Since wholesale natural gas prices were deregulated in 1986, Massachusetts domestic prices increased 28 per cent while those for industrial customers stayed below 1986 levels in most years and never increased as much as domestic prices. Most other states experienced a similar pattern. Nationally, on average, domestic prices increased 15 per cent (through 1999) while industrial prices dropped 4 per cent.[5]

Proponents of restructuring often cite the airline industry as evidence of the wisdom of deregulation.[6] And, indeed, it is true that prices per mile (adjusted for inflation) fell 1.7 per cent per year between 1978, when US airline price regulation ended, and 1994. However, prices per mile before deregulation had been falling faster – 2.5 per cent per year. Not only did price declines diminish after deregulation, but also service quality was substantially degraded as deregulated airlines scheduled fewer non-stop destinations, reduced the amount of seating space per passenger (as well as other amenities, such as meals) and served 141 fewer outlying airports.[7] Airline deregulation has also been characterized by severe market segmentation. For example, while the general price level has been declining, prices at airports dominated by one or two airlines have risen by as much as 26 per cent since deregulation. Fares for Pittsburgh (90 per cent of enplanements by US Airways), are up 21 per cent; for Chattanooga (76 per cent Delta, 20 per cent US Airways), up 26 per cent.[8] Prices for other captive market segments, such as last-minute travelers (typically business travelers, but also anyone with a personal emergency), have also risen sharply.[9] Similarly, airlines segment their customers by selectively providing to some but not others free travel, fewer carry-on baggage restrictions and more space around their seats.[10]

"Competition" for domestic customers

Another point that must be made about "competition" in electricity, gas, water and telephone distribution: it is simply not possible. With few exceptions, every home and business on every continent has one single electric wire connecting to the premises, one company's telephone wire, one water pipe and one sewerage line (where service exists at all). The term "natural monopoly" is out of fashion – and, indeed, there is nothing "natural" about a state-granted exclusive franchise to distribute services – but these are monopolies pure and simple. Domestic and commercial consumers, except in rarest circumstance, are captives of the single company which owns the pipe or wires.

Some nations, and some American states (such as California, discussed above), have declared "competition" in electricity supply. Prior to declarations of competition, utilities purchased power from the lowest cost generator. "Competition" permits independent buying agents ("suppliers") and some large individual consumers to purchase power directly from generators. But the number of generators has not increased – in fact, there has been much consolidation in ownership of generating plants – so the generation market remains in England (and the world over) under the control of regional oligopolies. It is axiomatic that one cannot break the power of a monopoly seller by increasing the number of buyers.

There is nothing wrong with a monopoly in distribution services: it is the only efficient, reasonable means of delivering electricity, gas and water services. What is wrong with the Californian and English "competition" models is that they make a false promise to consumers: that there is a true choice in electricity companies. In some cases, statements by regulators get perilously near to perpetrating fraud on the consumer. In England, the regulator's public relations office promised reductions in domestic charges of 10 per cent per kilowatt-hour at the launch of this ersatz "competition." After one year, the regulator conducted an independent audit and found that "competitors" offered prices to new customers that were, at most, 2 per cent below the monopolist's former charges – and in one case, the charges *increased* by more than 5 per cent. Of 15 suppliers, one offered the 2 per cent savings, two offered the same price, and the rest offered a price increase (see Figure 3).[11] Not surprisingly, only 6 per cent of consumers switched suppliers.[12] This is not unlike the experience in Pennsylvania, where utility prices were held higher than regulation would (or should) have allowed, after which modest decreases by non-utility suppliers were hailed as a success of competition.

One explanation for the lack of savings in the UK is that the introduction of competition was itself costly: £726 million (more than $1 billion) for computer systems, regulator Littlechild told the Trade and Industry Committee of the House of Commons.[13]

Yorkshire Electricity Region - Economy 7 rate, timely payment

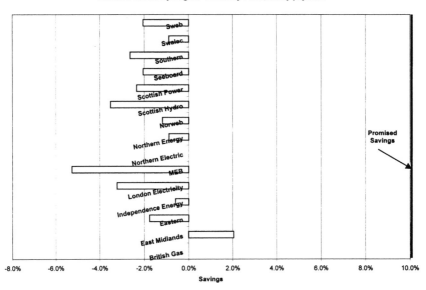

Figure 3   Press Release versus Actual Savings

The failure of electricity "competition" is no surprise. "Supply" accounts for 10 per cent of the total charge for electricity. It is not possible to cut prices by 10 per cent by reducing costs that total only 10 per cent of the bill.[14] The regulator seems to have confused markets with magic. The problem here is that regulators may be tempted to rely on fantasies of a chimerical free market to relieve themselves of the hard work of regulating prices. There is no such thing as a free lunch, no such thing as free electricity and, in utility distribution services, no such thing as a free market.

Telephones: the new marketplace is raising prices

After a century of traditional regulation of telephone service, the US has embarked on a partial-market experiment, which has produced dubious results to date. Cellular (mobile) telephones play Mozart, and the price of long distance calls (mostly used by business customers) has been cut by more than 50 per cent. But domestic local telephone service bills have increased by more than 50 per cent while complaints of fraud have mushroomed. In 13 years of deregulation of long-distance telephone service (1984–96), the price of local home telephone service jumped 52 per cent. For big business, long distance is the largest part of the bill, and those charges dropped at least 50 per cent.[15] Slamming and cramming have also become huge problems in the telephone industry – especially in low-income neighborhoods – and there is already some evidence that, without proper rules and vigilance, they will invade the competitive power markets as well. In a democratic environment, this may not be a sustainable change.

So-called "competition" has also driven up coin telephone prices to levels that are around double the amount telephone companies say it costs to provide the service.[16] Competition in the coin telephone business has only put extra money in the hands of location-owners, such as airports and all-night grocery stores, as telephone companies compete with each other – not to see who can provide the best and cheapest service, but for choice locations from which to exploit consumers with no effective choice at the moment they need to make a phone call.

Thus for business customers, who use mobile phones, fax machines and the internet, and who make many long distance calls, the new telephone regulatory regime has brought lower prices and new technologies – but at a cost to domestic customers of higher prices, considerable confusion and outright fraud.

Most domestic customers have very little need of long-distance service despite its sharply dropping prices. For 70 per cent of domestic customers, average monthly use of long-distance service is less than five minutes;[17] and a surprising number of households have no phone at home at all.

A home telephone is a social and economic necessity today to shop, look for a job, report an emergency or stay in touch with relatives thousands of miles away. (The US is about 3,000 miles wide.) Yet in some American low-income communities, more than one home in five has no telephone.[18] (Internet access is even more unevenly distributed, with about half of all homes on the internet as of 2000.[19]) The marketplace response to this failure is an entrepreneurial opportunity we call Phone Sharks – substandard service for almost triple the price, payable only in advance. For example, a telephone service offering that has so far been allowed in some states but not others charges $49.95 a month and provides no access to directory services, no access to long-distance services, no access to operator services, and violations of regulatory rules governing termination of service and other procedures. The standard service that is available to low-income customers from the regulated local telephone company provides all the missing services at a rate of $18 per month.[20] As a recent study for the National Regulatory Research Institute concluded:

Although it is irrational that a no-risk service could sustain a premium price for an extended period of time, that result is exactly what has

NOTE: Per minute rates and monthly fees include the percentage surcharge applied by each company for "universal service charge." We have not added the access (PICC) surcharge because we expect it to be eliminated.

SAMPLING OF RESIDENTIAL TELEPHONE RATES AS OF JULY 2000

COMPANY / FEATURED PLAN	One Star "Meridian A"		Qwest "5¢ Calling Plan" with online billing		Sprint "Nickel Night Anywhere"		VarTec "Fiveline Service"		Working Assets "7 Cent Round the Clock Plus"	
	Instate	Interstate	Instate	Interstate	Instate	Interstate	Instate	Interstate	Instate	Interstate
PER MINUTE RATE (including percentage-based surcharges)	8.4¢	7.4¢	12¢	5.34¢	10¢ day 5¢ night	10.84¢ day 5.42¢ night	5¢	5.25¢	10¢	7.41¢
Minimum	$3.00		None		None		50¢ per call		None	
Monthly Fee	$1.02*		$5.29*		$6.45*		None		$5.24	
CALLING CARD RATES										
- Rate Per Minute	13.9¢		49¢		59¢		19¢/minute + $1.95/month*		30¢	59¢
- Additional Charge Per Call			99¢		99¢				99¢	99¢
DIR. ASSIST. CHARGE PER CALL	$1.25		$1.40		$1.50		75¢	95¢	$1.40	

SAMPLE MONTHLY COSTS: Includes 50% instate/50% interstate minutes (50% peak, 50% off-peak) and monthly fees. Totals do not include directory assistance, calling card calls or international calls.

	One Star		Qwest		Sprint		VarTec		Working Assets	
LOW @ 10 mins. per month	$3.00		$6.16		$7.23		$1.00 to $5.12**		$6.11	
MEDIUM @ 100 mins. per month	$8.92		$13.96		$14.26		$5.12 to $51.23**		$13.95	
HIGH @ 500 mins. per month	$40.53		$48.65		$45.52		$25.61 to $256.13***		$48.77	
INTERNATIONAL RATES										
Canada	11.80¢		9.62¢		7.59¢	+ $5.95/mo.	5.25¢ (10 min. min)		7.41¢	
UK	10.73¢		10.69¢	+ $3/month	9.76¢	waived if usage	10.49¢ (1 min. min)		10.59¢	+ $2/month
France	16.10¢		17.10¢		16.26¢	over $30	12.59¢ (1 min. min.)		18.0¢	
Germany	15.02¢		17.10¢		16.26¢		12.59¢ (1 min. min.)		18.0¢	
UNIVERSAL SERVICE CHARGE (included in listed per-minute rate)	7.3%		6.85%		8.4%		4.9%		5.9%	
To Subscribe, Call:	1(800)482-0000		1(800)860-2255		1(800)746-3767		1(800)583-8811		1(800)788-8588	
ADDITIONAL DETAILS AND ALTERNATIVE PLANS	*No monthly fee if usage exceeds $50. Usage over $20/month gets 6-second billing. Totals do not reflect savings from 6-second billing.		*With credit card billing or online billing. Add $3/month for paper billing.		High-volume users should consider "Sprint 1000" plans: >1000 interstate night minutes - $20/month >1000 interstate weekend minutes - $20/month >1000 interstate anytime minutes - $40/month >1000 night instate and interstate - $30/month *For $8.95/month, Sprint offers 5¢/min. interstate at all times with 10¢/min. for instate calls or 5¢/min. nights & weekends instate and interstate.		*Higher calling card rates apply with no monthly fee. **Cost depends on average length of calls. Other more conventional rate plans also available.		Variety of other plans offered including "5¢ Evenings and Weekends" offering 5¢ off-peak, 10¢ peak for interstate calls and 12¢/min. for all instate calls. Promotion offers 60 free minutes for 6 months and pint of Ben & Jerry's per month for 12 months. 1% of phone charges donated to charities.	

Figure 4 Telephone Price Confusion (Source: *Ratewatchers Phone Guide*, State of Maine Public Advocate Office, July 2000.)

SAMPLING OF RESIDENTIAL TELEPHONE RATES AS OF JULY 2000

COMPANY / FEATURED PLAN	AT&T "One Rate 7¢ Plan" with 5¢ off/peak		Bell Atlantic "Pine Tree State Calling Plan"	Excel "Option B" / "Simply 7"		GTC TELECOM		MCI/WorldCom "5¢ Everyday Plus"	
	Instate	*Interstate*	*Instate Only****	*Instate*	*Interstate*	*Instate*	*Interstate*	*Instate*	*Interstate*
PER MINUTE RATE (including percentage-based surcharges)	8¢	7.6¢ peak 5.43¢ off-peak*	9¢	13¢	7¢	8¢*	5.3¢	.08¢	7.6¢ peak 5.42¢ off-peak
Minimum	None		$5.40*	None		None		None	
Monthly Fee	$5.38*		None	$6.15		None***		$5.36	
CALLING CARD RATES									
- Rate Per Minute	25¢		Regular rates of 5.5¢ to 45¢/minute depending on time and distance minus 25%	29¢	25¢	No Calling Card Service		55¢	69¢
- Additional Charge Per Call	25¢		58¢	89¢	75¢	Not Applicable		89¢	$1.25
DIR. ASSIST. CHARGE PER CALL	80¢	99¢	3 free - 40¢** each additional call	85¢	$1.60	85¢	85¢	90¢	$1.49

SAMPLE MONTHLY COSTS: Includes 50% instate/50% interstate minutes (50% peak, 50% off-peak) and monthly fees. Totals do not include directory assistance, calling card calls or international calls.

	AT&T	Bell Atlantic	Excel	GTC	MCI
LOW @ 10 mins. per month	$6.10	$5.40***	$7.15	$6.09	$6.09
MEDIUM @ 100 mins. per month	$12.63	$9.00	$16.15	$6.65	$12.61
HIGH @ 500 mins. per month	$41.67	$45.00	$56.15	$33.24	$41.61

INTERNATIONAL RATES	AT&T	Bell Atlantic	Excel	GTC	MCI
Canada	7.60¢	No International Rates	8¢	12.71¢***	7.58¢ (5¢ wkend)
UK	10.86¢ + $3/month		10¢ + $3/month +	13.77¢	10.83¢ (9¢ wkend) + $3/month
France	18.46¢		19¢ $1.20 USF	23.30¢	18.41¢ (9¢ wkend)
Germany	18.46¢		19¢	23.30¢	18.41¢ (9¢ wkend)

	AT&T	Bell Atlantic	Excel	GTC	MCI
UNIVERSAL SERVICE CHARGE (included in listed per-minute rate)	8.6%	None - no interstate service	$1.20/mon.	5.9%	8.3%
To Subscribe, Call:	1(800)222-0300	1(800)585-4466	1(800)875-9235	1(800)486-4030	1(800)444-3333

ADDITIONAL DETAILS AND ALTERNATIVE PLANS

AT&T: Low-volume customers using AT&T should consider the "Nineteen Sense Plan" (19¢/minute) with no monthly fee or minimum. High volume users should consider AT&T's "One-Rate 5¢ Plan" (8¢/minute instate) with a $7.95 monthly fee. *Monthly fees drop by $1 with on-line billing. **Must request 5¢ off-peak add-on.

Bell Atlantic: *Low volume customers should consider Sensible Minute Plan at 15¢ per minute with no monthly minimum. **National 411 directory service is 95¢ per call. ***Totals do not reflect monthly costs associated with an interstate plan which is also required by most customers.

Excel: Three Penny Plan offers 3¢ evenings and 10¢ daytime for interstate calls and 13¢ for all instate calls - monthly fee of $7.15.

GTC: *GTC has not filed this rate with the Maine PUC as of June 15, 2000. However, GTC assures us that this rate is in effect. **Add $1.95/month for paper billing. ***Lower rates available with $3/mo. international plan. Note 5¢ rate drops to 4.75¢ if you sign up online with www.onlinechoice.com

MCI: Other plans are available including "MCI One Savings II" - 15¢/min interstate Mon.-Sat., 5¢ interstate on Sunday, 8¢/min. off-peak instate (15¢ peak), no monthly fee and $5 minimum, and "5¢ Everyday Savings," - 5¢/min. all evenings and weekends interstate, (15¢/min. daytime) for $2.95/month, instate 6¢ off-peak, 15¢ peak with $5 minimum.

happened for at least two years. Apparently the convergence of disconnection rules and informational problems creates an opportunity for
resellers in the name of competition to price discriminate against low
income and transient populations who are desperate enough for
telephone service that they will pay extraordinary rates for substandard
service . . . Something is plainly wrong here . . .[21]

Another marketplace response is long-distance pricing at coin telephones,
where some sellers take advantage of the usual lack of disclosure of prices
and the fact that their customers are, at least for a moment, monopolized.
One extreme example of this is in prisons, where international calls are
often priced at as much as 14 times the standard rate.[22] The victims of this
joint government–private enterprise scam are the families of the prisoners,
since all calls are required to be "collect" (receiver pays).

While Phone Sharks and prison pay phones are nominally lawful, the
new marketplace has also spawned a mushrooming amount of outright
fraud. American consumers now take for granted the possibility that their
long-distance service may be reassigned without their consent. One
woman was told the change had been authorized by her husband, who
had died six years before.[23] There is even a name for the practice –
"slamming" – named for what consumers do with their telephone receiver
when their dinner is interrupted by an uninvited solicitation. Until the
Florida regulator stopped it, one seller signed up customers by naming itself
"I Don't Know" and enrolling all those who gave that answer to the
question: "What long-distance service do you want?"[24]

Another increasingly common practice, called "cramming," is adding
services to a utility bill even though they have not been ordered – such as
the internet service added to the telephone bill of a 72-year-old with no
computer.[25]

Even those domestic consumers who avoid fraud can be utterly confused
by the array of pricing schemes for the relatively simple service of long-
distance calling. Rather than lowering prices, much of the domestic
long-distance competition has focused on each telephone company
creating a unique pricing structure that cannot be compared to any other.
In order to make an intelligent choice of carriers, consumers must know in
advance how many calls they will make in a month, at what time of day
and over what distances. One well-meaning consumer advocate's effort to
sort out the confusing claims is the almost unreadable Figure 4.[26]

While it is too soon to predict the details of the remedies, it is unlikely
that US regulators will be permitted much longer to tolerate utility abuses

that are not allowed when practiced by used car dealers or door-to-door salesmen. Government commonly regulates to prevent consumer abuses,[27] in part because the resulting consumer trust benefits honest participants in the marketplace. Businesses honestly run are better off when the crooks competing against them are closed down. Indeed, Federal law specifically permits state regulators to "impose, on a competitively neutral basis . . . requirements necessary to preserve and advance universal service, protect the public safety and welfare, ensure the continued quality of telecommunications services and safeguard the rights of consumers."[28] Those requirements are likely to become the platform for the next round of regulatory challenges in the US telephone industry.

5   The Open Regulatory Process

The process

In contrast to the marketplace secrecy and manipulation described above, this chapter describes, step-by-step, the democratic process by which US public utility prices[1] are set under regulation. The vast majority of gas, electric and telephone customers are served by investor-owned utilities; they are not government-owned. (By contrast, almost all water and sewerage customers are served by government-owned utilities.) These investor-owned utilities do not set their own prices. They must first ask a regulator for permission. Usually, the utility does not get to set its prices as high as it asks. Sometimes, it receives no increase at all. To a casual observer, in many ways the process resembles a civil trial.

A utility unhappy with its current prices must put together for a regulator more than a list of the price increases it wants to impose. It must justify each price proposal, and the total amount of revenue it would generate. Sometimes the filing is the size of an encyclopedia. This filing is then picked apart in public by regulatory staff and anyone else with the time and interest to do so. The regulator's decision is equally public and must be explicitly based on this public debate.

A utility rate filing begins with proposed new prices and terms of conditions, contained in tariff sheets that must be open to the public at all utility offices, the offices of the regulator and often also at municipal buildings and libraries across the utility's service territory. The public rate filing also contains written sworn testimony of utility executives and experts that includes reams of cost accounts and studies.

Other filings may include fuel or power purchase contracts, conservation program descriptions, low-income price protections, service quality maintenance and improvement plans, environmental compliance plans, emergency preparedness plans, nuclear decommissioning fund studies, economic development program descriptions and details of transactions with affiliates, to which regulators pay particular attention (see Appendix 2).

Immediately after these filings, both the utility and the regulator notify the public of the opportunity to oppose the utility's proposal. The utility must publish large advertisements in major newspapers announcing its

Steps of a Price-Setting Case
1. Public filing by utility and deposit for review at designated locations.
2. Public notice of filing.
3. Notices of formal participation (petitions to intervene) filed by anyone affected.
4. Public hearing for statements by anyone.
5. Procedural meeting to set schedule and other matters.
6. Formal written questions to utility by all participants (discovery by parties); parties also conduct independent research and negotiation.
7. Filings by parties (e.g., expert testimony and counter-proposals).
8. Discovery by utility and other participants concerning filings by parties.
9. Public hearings for cross-examination by all participants of filings and discovery responses filed by utilities and all other participants.
10. Written briefs and reply briefs summarizing evidence and arguments and responding to others, filed by utility and all parties.
11. In some places, tentative decision or proposed order circulated by judge or commission, followed by another round of briefs and reply briefs.
12. Sometimes, oral argument.
13. Decision (order).
14. Post-order motions to clarify or reconsider (if any).
15. Filing by utility to comply with order; e.g., new tariff sheets.
16. Appeal (if any).

proposal. In addition, the regulator sends out notices to people likely to be interested, including city and town officials, legislators, people who have asked to be notified, and people who participated in recent cases involving the utility.

Anyone with an interest in the utility's prices or practices may then "intervene" to become part of the case that will determine future prices and practices. In some cases, as many as 70 organizations may formally participate. Broad economic interests such as domestic and industrial customers are usually represented by self-chosen advocacy organizations.

Particular interests often also participate, including environmentalists, advocates for poor people, proponents of particular technologies (such as renewable resources or nuclear power), stewards of economic development and representatives of labor. Representatives choose themselves – they are not chosen by the government (although, uniquely in the US, local and state government agencies may participate as adversaries in their roles as both customers and policy-makers, as well as representatives of their constituents' interests.) In some states, staff of the regulators are designated to intervene as a party as well. Many of these interests, such as industrial customers, can easily raise the funding they need to participate in utility rate cases. Sometimes even federal government agencies, such as the US Army, participate. Other interests, such as environmentalists, raise funds through public appeals and charitable foundations. Domestic consumers are usually represented by a state agency. Low-income advocacy groups are funded through governmental or charitable means.

In a few states, domestic consumers are represented also by a Citizens Utility Board, a self-supporting non-governmental organization (NGO) that receives its initial funding as a result of a direct mail solicitation of utility customers through their monthly bills. Other grass-roots NGOs support themselves by house-to-house soliciting for funds.

Soon after the utility's first filing, there is usually a public hearing before the regulator in the utility's service territory, not at the seat of government where later hearings are usually held. This is the chance for everyone to give their opinion about the utility and its proposal – customer or not, intervenor or not, in writing or not, sworn testimony or not. This is also where the regulator takes the utility's political temperature. The authors have represented groups that produce large, angry crowds that draw television news cameras to these public hearings. Such scenes are usually not cited in the regulator's written decision, but they remain a vivid memory each time the regulator makes a choice and thinks about returning to the next public hearing.

Then the investigation begins, again all in public. In a process called "discovery," regulatory staff probes details as tiny as how and when the utility decides to make a charitable contribution and as large as the choice of generator fuels. Every "intervenor" (public party) may do the same. Hundreds of questions are asked; thousands of documents are produced in response. In a general price-setting review, or rate case, all aspects of utility rates and operations are open to scrutiny. Utilities must answer citizen questions in writing and must answer them truthfully.[2] A price review covers such issues as the utility's rate of return on equity, accounting methods, cost of service, investments in plant and equipment, and documentation of all costs. In rate cases we have also delved into such issues as quality of service, fraudulent or unfair marketing practices, "redlining" (discrimination against racial or economic minorities), conservation investments, favored treatment of utility affiliates and discrimination against some customers in assessment of deposits before service is begun.

Consumers use the utility's own documents to challenge utility prices and practices. For example:

- By combing through internal company maintenance records obtained in discovery, one of us (for a consumer protection agency) learned of an unlawful shift of funds by a telephone company. When we secured a regulatory finding that "the [Telephone] Company has directed investment toward modernization of the network and away from maintenance of existing plant" in a low-income community, the regulator ordered that the Company restore service more than twice as quickly as the Company had proposed.[3]

- By analyzing internal telephone company records of service sales, we also learned of a strategy to target unsophisticated customers with extra, unneeded services. After our investigation showed that the company was selling proportionately two to three times more high-priced "Custom Calling" services in certain low-income neighborhoods than any place else, the utility agreed to limit its efforts to sell extra-cost optional services to such subscribers.[4]

- In other cases, we (on behalf of another consumer protection agency) successfully challenged the right of a company to compete in the utility marketplace at all because of its excessive, unreasonable prices. A company proposed a competitive local telephone service, charging about 2.5 times the price for sub-standard service, to be marketed primarily to low-income customers. The regulatory commission rejected the application.[5]

During the investigation stage of the price review, all costs are subject to scrutiny, whether or not they remain at issue later. Consumers and unions may demand that the utility produce internal documents. Consumers and other intervenors can ask questions about CEO salaries, travel and entertainment vouchers, favorite charities, executive perks, sweetheart deals, lobbying, advertising (a questionable need for a monopoly), credit and collection policies (including special treatment for elected politicians),

---

Seabrook Nuclear Power Plant

In one long-running battle involving several New England utilities, which owned the Seabrook Nuclear Power Plant, the utilities were seeking to raise prices to cover cost-overruns at the nuclear plant then under construction. Perhaps to dramatize the claimed need for the new unit, the utilities arranged their maintenance schedule one summer so that three of the largest generating plants were all off-line at the time of greatest demand for electricity. We learned of the maintenance scheduling chicanery by reviewing internal maintenance documents obtained in discovery. When one of us challenged the maintenance practice on behalf of the Attorney-General, the utilities were slapped with a regulatory finding that "operational planning and long-term capability planning are flawed, and that continued reliance on the process as currently designed could lead to unreliable service." The utilities changed their forecasting and maintenance scheduling in accordance with our recommendations.[6] The nuclear unit did ultimately come on line, but price increases denied by the regulator ultimately forced two of its owners into bankruptcy.[7]

---

training scripts, employment projections, geographical distribution of outages and maintenance investments. When questioning has revealed corporate yachts or jets,[8] wild parties in out-of-state resorts,[9] and sweetheart agreements with corporate executives,[10] regulators trimmed rates and ordered operational changes. When questioning revealed failure to abide by regulatory orders to make certain investments, regulators cut the utility's allowed profit.[11] When questioning revealed that the need for a $2.5 million plant repair was caused by utility laxness, the utility was not allowed to recover the cost in rates.[12]

A considerable amount of information is available to all members of the public even before the discovery process. Every US utility must file detailed annual reports with federal rate regulators (Federal Energy Regulatory Commission (FERC), Federal Communications Commission (FCC), Department of Energy's Energy Information Administration (DOE EIA)); state rate regulators and energy offices; the Securities and Exchange Commission (which also requires annual "proxy statements" with executive compensation and conflict of interest information); environmental regulators (Nuclear Regulatory Commission, the Federal Environmental Protection Agency, state environmental protection

```
FIFTH SET OF INFORMATION REQUESTS OF THE ATTORNEY GENERAL
WESTERN MASSACHUSETTS ELECTRIC COMPANY, D.P.U. 270
JANUARY 23, 1985
PAGE 2
```

Load Patterns

AG-5-5   Please provide system and class coincident demands,
          kwh sales and revenues for the last 10 years and
          forecasts thereof for the next 10 years. Please also
          provide this data for subclasses of large and small
          residential customers.

AG-5-6   Please provide monthly bill frequency analyses, for
          the last 12 months, in bands of 10 kwh or less,
          showing for each band the number and percentage of
          bills, current and proposed revenue, proposed revenue
          increase and cumulative totals thereof.

AG-5-7   Please provide a copy of the company's most recent
          appliance saturation survey.

AG-5-8   Please provide a copy of the company's most recent
          brochure or pamphlet listing typical consumption (in
          kwh and dollars per month) for common residential
          appliances and usages. Please state the source(s) of
          the data therein.

AG-5-9   Please provide your latest class load studies showing
          residential demand by usage strata, including strata
          contributions to peak and maximum diversified demand.
          Please include your data of hourly peak demand by
          class and residential stratum.

Customer Costs

AG-5-10   Please state the number of existing residential (a)
          meters and (b) services that the company replaces per
          year.

AG-5-11   Please state the number of new residential (a) meters
          and (b) services that the company adds per year.

AG-5-12   Please state the cost of a new residential (a) meter
          and (b) service.

AG-5-13   Please provide the decremental costs of service for
          residential customer costs (i.e., the costs that would
          be saved by the loss of a residential customer).

Figure 5   Discovery on Western Massachusetts Electric Company

agencies); and labor regulators (Occupational Safety and Health
Administration or OSHA). Much of this information is now on the World
Wide Web and all of it can also be obtained in discovery.

These public documents include:

• compensation of and inside dealing with high-level executives;

- amount invested in the utility, by category of investment (generating plant, transmission lines, supplies, etc.);
- profits;
- amount of pollution emitted, by pollutant; and
- hours of labor lost due to injury.

Additional public information is available from the files of public agencies under state and federal Freedom of Information Acts (FOIA).

After several months of poring over the utility's testimony, data tables and answers, intervening members of the public may file their own proposals for what utility prices and practices should be. These proposals can include expert testimony, analyses and supporting tables and studies. The utility is then given time to ask discovery questions of the intervenors regarding their proposals.

		BRIDGE STREET, NEW YORK		RFQ 8823 A
Invoice #	Scrap Vendor Truck			Amount
63720	Charged 47,750# X 7.25 CWT Correct to 47,750# X 6.50 CWT Check # 128522 dtd 5/1/89		Credit	$3,461.87 3,103.75 358.12
63772	Charged 25,640# X 7.25 Correct to 25,640# X 6.50 Check # 128522 dtd 5/1/89 *Minimum charge 30,000		Credit	$2,175.00 1,950.00 225.00
63689	Charged 44,8... Correct to 44,8... Check # 128522 dt...		Credit	$3,248.72 2,912.65 336.07
63787	Charged 38,100 X 7.2... Correct to 38,100 X 6.50 Check # 128109 dtd 4/26/89		Credit	$2,762.25 2,476.50 285.75
63261	Charged 30,000 X 7.25 CWT Correct to 30,000 X 6.50 CWT Check # 125021 dtd 3/17/89 *Minimum charge 30,000		Credit	$2,175.00 1,950.00 225.00

Figure 6 Discovery Response by NYNEX – Public Disclosure of Commercially Confidential Information

Name of Respondent	This Report Is:	Date of Report	Year of Report
Entergy Arkansas, Inc.	(1) [X]An Original (2) [ ]A Resubmission	(Mo, Da, Yr) 04/30/2000	Dec. 31, 1999

ELECTRIC OPERATION AND MAINTENANCE EXPENSES

If the amount for previous year is not derived from previously reported figures, explain in footnote.

Line No.	Account (a)	Amount for Current Year (b)	Amount for Previous Year (c)
1	1. POWER PRODUCTION EXPENSES		
2	A. Steam Power Generation		
3	Operation		
4	(500) Operation Supervision and Engineering	3,955,173	3,863,799
5	(501) Fuel	197,651,690	180,324,249
6	(502) Steam Expenses	3,125,735	2,430,319
7	(503) Steam from Other Sources		
8	(Less) (504) Steam Transferred-Cr.	-10,955	-35,785
9	(505) Electric Expenses	1,049,876	795,122
10	(506) Miscellaneous Steam Power Expenses	4,797,944	5,537,760
11	(507) Rents	4,619,963	4,543,823
12	(509) Allowances		
13	TOTAL Operation (Enter Total of Lines 4 thru 12)	215,211,336	197,530,857
14	Maintenance		
15	(510) Maintenance Supervision and Engineering	482,726	552,260
16	(511) Maintenance of Structures	835,970	471,699
17	(512) Maintenance of Boiler Plant	6,656,968	6,941,538
18	(513) Maintenance of Electric Plant	4,142,662	3,648,416
19	(514) Maintenance of Miscellaneous Steam Plant	992,997	1,248,957
20	TOTAL Maintenance (Enter Total of Lines 15 thru 19)	13,111,323	12,862,870
21	TOTAL Power Production Expenses-Steam Power (Entr Tot lines 13 & 20)	228,322,659	210,393,727
22	B. Nuclear Power Generation		
23	Operation		
24	(517) Operation Supervision and Engineering	13,367,527	11,922,954
25	(518) Fuel	68,672,817	69,345,986
26	(519) Coolants and Water	5,340,407	5,337,619
27	(520) Steam Expenses	22,656,331	16,194,352
28	(521) Steam from Other Sources		
29	(Less) (522) Steam Transferred-Cr.		
30	(523) Electric Expenses	·	
31	(524) Miscellaneous Nuclear Power Expenses	21,369,427	30,012,403
32	(525) Rents	2,012,400	1,875,642
33	TOTAL Operation (Enter Total of lines 24 thru 32)	133,418,909	134,688,956
34	Maintenance		
35	(528) Maintenance Supervision and Engineering	15,432,135	14,296,274
36	(529) Maintenance of Structures	10,361,358	8,356,639
37	(530) Maintenance of Reactor Plant Equipment	8,360,853	7,643,818
38	(531) Maintenance of Electric Plant	4,897,293	4,239,343
39	(532) Maintenance of Miscellaneous Nuclear Plant	48,446,740	47,067,444
40	TOTAL Maintenance (Enter Total of lines 35 thru 39)	87,498,379	81,603,518
41	TOTAL Power Production Expenses-Nuc. Power (Entr tot lines 33 & 40)	220,917,288	216,292,474
42	C. Hydraulic Power Generation		
43	Operation		
44	(535) Operation Supervision and Engineering	87,120	82,661
45	(536) Water for Power	232,785	252,756
46	(537) Hydraulic Expenses	97,126	131,461
47	(538) Electric Expenses	521,893	588,587
48	(539) Miscellaneous Hydraulic Power Generation Expenses	231,933	154,976
49	(540) Rents	4,641	5,647
50	TOTAL Operation (Enter Total of Lines 44 thru 49)	1,175,498	1,216,088

Figure 7   Page from Entergy Annual Report to FERC

Finally, everyone presents their case in public hearings conducted by a hearing officer, administrative law judge or a regulator. In ordinary civil or criminal trials, discovery precedes all testimony; witnesses give sworn, direct oral testimony at the trial and are cross-examined immediately thereafter. "Utility trials" elicit much more probing information by reversing the sequence. Direct testimony is filed first and in writing and must include the boxes of quantitative information described above; then detailed discovery is conducted for months on the written testimony; finally, the direct testimony is sworn and cross-examination takes place at trial. Every witness, including utility executives, is subject to sworn cross-examination not only by government, but also by members of the public. For example, a union official or union lawyer may ask detailed questions about employment programs; industrial customers may ask about complex

Page 108

[1] A: I'm sure I did. I reviewed the testimony that I filed
[2] in previous cases, and this is very similar to previous cases.
[3] I reviewed, of course, the – and prepared the pro forma
[4] financial statements that are attached, as well as all the other
[5] exhibits that were attached.
[6] Q: That were attached to the application?
[7] A: That's correct.
[8] Q: Did you review any other documents, though, for this
[9] testimony that was filed on August 11th?
[10] A: I don't recall. I'm sure I reviewed documents, but if
[11] you have a specific document, I can tell you whether I reviewed
[12] it or not, but I don't –
[13] Q: For example, on Page 7 of your prefiled testimony, you
[14] have a citation there to Section 253(a) of the
[15] Telecommunications Act of '96.
[16] MR. HART: Could you –
[17] MR. ETTER: Page 7.
[18] THE WITNESS: Page 7.
[19]   BY MR. ETTER:
[20] Q: Yes. It's starting on Line 4 going through Line 6.
[21] Did you review the Telecom Act of '96 before filing
[22] this testimony?
[23] A: Not in relation to this testimony, but I've read the
[24] Telecommunications Act several times, yes.
[25] Q: Okay. And did you read Section 253(a)?

Page 109

[1] A: Yes.
[2] Q: How about Section 253(b), did you read that section
[3] before filing this testimony?
[4] A: I read the complete Act, but if you'll tell me the –
[5] if you'll quote those sections, I can tell you whether I
[6] remember specifically what they say or not.
[7] MR. ETTER: May I approach the witness, your Honor?
[8] THE EXAMINER: Yes.
[9] MR. ETTER: I'm not sure if we need to mark this as an
[10] exhibit since it is a public document.
[11] THE EXAMINER: What is it?
[12] MR. ETTER: It's a – It's Section 253, or at least a
[13] portion thereof, of the Telecommunications Act.
[14] THE EXAMINER: If you want to mark it, that's fine.
[15] MR. ETTER: Yeah. We can mark this then as OCC
[16] Exhibit 5, I believe.
[17]
[18] Thereupon, OCC Exhibit No. 5 was marked
[19] for purposes of identification.
[20]
[21]   BY MR. ETTER:
[22] Q: Now, is that the same Section 253 that you reviewed
[23] prior to filing your testimony?
[24] A: Yes, it appears to be.
[25] Q: Okay. And Section 253(a) states that, "No State or

Page 110

[1] local statute or regulation, or other State or local legal
[2] requirement, may prohibit or have the effect of prohibiting the
[3] ability of any entity to provide any interstate or intrastate
[4] telecommunications service"; is that right?
[5] A: Yes.
[6] Q: Did you read Section 253(b) prior to filing your
[7] testimony?
[8] A: Yes.
[9] Q: And you have it there in front of you.
[10] Does it not state that – Well, quoting this, "(b)
[11] State Regulatory Authority. Nothing in this section shall
[12] affect the ability of a State to impose, on a competitive
[13] neutral – competitively neutral basis and consistent with
[14] Section 254, requirements necessary to preserve and advance
[15] universal service, protect the public safety and welfare, ensure
[16] the continued quality of telecommunications services, and
[17] safeguard the rights of consumers". Is that not what it says?
[18] A: That's what it says.
[19] Q: Okay. So are you a lawyer, sir?
[20] A: No, I'm not.
[21] Q: So in your opinion, as a nonlawyer, what does
[22] Section 253(b) allow state governments or state regulatory
[23] agencies to do?
[24] MR. HART: I would object, your Honor. He's not a
[25] lawyer.

Page 111

[1] MR. ETTER: Well, I'm not asking for a legal opinion.
[2] MR. HART: Opinion of a nonlawyer as to a statute is
[3] improper.
[4] MR. ETTER: But, your Honor, he brought in
[5] Section 253(a) and gave an opinion about that, at least cited to
[6] it, and so – and he has read the Telecom Act, so his opinion as
[7] to what Section 253(b) would be is just as valid as a nonlawyer.
[8] THE EXAMINER: All right. I'll let him answer the
[9] question.
[10] THE WITNESS: In my opinion, what does it say?
[11]   BY MR. ETTER:
[12] Q: Yeah. In your opinion, what would it allow state
[13] regulatory bodies to do?
[14] A: It allows a public regulatory authority to, on a – on
[15] a competitively neutral basis, which means treat all CLECs, or
[16] ALECs, or incumbent LECs the same, on a neutral basis,
[17] consistent with Section 254.
[18] I don't know what Section 254 is without you handing
[19] it to me, but assuming that it's consistent with 254, the state
[20] regulatory authority can set requirements necessary to advance
[21] and preserve the universal service, protect the public safety
[22] and welfare, ensure the continued – continued quality of
[23] telecommunications services, and safeguard the rights of
[24] consumers.
[25] You want me to tell you what that means? I mean, I

Figure 8   Cross-Examination of Telephone Company CEO

accounting practices. In one controversial case, cross-examination took weeks and the transcript ran to over 1,000 pages. Time is set aside for all to be heard. Anyone can testify.

Often, the utility loses. Experts for the other parties (consumer groups, industrial customers, unions, local governments) often prevail. Regulators almost never give utilities the amount of profit their experts say they need.[13] After an expert one of us sponsored on behalf of residential consumers testified that cheaper investments in power plants had been available, the regulator in Massachusetts decided that some of the investment in the aptly named Millstone 3 nuclear power plant was not economically useful and denied Western Massachusetts Electric Company a profit on it.[14] In a case involving New England Telephone, a consumer group's expert (sponsored by one of the authors), in combing through the Company's "cost studies," found that some claimed expenses had been counted twice. Largely because of this discovery, the regulator denied the Company's petition to increase the pay telephone rate.[15] In another case, cost recovery for expense was disallowed when wages were claimed to have been paid, but employees had actually not been working because of a strike (presented by one of the authors, sponsored by a citizens' group). In yet another case, the regulator denied recovery of a portion of the investment in a nuclear power plant that was in excess of what a less costly available alternative would have cost (also proven by a citizens' group).[16]

Non-expert and even unsworn opinion is also given credence in such areas as the effect of a price increase on society, service quality and fraudulent marketing. In a case involving Illinois Bell Telephone Company, one of us challenged the Company's practice of denying credit to a customer (a member of a racial minority) who had already qualified for an American Express credit card. We sponsored the testimony of that consumer. This demonstration that the Company's policy imposed a hardship on minority customers was enough, with an expert analysis of racial patterns, for the Illinois regulator to abolish domestic deposit requirements statewide because they were discriminatory.[17] In another case, a local fireman who was worried about water pressure for fire fighting, together with one of the authors, used discovery to uncover the fact that there was not enough water available to support operation of a utility's planned new power plant. The building and siting application process was halted.[18]

Every party can file a legal brief summarizing their positions and the facts that support them. Usually, there is opportunity for Reply. Sometimes there is Oral Argument before the regulators. Once the hearing, or trial, phase is over, the regulator issues a decision on the utility's petition.

The regulator's final decision – called the "order" in some states – is limited by what appears on the public record.[19] The order must recite the facts on which it is based and is subject to appeal to the courts by any intervenor. In addition, if a utility or one intervenor appeals, all other intervenors may participate or cross-appeal. There is a strong tendency by the courts to defer to regulators, especially on factual matters, because of their expertise in technical matters such as utility price-setting.[20] However, any anti-utility impulses are held in check by the US Constitution's pro-hibition on arbitrary confiscation of utility property.[21] Nevertheless, appeals of regulator decisions by non-utilities can prevail. For example, large utility price increases to pay for nuclear power plants to serve Chicago and New Orleans were overturned by citizen appeals. In the Chicago case, the court found that the regulator's finding that certain investments were prudent could not be justified from the public record. In New Orleans, the regulator had found imprudence but awarded an increase to prevent insolvency; the court rejected that objective as the basis for a price increase and consumers received a refund of several million dollars.[22]

Principles

Five essential principles guide utility price-setting in the United States:[23]

1. Rights of transparency and participation, or "due process," must be observed. (This is the principle that guarantees application of all of the others.)
2. All prices must be "just and reasonable."
3. Investments by utilities must not be arbitrarily confiscated.
4. Conflicting interests must be balanced against each other.
5. Prices must be related to costs.

1. Transparency and participation

The word "transparency" in this context means "no secrets." In the US, utility prices are set in a glass bowl. Anyone with an interest in utility prices can join the process. This includes all customers – domestic and industrial alike – as well as those with particular agendas, such as protection of the environment, protection of poor people, development of the economy and advancement of labor. Upon joining the price-setting process, a party can obtain from the utility any scrap of information that pertains to its interest. Parties dig deep into the utility bureaucracy and uncover such internal corporate documents as construction plans and their economic justification, reports showing how utility performance varies between rich and poor neighborhoods, and employee safety records.

Each party is allowed to place the facts it has learned on the public record. Cross-examination of utility executives under oath is conducted in public. Statutes setting out rules of administrative procedure[24] and the US Constitution's written guarantee of due process under the law[25] ensure that the factual and legal rationale of every decision is out in the open and that every participant has an opportunity to ask questions of utility executives under oath and an opportunity to present his or her facts. The regulator's decision cannot be "arbitrary" or "capricious," but rather it must square with the facts on the public record, must be explained sufficiently well for a court to review it, and may then in fact be reviewed by a court for consistency with the facts as well as with the other principles outlined here.

2. Just and reasonable prices

Virtually every regulatory statute requires that prices (rates or tariffs) and practices be "just and reasonable."[26] Indeed, part of the point of utility regulation is to keep prices low by keeping the cost of capital (i.e., profits to investors) low by minimizing risks to those investors, which is done by assuring recovery of prudently and reasonably incurred expenses. This is known as the "regulatory bargain."

Prices must not only be reasonable, they must be just. Justice permits social rates that are discounted to make it possible for poor families to more easily afford utility service. Indeed, the goal of reaching every home – rich and poor – with a telephone line is written into the federal communications regulatory statute.[27] Similarly, justice requires procedural protections before service is terminated, such as a notice sent a specified number of days in advance. Typically, service cannot be terminated at a time that does not permit payment to restore service within a few hours (such as when utility offices are closed).

Although prices are set on the basis of costs actually expended, those costs are examined to be sure they are reasonable.[28] More than once, multi-billion-dollar investments in unnecessarily expensive nuclear power plants have been denied recovery through electric utility prices because they were not necessary, economic, or prudent.[29] In New York, for example, the Long Island Lighting Company (LILCo) was denied recovery of imprudent expenditure on a nuclear plant. Company shareholders bore this $1.7 billion loss; consumers paid the balance of the plant's cost.[30] In every rate examination, the level of profit to investors is reviewed and held to a level deemed reasonable given the low levels of risk assumed by utility investors. As this is written, for example, allowed nominal rates of return on utility equity are in the range 9.56–12.25 per cent per annum[31] (about 6.5–9.25 per cent in real terms).

3. No arbitrary confiscation

Utilities do have one giant advantage in the price-setting process. In exchange for submitting their investments to scrutiny and a limited profit, utility investors are promised that they will have the opportunity (but not a guarantee) to earn a reasonable rate of return on investments prudently made in the public service.[32] This is a specialized application of the more general rule written into the US Constitution that no property can be taken from its owner without due process of law. It is not, however, a protection against bankruptcy resulting from improvident decisions, as shareholders in Public Service of New Hampshire discovered when their utility was forced into bankruptcy. The utility had invested billions more dollars in the Seabrook nuclear power plant than the plant could ever return in the value of electricity generation.[33]

4. Balancing conflicting interests

Seabrook is a good example of the principle that regulatory orders must balance the interests of utility consumers with those of utility investors.[34] Among the competing interests are social equity, environmental protection and labor issues. It is typical to have several governmental agencies that have varying concerns: environmental; consumer protection; economic development; municipal services; and energy policy, to name a few. Those interests that participate in the formal process are delineated in the regulators' decisions. In the US, domestic and industrial customer classes are usually represented in price-setting cases and therefore often fare better in decisions than do small business customers, who are typically poorly organized and unrepresented at hearings.

Utility investors are on the other end of the balancing seesaw. What they are guaranteed is not any particular profit, or even any profit at all, but rather the *opportunity* to earn a reasonable rate of return on the capital they prudently and usefully devote to public service.

Thus it is that a utility such as Seabrook's principal owner, Public Service of New Hampshire, whose investors devoted substantially more than was prudent or economic, assumed the risk of losing their investment in the regulatory balancing between shareholders and ratepayers.

5. Prices related to costs

Under US regulation, prices are based on cost.[35] Thus total revenues are designed to meet, but not exceed, total costs. (Costs in this context include the cost of invested capital, i.e., bond interest and fair profit to equity shareholders.) Indeed, regulators and customer advocates scrutinize the annual reports of utilities and begin investigations designed to reduce prices where earnings are meaningfully above authorized levels.

For example, the utility may charge prices that recover documented wages paid for the year: no more and no less. Utilities across the US are required to post all expenses in a Uniform System of Accounts (a document of several hundred pages), which must be made available for review by the regulators and the public in a price-setting case. Costs that are allowed to be included when prices are set must be spent on the agreed project or other expense, or prices will be cut during the next review. A review can be required by the regulators or requested by the public or the utility as soon as it becomes known that prices do not match costs.

Thus, there is a three-stage mechanism to ensure that funds collected from the public match expenditures by the utility – forecast, monitor and adjust:

- a detailed public advance review of proposed expenditures;
- a detailed public accounting of all expenditures and investments as incurred, in accordance with a Uniform System of Accounts; and
- when prices and costs do not match, reset prices.

Expenditures such as wages and fuel are recovered dollar-for-dollar in the year incurred. Investments in new plant and equipment are also recovered at cost, not more nor less. The value of plant and equipment in the companies' account books is not adjusted for "replacement value" nor adjusted for inflation; that is, the accounts remain at actual cost: they are not changed to reflect what is sometimes termed "economic" value.

In setting prices, regulators also make a crucial distinction between current expenditures (such as wages and fuel) and spending on plant and equipment that last longer than a year, such as water pipes. Such plant expenditures must be depreciated over the useful life of the item. For example, if a transmission tower is expected to last 20 years, then only 1/20th of the tower's cost may be charged in a single year, as a depreciation expense.

"Useful-life depreciation" keeps down prices. A utility cannot charge customers for plant and equipment investments until they go into service.

For example, a new water treatment plant cannot be charged to the public until it is in operation.

The price formula is as follows:

(Plant investment × profit rate) + current expenses = annual revenue allowed

Plant investment, often called "rate base," equals the cost of the plant minus previous charges to customers for depreciation.

Profit rate, often called "rate of return," is the amount the regulator has decided is a fair profit for investors. Determining a reasonable rate of return is more art than science and is therefore highly subjective. However, there is a basic rule: rate of return must be related to risk.

Current expense includes interest, the current year's depreciation and all other out-of-pocket expenses such as wages that are allowed by the regulator.

The great benefit of regulating prices by the price formula above is that, by effectively guaranteeing the opportunity to earn a certain and consistent level of profit, risk (and therefore the rate of return) can be kept relatively low.

In principle, this rate of return computation is based on the same factors as performance-based rate-making (PBR) (RPI-X) and results in the same set of rates. Indeed, a PBR review requires a cost-of-service review as a starting point. The main difference is that the PBR method allows utilities to maintain rate levels while pocketing the "savings" from cuts in service levels and investment from those that were projected to the regulator. In practice, both methods depend heavily on regulator expertise to ferret out phantom expenses from real ones. (See Appendix 1.)

The price formula determines the total revenues a company will receive during a year. The next step is to divide this total amount among customer groups – domestic, commercial and industrial customers. There are other divisions within these groups, principally dividing large and small users in each category.

Once again, cost is the primary determinant. This is the focus of much debate as the different customer groups battle (in public) about responsibility for costs; for example, who should pay for a new power plant. While cost may be the primary determinant of cost allocation among customer groups, it is modified by other social and economic concerns such as price impact, customer retention, economic development and social equity. Regarding social equity, poor people's organizations have successfully argued in favor of price discounts for low energy use, often called "Lifeline rates," or reduced standing charges. (More on this in Chapter 6.) Some rates have been limited by a concern for the impact on area employment, requiring a "phase-in" of price increases over time.

The regulators

The regulators that strike these balances and set prices are commissions that are appointed or elected in each of the 50 states. Usually they consist of panels of three to five members. With more than one regulator to set and implement policies, multiple points of view are aired, and more balanced and reasoned decisions are possible. However, whether appointed or elected, regulators are subject to the political system in various ways. How directly regulators respond to political initiatives is a function of many factors, including:

- the nature of the administration that appointed them or the political culture of the electorate;
- the dominant political party at the moment;
- individual personalities and philosophies;
- legislative attention;
- the quality of intervention;
- economic factors; and
- utility leadership and culture.

Thus, from the point of view of each interested party, there have been terrific and horrible examples of both appointed and elected regulatory panels.

While most electricity, natural gas, and telephone customers in the US are served by investor-owned utilities (IOUs), many are served by cooperatives, municipal and publicly owned systems.[36] For example, the city of Los Angeles is served by a municipal electric and water system. Government and cooperative systems are responsible for 26 per cent of electricity generation, including a large fraction of hydro generation, and 85 per cent of water customers.[37]

The US system of regulation of IOUs is substantially decentralized. For example, state regulators set the price to final customers for natural gas, electricity and local telephone service. The national regulators, the Federal Energy Regulatory Commission (FERC) and the Federal Communications

Commission (FCC), regulate wholesale energy prices and long-distance telephone prices, respectively. State commissions tend to be more responsive to public pressures because they are geographically and politically closer to the people.

State or federal, elected or appointed, what all US utility regulators have in common is that their decisions, and all the facts on which they base their decisions, are transparent to all and open to binding challenge by any.

6 Social Pricing

One of the most difficult burdens faced by poor people everywhere is income that is inadequate to cover all basic necessities. Even in the US, every day, poor people must choose between heating their houses and feeding their children, between electricity and medicine, even with relatively low regulated prices. One reason for this income gap is the fraction of income demanded by modern utility bills.

US regulation requires universal, reliable service at affordable prices. There is a recognition that utility services are basic necessities, and that poor customers are rightfully entitled to these necessities, despite their lack of market power. This policy recognizes also that benefits accrue to all customers and to society as a whole when the poorest members of society have access to affordable utilities.

Social rate-making in the US goes back over 100 years.[1] This traditional concept stems from the principle that public utilities provide benefits in many ways to their customers and to the community at large. Many of these benefits are not transparent or explicitly accounted for, but their costs are embedded in prices and all customers support them, even though they may directly benefit some customers more than others. Such benefits include community relations and economic development services traditionally provided by utilities to the communities they serve. The general principle is that everyone on the system benefits in some ways; thus, everyone contributes to the costs.

For at least the last 20 years US utilities have, for example, adopted policies and programs to promote energy efficiency for low-income customers and others; to support research and development on reliability, efficiency and environmental benefits; and to provide payment assistance to poor people for whom the energy burden is high. In some instances, payments are made to specific funds for a program administered outside the utility. Often, the fund appears as an accounting entry or is simply rolled into prices.

Another example is average-cost rate-making for distribution services. High costs of additions to the distribution system in suburban or rural areas (where new lines or substations must be built) are paid for by all, including residents and businesses in older, urban areas. This concept is fundamental to traditional regulation of monopoly utility services: everyone pays because everyone ultimately benefits.

There is no single US model of assistance to poor consumers; rather, each state has adopted assistance programs that meet its particular circumstances. However, while the details vary considerably from state to state, there are four broad categories of programs that regulators have mandated as part of the regulatory hearing process.

Affordability programs

Affordability programs provide direct assistance in paying utility bills.[2] A benchmark often referred to, if not relied on exclusively, is that the fraction of income a low-income household must devote to its utility bills (energy burden) should not exceed twice that of the median-income household. This is related to the UK concept of fuel poverty.[3]

Generally, assistance is either a fixed dollar amount or a fixed percentage of the bill. The cost to fund this assistance is added to other customers' bills as a cost of service. For example, in Massachusetts, "Lifeline" rates for poor people for local telephone service are $1.39 a month (plus usage), while average local service costs $15.24. Installation of a new line costs $19.47, half the usual $38.92. Many programs include a component which reduces unpaid balances if timely payments are made on new, discounted bills. In some programs, benefits are targeted depending on income, giving the greatest help to the poorest of the poor. In others, benefits are targeted according to special needs such as a physical or mental disability.

Affordability programs have resulted in discounts ranging from 7 to 40 per cent, depending on the state and utility company (e.g., California provides a 20 per cent discount on electricity prices; Massachusetts discounts range up to 40 per cent for natural gas). One way some states have structured the discount is to waive the tax on energy, which is by nature a fixed per cent of the bill. In a small number of states, the discounts apply only during the costliest part of the year (e.g., West Virginia provides a 20 per cent discount in the winter months).

Other states provide a fixed dollar discount, most typically by waiving the standing, or customer, charge for low-income customers (e.g., Alabama, $7.65 per month; Mississippi, $8.65). Others provide a fixed credit amount that has been determined in a price-setting case to be sufficient to the state's purposes (e.g., New Jersey, up to $18.75 per month).

A percentage discount may also vary with a customer's usage, as in the original California Lifeline rate. This could take the form of a discount that applies only to a lifeline block – i.e., the minimum amount of electricity deemed to be necessary to sustain life in today's society. Usage beyond this amount is priced at the regular residential rate. Thus, for example, usage up to 500 kilowatt-hours (kWh) per month in Minnesota is discounted 50 per cent. In the District of Columbia, a 28 per cent discount is applied to the first 400 kWh per month. Alternatively, the discount could decline, but still exist, as usage increases. Thus in Arizona the discount is 30 per cent for usage at or below 400 kWh per month, 20 per cent on usage between 401 and 800 kWh, 10 per cent on usage between 801 and 1,200 kWh, and there is a $10 credit for higher usage.

Fixed per centage and fixed dollar discounts are simple for the utility to administer and for customers to understand. On the other hand, a discount that varies with usage is preferred by some because it encourages conservation – or at least does not encourage consumption. However, these effects are probably very small, if not zero, because low-income consumers have so little income relative to their needs that decreasing the price of one necessity tends to result in larger consumption of another scarce necessity rather than an increase in discretionary consumption.

Consumer protections

Consumer protections, such as collection practices and installment billing requirements, make it easier to pay utility bills on time.[4] Most states prohibit or restrict late payment penalties and reconnection fees, limit the size of deposits, mandate levelized billing plans and protect the most vulnerable customers from service disconnection. In most cold, northern states, utilities cannot be shut off during the winter.

For example, charges for late payments and reconnection fees, if allowed, must generally be based on cost (for late charges, this is rarely found to be higher than 1 per cent or 1.5 per cent per month). Deposits, if allowed, are generally limited in size and to those who cannot establish credit any other way.

In most states with long periods of extreme weather causing large seasonal changes in utility service consumption for heating and/or cooling, levelized billing plans are provided to make it possible for customers to budget the same payment each month. A true-up adjustment is made at least annually. Some states allow customers to choose the date each month that they would prefer to have their bills come due, thus letting customers align bill payment with revenue streams. Similarly, many states provide for deferred payment arrangements of accumulated overdue payments. In some states, these arrangements are coupled with debt forgiveness and discount plans. In any event, the most successful programs tailor the payments in some way to make it more likely that the customer will be able to make the payments.

Most states also recognize situations where the need to protect the most vulnerable customers mandates that disconnection for non-payment not be allowed. Budget counseling and payment arrangements can be effective in making payment possible in these difficult situations. Shut-off moratorium conditions include extreme weather, medical emergencies and serious medical conditions, and presence of elderly people or infants in the home. This is similar to the rule in nations that guarantee a minimal amount of current even to those who cannot pay for electricity.

Education programs

Education programs teach consumers about prudent energy use and counsel them about budgeting. Education programs are often combined with payment assistance and energy conservation programs to increase their effectiveness.[5] For example, in Connecticut, when contractors install new, efficient refrigerators in poor people's homes, they also explain how to use all of their energy-consuming appliances in the most energy-efficient way.

In another example, budget counseling has been provided at the same time as, and in conjunction with, payment assistance or made a condition of debt forgiveness. Sometimes, a utility company will have on staff community relations people who can provide budget counseling as well as other community interface activities such as outreach to human service agencies. At other times, community service agency personnel provide budget counseling as part of a comprehensive weatherization and energy conservation package. It is probably most effective to have both systems in place because not every customer who needs payment assistance will be eligible for weatherization, and even when they are, not every customer can be served immediately.

The most successful education materials are consistent, easy to use and understand, clear, humorous and useful. Obviously, to maximize their value, they are provided in all the major languages spoken in the service territory. Utilities have put helpful hints on sticky notes, refrigerator magnets or other useful places to help reinforce the messages.

Utilities conduct workshops for local community action or other service agencies in order to disseminate consistent information. Since these agencies are often known and trusted by members of the community, this avenue is often the most effective avenue of communication to low-income families.

Efficiency and weatherization programs

Efficiency and weatherization programs make investments to help consumers control their energy bills by reducing their need for energy. Investments are made as long as they are cost-effective. Benefits that are counted against costs include utility benefits (such as increased payments due to lower bills at weatherized homes) and participant benefits (such as increased comfort and reduced illnesses caused by drafts that have been sealed). These programs often include an energy audit of the customer's house to determine which appliances or equipment are the largest users of energy (such as old refrigerators) and direct installation of energy-saving measures such as wall and attic insulation, air sealing measures, hot water tank wraps, efficient refrigerators, low-flow showerheads and faucets, new water heaters, energy-efficient clothes washers, light fixtures and bulbs. For example, Massachusetts Electric Company runs a relatively aggressive low-income base-load efficiency program (the Appliance Management Program, AMP), which includes replacing refrigerators and that achieves an average reduction in energy use of 15 per cent.[6] The US Department of Energy's evaluation of weatherization programs found a 23 per cent reduction in natural gas consumption, with a 34 per cent reduction in consumption of natural gas for space heating.[7]

Total budgets for these programs are based on a utility's total revenues. For example, one of the authors successfully lobbied for an electricity efficiency program in Massachusetts funded at about 0.4 per cent of utility revenues, including about 0.03 per cent set aside for low-income households. In another example, the New York Public Service Commission has established an account funded by a fraction of a penny surcharge on each kWh of electricity sold, to finance energy efficiency, research and development, and renewable energy resources.[8]

Benefits

As is true of price-setting, all these programs are designed in a public regulatory process and not imposed unilaterally by either a utility or a government agency. Programs usually include more than one of these four components. All programs also include outreach and evaluation components. Outreach to the eligible population takes place (among other ways) through community meetings and workshops, bill inserts, toll-free telephone lines dedicated to the effort, and automatic enrollment for anyone receiving public assistance. Evaluation is necessary to assess the effectiveness of a program, as well as to ensure that it meets the goals set at the outset and to maintain public support for the program.

Social programs, such as "Lifeline," to help poor people pay their telephone bills are designed to increase the number of people who connect to, and stay connected to, the network. This policy benefits everyone because the value of the network is based partly on the number of people that can be reached on it.

Natural gas and electric social programs are aimed at reducing the "energy burden" (the amount that a household spends on all forms of energy as a per cent of total income), which is much higher for poor families than it is for most families.[9] Whereas the energy burden for families with median incomes across the United States is approximately 5 per cent, for poor families it averages 22 per cent, depending on their source and amount of income.[10] In general, a family earning the median income has at least ten times more income to live on (and in some states, over 20 times as much) as does a family receiving welfare assistance.[11] Studies have also shown that, on average nationally, roughly 64 per cent of the energy burden for poor customers goes toward electricity.[12]

A number of studies have made the connection between the inability to pay utility bills and homelessness; as well as the connection between the loss of central heat and increased heart disease; between malnutrition and the heating season; and between utility shut-offs and children being placed in foster care.[13] A sickly poor child is put at risk by a system that requires a parent to choose between nutrition and electricity for refrigeration.

The high energy burden faced by poor customers has led many to fall behind on their utility bill payments, often resulting in high levels of arrearages, collections actions by the utility, payment negotiations, service terminations, and reconnections – all costly to the utility and all other customers. In order to alleviate this high energy burden on poor consumers and save substantial costs to other customers, many states have instituted programs to make energy more affordable.

In most cases, other customers of the utilities, once they have been informed of the costs and benefits of these programs – both to the customers who benefit directly and to all other customers because of reduced utility costs – have supported them. The primary economic benefit to non-participants is reduced utility bill collection expenses that all customers would otherwise have to shoulder, such as the following:

- carrying costs on late payments (arrearages);
- termination and reconnection costs;
- costs of collection notices, termination notices, collection calls, and related activities;
- administrative and regulatory costs of disputed bills and other complaints;
- theft of service;
- costs of establishing and administering payment plans; and
- uncollectibles and bad debt.

In addition, programs to assist low-income customers reduce taxpayer costs for such functions as shelters for the homeless and responses to fires caused by dangerous alternative heating systems. Further, they help maintain a community's property values by contributing to housing maintenance and preventing housing abandonment and homelessness; and they contribute to social equity.

Regulators and utility companies throughout the US have recognized that they have an obligation to provide public services to all members of the public, but especially to the most vulnerable who can least afford to provide for themselves. But they also recognize that by helping the neediest families obtain reliable services at affordable prices, everyone reaps benefits far beyond the costs.

7   Issues that are Publicly Decided

There is space here to sketch only a few of the myriad issues besides pricing that are debated as part of US price regulation. Among those issues that we touch on are service quality and employment, choice of utility ownership, universal service, choice of technology and other regulatory agencies.

Service quality, safety, prices and employment

Employees have a direct interest in the extension of service to all who request it, system reliability and safety. Every improvement in quality has an obvious and direct effect on utility workers: the expansion of networks creates jobs; the refurbishment of systems creates more work; higher safety standards create the demand for workers with increased skills. For example, the US Nuclear Regulatory Commission (NRC) establishes the minimum levels of staffing at key positions in a nuclear plant. Many state commissions have adopted requirements for reliability (frequency and duration of outages) and customer service (e.g., telephone answering, complaint resolution). Utilities failing to meet the standards are punished financially, on the principle that they have not provided the level of service that corresponds to the prices that have been set for them.[1]

Service and safety are where public and employee interests meet – and sometimes conflict with the interests of the owner of the distribution network. In the case of the Chicago gas workers (see Chapter 2), utility unions joined with organizations representing the poor to push for the replacement of the city's deteriorated piping system.[2] In addition, poor customers, concerned about high "estimated" bills, won an increase in the number of meter readings, which led directly to the gas company's hiring more meter readers to assure that meters were read every month.[3] Citizens successfully argued for retention of local offices and improved storm outage response.[4] In each of these cases, the union's experts had the right to analyze detailed gas company records of leaks (the safety issue), employment projections and record of meter readers (the service issue) and cross-examine utility executives on the record. The cases were brought before the regulator, not by the union itself, but by the organizations advocating for the poor.

Note that in the US, as elsewhere, regulators are seldom swayed by arguments about saving jobs of utility workers. However, the US is unique in allowing unions unlimited access to information and the right to institute complaints based on public interest concerns. For example, the Communications Workers of America AFL-CIO (CWA) fiercely challenged the institution of customer charges for telephone directory inquiries that was proposed by the phone company and regulators. The union had found that calls – and therefore operator jobs – plummeted in states that adopted charges for the calls. The CWA (joined by a coalition of government and consumer groups) successfully argued in Illinois and other states that customers should be given several free directory calls each month.[5] As a result, the union protected its operators' jobs by helping the public win no-cost directory information calls.

In Massachusetts, labor unions won a series of detailed minimum standards of quality for telephone service. Again, the appeal to the regulator was not to save utility workers' jobs, but to improve the provision of services – which has the *effect of* saving jobs.[6] Similarly, coalitions of consumer groups, low-income organizations, environmental advocates and trade unions assured that service quality standards are required of electricity utilities as part of the statutory restructuring of the electricity industry.[7]

A few American labor unions have become quite adept at using the regulatory process in industrial disputes. When Brooklyn Union Gas, a private New York gas company, locked out its union workers in a wage dispute, the union appealed to the regulator to reduce the company's prices on grounds that the rates included a provision for workers locked out. Rather than face the reduction, the company agreed to settle the wage dispute with the union. That union (Transport Workers Union Local 1) also used its right to access company information to find that the company had overstated to the regulator its cost for health insurance for union workers. A US Department of Labor arbitration then ruled the company owed the money to the workers' health fund.

Choice of utility ownership form

The vast majority of US customers (74 per cent of sales in 1999) are served by investor-owned electric utilities; that is, utilities that are privately owned by shareholders. However, 17 per cent of US electricity is sold by government-owned utilities, nearly all of which are owned and operated by municipalities. (A handful are run by state or federal agencies.) While most government-owned utilities are small, the cities of Los Angeles and

California Regulator Rescinds Layoffs

In response to the recent debacle in California, and the near-bankruptcy of the investor-owned electric utilities there, two companies – Pacific Gas and Electric Company (PG&E) and Southern California Edison Company (SCE) – began laying off workers in order to recoup some of the losses incurred by paying inflated prices for wholesale power. The Coalition of California Utility Employees (CCUE) petitioned the regulator to prevent these layoffs, based on the premise that cuts in workers would lead to cuts in service quality.

CCUE charged that the proposed layoffs would "affect the utilities' obligation to furnish and maintain adequate, efficient, just and reasonable service" and also "the safety, service and reliability of the electricity system."[8] The unions were joined in their petition by a consumer advocate group, The Utility Reform Network (TURN). TURN contended that, if the layoffs occurred, SCE's customers would be paying for services they would no longer be receiving. TURN also requested that the regulator require SCE to establish an accounting mechanism that would track the costs and savings associated with a major workforce reduction.[9]

After taking input from the utilities, CCUE, TURN and another interested ratepayer, the Administrative Law Judge (ALJ) found, among other things, that the "practices and services resulting from the layoffs and the cutback in overtime have resulted in inadequate, unjust and unreasonable service and practices." Further, the ALJ concluded that CCUE's motion should be granted, and that "the layoffs that have already been implemented should be rescinded, and the utilities should be ordered to restore and staff the positions to the extent that the terminated positions affect the utilities' ability to fully staff their customer call centers, read meters on a monthly basis, and to timely respond to service calls and outages and to connect new customers." Further: "All future layoffs which affect the aforementioned services and practices shall be barred unless the utilities can substantiate that the layoffs will not prevent the utilities from furnishing and maintaining adequate, efficient, just and reasonable service." And finally: "SCE and PG&E should establish . . . accounts to record the costs and savings associated with the permitted layoffs and cost cutting measures that have already been implemented, and which will be implemented by the utilities."[10]

Austin, Texas as well as the state of Nebraska and the national government (e.g., the Tennessee Valley Authority) own large systems, And 9 per cent of US electricity is sold by utilities owned by customers themselves, organized as cooperatives. Most of these are in rural areas, where residents organized their own systems (mostly in the 1930s) when no one else would bring electricity to them. As a result of the cooperative movement, the fraction of farm homes with electricity rose from about 11 per cent in 1932 to still only about 35 per cent in 1941.[11]

The proportions are reversed for water supply, where government ownership is the norm in the US. Government-owned telephone systems also exist (e.g., in Lincoln, Nebraska), but they are rare.

The form of utility ownership – shareholder-owned, government-owned or customer-owned – is democratically decided. No utility can place its equipment in public streets without first negotiating a municipal franchise, which is a contract that sets out the conditions on the utility's work. In many places, price regulation was first undertaken under such a franchise and later taken over by a state regulatory commission. Other terms include street repair after the utility work is performed, service quality and obligations to connect all applicants for service. These regulations have also been taken over by state commissions, except in New Orleans and Washington, DC. Often, granting a franchise also involved choosing among competing investor-owned utilities – or deciding against all of them in favor of a municipality-owned system.

Advantages perceived for government-owned systems include the fact that they are exempt from taxation; their lack of a profit motive may result in less financial abuse; and their local government ownership makes them more responsive to democratic control. Government ownership is also relied on to exploit hydropower resources on public lands, such as the New York Power Authority's operations at Niagara Falls, the Lower Colorado River Authority in Texas, and the federal Bonneville Power Administration's Hoover Dam on the Columbia River.

In the early years of electricity development, investor-owned utilities preferred densely populated urban areas to rural communities, so there often were no franchise requests for rural areas. In many such places, groups of homeowners and businesses banded together and created customer-owned cooperative electric utilities.

Public decisions about the form of utility ownership can be changed. For example, a municipality or cooperative may agree to sell its system to an investor-owned utility. And a community can decide that a private utility has performed so unacceptably that it should be replaced by a public agency. Under conventional US law, for example, a municipality can take over private property for public use if it pays the fair value of the property that a court sets.

The primary recent example of a private utility replaced by a government-owned one is Long Island Lighting Co. (LILCo) in New York. In a complicated public negotiation, led by the State Governor, LILCo was replaced by a government authority after LILCo had insisted on building a hugely expensive and unpopular nuclear power plant near the distant end of a narrow 50-mile-long island that has only one major highway down its length. Many residents worried about the safety of the plant after the nearby Three Mile Island nuclear plant accident had made local milk questionable to drink. They were skeptical that, in the event of a local accident, the island could be evacuated along its one highway, which had already proven itself inadequate to an ordinary rush hour.

Decades of battling ensued in the courts and the regulatory commission by local towns and counties, state officials and non-government agencies. The regulatory commission had considerable leverage from its ability to set the utility's prices. The courts, among other things, declared that the utility had lied to the regulator. Finally, a complex transaction was negotiated by which the public authority was created to buy the utility's transmission and distribution facilities. LILCo was also forced to sell its generators (and gas distribution system) to a nearby utility and dissolve.[12]

Universal service, including extension of service

Universality of utility service, geographic and economic, is a goal of US utility regulation. This is accomplished in a number of ways.

Economic universal service has been an explicit objective of the national telephone statute since 1934 and is explicitly or implicitly included in every state's utility regulatory structure.[13] When the 1934 telephone statute was passed, home telephones were still relatively rare. A national policy was adopted of charging businesses for the extra economic value they received from telephone service, in large part as a way to keep domestic telephone prices low enough to encourage their use. Other universal strategies are described in Chapter 6.

In some cases, geographic universal service is made an explicit term of the franchise contract under which the utility is allowed to occupy city streets. Most cable television franchises in the US, for example, contain a schedule by which each part of the franchised territory must be sufficiently wired that anyone who wants service can order it.

A hallmark of US utility regulation is the obligation to serve. Once a franchise area is designated, and accepted by the utility, there is an obligation to serve every person or business in that area. (For natural gas, since there are alternative heating fuels, this obligation is usually limited to the areas actually served by gas mains. For cable TV a schedule is often set out.) This is not to say that service may not come at a price. Utilities are generally allowed, beyond a specified distance, to charge for extending their lines into remote areas. Usually the utility will be required to finance this cost over 10 or 20 years. Utilities may not, however, refuse to serve areas just because they do not expect much revenue. The American term for such refusal is "redlining," and it is prohibited. Redlining neighborhoods because they are predominately low-income or of a particular race is often prohibited by statute.

Other regulatory agencies

So far, we have focused on America's utility regulators, the 53 federal, state and city "public service commissions" that establish prices and services standards for utilities. Other agencies also must adhere to the open process, inviting all interested parties to participate, with all information made available to the public. Employees and employers have a special interest in the Occupational Health and Safety Administration, the Nuclear Regulatory Commission (whose sole work is establishing and enforcing nuclear power plant safety regulations), the National Transportation Safety Board (concerned with gas pipeline safety) and the Environmental Protection Agency. All nations have agencies that set safety standards, but most rely on expert civil servants, consultants or appointed committees to determine the rules and their enforcement. At most, parties such as labor unions or consumer organizations are given an opportunity to "comment" or are asked for "input," which is then reviewed by the committee in private. The US model differs from others in the extent to which the public (which includes unions and industry) may have an active role.

In the case of the Nuclear Regulatory Commission, the license to operate a nuclear plant is reviewed in the same type of court-like proceedings used to set electricity prices. In the largest case on record – the contentious fight over the license to operate the Shoreham, New York, nuclear power plant – hearings lasted ten years and the records (all available for public inspection) totaled *20 million* pages of transcripts of debate, investigative reports and evidence. All groups, from the plant's builder to environmental groups, had the right to question every aspect of the plant's future operation. These hearings (among other issues) led to the dissolution of the Long Island Lighting Company (LILCo) described above.

Choice of technology

Power plant construction requires approval of a public siting agency, usually after a process similar to the price approvals described earlier. Among the decisions subject to this process are:

- *Location.* For example, consideration may be given to whether the proposed plant is too close to a residential neighborhood or whether a particular geographical area is bearing an unfair concentration of such plants.
- *Environmental impacts.* For example, noise, water use and air pollution are analyzed in detail and compared to similar impacts at other sites.
- *Need.* In most jurisdictions, a regulator will decide whether the plant should be built at all. (The few systems relying on markets leave this decision to market players, with adverse consequences that are described elsewhere in this volume.)

One of the most important decisions to be made is the choice of the technology to be employed. Public subsidies to various technologies are one means of influencing this choice. For example, oil prices in the US do not include a proxy for the military costs of maintaining the oil supply from the Middle East. Various public funds have been established to encourage the development and use of renewable fuels, such as wind, biomass and solar power, and relatively low-emission technologies, such as cogeneration and gas-fired fuel cells. As described earlier, public and utility funds are set aside for energy efficiency measures.

Public reviews of plant investment decisions also mandate certain technology decisions. For example, the criterion of least-cost choice of generation generally leads to the choice of natural gas combined cycle generators when lifecycle costs, including the cost of air and water pollution, are considered.

Using such a plant in co-generation is even more efficient where there is a separate need for steam, which can be used for heat or industrial processes. Heat can be used in a local facility or, in many cities (New York City's Consolidated Edison Company is the largest co-generator in the country) for piped district heating. A plant that can use the same fuel to produce steam that both drives electricity turbines and then provides heat or motive energy is obviously more efficient than a plant serving only one of those functions alone.

Similarly, review of an investment to buttress a distribution system may determine that it would be less costly to invest in local efficiency to reduce demand in the affected area. Or it may be less costly to invest in a distributed generating resource to meet the demand. Distributed generation is placed at a specific customer location, or a specific neighborhood, and thereby obviates the need for distribution investment since the power is already located where it is needed. These technologies include micro-turbines, gas-fired fuel cells and photovoltaic panels.

The siting of a power plant is a particularly long-lived decision with impacts that can be unusually harsh. It is therefore particularly appropriate for a transparent process with broad public participation.

8 An Alternative: Democratic Negotiations

The formal price-setting process described in Chapter 5, from initial filing through final decision and before possible appeals to the courts, can take from six months to a year. At the end of the process, few are fully satisfied with the results – everyone who shows up usually wins at least a little bit, but everyone also loses something. The utility and other parties have made their cases and presented their arguments – often diametrically opposed. The regulator has issued its ruling on each item of contention – sometimes splitting the difference between two opposing positions – and reached a decision that often pleases no one.

This system of litigation developed because it was seen as the best way to resolve most issues that arise in a price-setting case, because it was transparent and democratic. However, some kinds of utility cases can be better resolved through negotiation than litigation. These include energy conservation or efficiency programs, and payment and other assistance to the poorest citizens of society, a topic dealt with in Chapter 6. Negotiation allows the parties themselves to make the trade-offs, instead of leaving it to the regulator to split the difference. A group or party's standing in the negotiations is related to its standing in the formal hearing process; that is, any party with intervenor status has the ability to litigate any issue that is not resolved through negotiation. This ability confers a balance of power between the utility and all other negotiators. This chapter will present an anatomy of a negotiated settlement based on the experience of two of the authors with such settlements in Massachusetts.

The filing

The filing in a negotiated settlement can be the same as that in a litigated case; that is, it can include all the elements described in earlier chapters. A utility proposing an energy conservation program for approval would likely, in addition to those elements, file the following:

- the overall goal and specific objectives of the conservation program;

- detailed descriptions of the proposed program components; a funding mechanism and associated rate impacts on each of the various customer groups;
- an analysis of the costs and benefits (a cost-effectiveness analysis) that includes a projection of the energy and other savings to be achieved through the program; a plan to evaluate and monitor the implementation and savings achieved;
- a projection of any fixed revenues that might be lost because of energy not sold; and
- any financial incentive the utility is requesting it be awarded upon achieving the goals of the program.

Intervention

Once the filing is made, all interested parties may intervene, just as in a litigated case. These include environmental advocates, energy service companies (who install energy saving measures in houses or business facilities) and advocates for poor people (who have specific energy conservation needs). In addition, most of those who intervene in rate cases would also intervene in a conservation case, such as consumer advocates, large and small commercial and industrial customers, municipalities, other government agencies and NGOs. As noted earlier, the US system is radically different from the British system. In the UK, prices are often negotiated between the regulator and the utility. Consumers may not participate or even attend the secret sessions.

Mediation

Often it is at this point in the process – once the parties and issues have been identified – that the parties may decide to try to resolve the issues through negotiation rather than litigation. They may choose an independent mediator or the regulator may appoint one from its staff. The mediator does not have the power to make decisions or to force the parties to accept an outcome. Rather, the mediator's role is to ensure that all parties have an opportunity to be heard during negotiations and to provide an objective sounding board for issues and ideas. (If a regulator's staff person is designated as the mediator, that person will be barred from sharing confidential information gained from settlement discussions with the regulator or with other staff members.)

Boston Edison Company

In 1991, a Massachusetts utility filed a proposal to implement an energy conservation program. The filing contained all the elements required by the regulator. However, this particular utility had developed an adversarial relationship (to the point of deep mistrust on all sides) with a group of intervenors called the "Non-Utility Parties" (NUPs). No one believed that this group could reach an agreement with this particular company, and all were prepared to litigate. Formally arrayed against the utility were the Attorney-General of Massachusetts (a consumer advocate who intervenes by law on behalf of domestic consumers in every rate case), the Conservation Law Foundation of New England (an environmental advocate), the Massachusetts Division of Energy Resources (a state energy policy agency), the Massachusetts Public Interest Research Group (an NGO advocate for consumer and environmental interests), a representative of large industrial customers and a group of state legislators.

The Massachusetts regulator appointed a staff person (one of the authors) to mediate settlement negotiations. The NUPs chose a lead negotiator (another of the authors). Negotiations began in an atmosphere of hostility and mistrust, but with the clear understanding that, if no agreement were reached, the regulator would issue a decision that was sure to please none of the parties – including the utility. The first three weeks were spent in an effort to determine whether these parties could even hope to reach agreement on the issues. It took another six weeks of intensive negotiation (including one twelve-hour stint in a stuffy room with the air conditioner turned off and no dinner) before an agreement was hammered out. But agreement was finally reached, and it was ratified by the regulator.

Ultimately, in Massachusetts, the negotiations took on a life of their own and, even without a mediator, have continued successfully ever since. Other parties have joined the discussions – including energy service companies and advocates for poor people. These groups, working with the utilities and often with input from regulatory staff, have developed detailed conservation program agreements that the regulator has only had to oversee and ratify. (Of course, this process depends on a regulator who can understand the value of negotiated settlements over litigation and is willing to give up a small measure of control. Frustratingly, sometimes a regulator will reject a unanimous settlement and force a hearing process on reluctant participants.)

Discovery

All parties can ask questions about any aspect of the filing, as described in chapter 5. However, parties to negotiations can agree to hold in confidence any information shared within the context of settlement negotiations. Thus, the utility (and any other party that might put forth a counter-proposal or modifications to the utility's proposal) can share information and develop a more thorough understanding of other parties' positions without fear of that information or positions becoming a part of the public record. Once a settlement is reached, all parties to the agreement decide which information should be included as support for the final agreement that goes to the regulator for approval. A caveat here, though, is that if all parties do not reach an agreement on all issues, they may yet be litigated, and any information not filed will be subject to formal discovery rules.

An energy conservation case

In about half the states, electric or gas companies invest in energy efficient equipment or processes on behalf of their customers in order to lower energy consumption. Participating customers generally contribute a portion of the cost of the efficiency measures, but the balance is paid by the utility, i.e., by all of the utility's customers. In most cases, the utility offers a program that can provide energy conservation to all customer sectors – business, domestic and government. Among many issues that arise in an energy conservation case, the following illustrate some that are the subject of negotiations:

- economic rationale;
- environmental considerations;
- customer sector interests;
- labor benefits; and
- funding.

Economic rationale

Why would a utility whose purpose is to sell electricity or natural gas spend some of its revenues to *save* energy? What is the economic rationale for a utility to undertake energy conservation? As electricity generation costs rose during the late 1970s and 1980s, utilities were asked to justify their expenditures on new generation – especially extremely costly nuclear power plants. Some regulators (usually at the urging of consumer and environmental advocates) directed the utilities to assess the value of energy conservation as an alternative to building new generation.

Several tests have been developed by which to analyze the cost-effectiveness of investments in energy conservation. In each of the tests, if the projected benefits are greater than the projected costs to implement the program, the program is deemed cost-effective. Categories of costs and benefits vary with the test employed. The cost-effectiveness of most traditional energy efficiency programs has been estimated using either the "utility cost test" or the "total resource cost test" (or both). However, some states have used a "societal test," which includes benefits not captured in the former two but very real, nonetheless.

Briefly, the utility cost test evaluates the costs and benefits of a program to determine its net economic value to an electric or gas company; it does not take into account customer costs and benefits that are unrelated to a utility company's system. The total resource cost test estimates the net economic value of all direct costs and benefits to customers as well as to the utility company, although in most cases the direct benefits are limited to easily quantifiable elements such as amount of water saved, or lower repair and maintenance bills.

Over the years, different states accepted different tests, but recently in Massachusetts a consensus of 20 different entities, including gas and electric utilities, municipal governments, consumer and environmental advocates, low-income advocates, energy service companies and energy efficiency advocates all agreed that the most appropriate test to use is the societal test.[1] The societal test incorporates all the costs and benefits to the utility and to customers of implementing an energy conservation program and adds benefits that affect society as a whole (such as avoiding air pollution or lowering health-care costs), or particular segments of society (such as assisting economically disadvantaged neighborhoods, creating jobs, or lowering energy bills).

For instance, the societal test used to determine the cost-effectiveness of a commercial-industrial conservation program could include the benefit of reducing the energy bill of a manufacturing firm enough to enable it to stay in business and provide jobs for 100 people, who might otherwise become unemployed. The societal test for a program targeting poor people (such as weatherizing their homes and providing energy efficient lighting) could include the value of reducing fire damage from people using dangerous alternative heat sources such as stoves or kerosene heaters.

The societal test for all programs also takes into account three types of potential economic impacts:

1. net increase in labor employment (i.e., new jobs created in the energy conservation field, and jobs retained in industry that would otherwise have been lost);
2. indirect "economic multiplier" effects (money saved from lower energy bills recycled back into the economy in myriad ways, multiplying several times over the investment spent on conservation); and
3. indirect price effects of lowering demand for energy supply with conservation (i.e., resource price stabilization effects that result from reduced demand for the resource). Because these types of benefits are difficult to quantify with a high level of precision, they lend themselves to negotiation to set a value for them to be used in a cost-effectiveness analysis.

Table 8.1   Elements of a Societal Cost-Effectiveness Test

Costs	Benefits
Program administration Program implementation, including financial incentives to customers Marketing Customer costs Evaluation	Avoided generation or gas supply costs Avoided transmission and distribution or transportation costs Other energy resources (gas, oil) saved Non-energy resources (water, land) saved Non-resources (health, comfort, safety, lower bills, economic growth, job creation/retention)

Environmental considerations

As energy is saved, depending on the fuel source used for the generation of electricity, in many cases less coal, oil or natural gas is burned. A societal test would include the value of pollution not emitted by power plants burning these fossil fuels – a concept called "environmental externalities" because the costs are external to the price of the fuel. Although the costs from this pollution are not usually calculated and are not included in the price paid for electricity or gas, we all pay in increased health-care costs, in damaged lakes and forests and in global warming. The benefits of lowering the rates of pollution are very real and are included in societal cost-effectiveness analyses of energy conservation programs. Because they are also difficult to quantify with precision, these are also among the types of benefits that lend themselves to a negotiated agreement on their value.

The consensus group of 20 in Massachusetts described above proposed that an additional 25 per cent of the value of the avoided cost of energy be added to the benefit side of the cost-effectiveness equation to reflect combined general economic benefits and environmental benefits not already captured in fuel prices.

Benefits specific to low-income customers

There are numerous benefits that accrue to society and to low-income customers in addition to the benefits that are associated with all energy conservation programs. Many of these, such as increasing energy afford-ability, are described in Chapter 6. They include reduced costs to the utility from lower collection, disconnect and reconnect costs; termination notice expense; carrying charges on late payments; determination of payment plans; and uncollectible and bad debt costs. Benefits also include lower societal costs from reduced health-care expenses, fewer homeless shelters, fewer fires and higher property values. These programs also provide direct benefits to the low-income customers themselves in the form of more money available for food, medicine and other necessities; fewer termin-ations of service; and increased comfort and safety in their homes.

Some of these benefits can be quantified by the utility (such as reduced carrying charges from late payments), but others are difficult to measure with precision. However, there is general agreement that lowering energy bills for poor people through energy conservation – especially if combined with education on how to manage energy use most efficiently – will provide all of the benefits described and should not be valued at zero. Thus, the value of low-income benefits in an energy conservation program's cost-effectiveness analysis is best determined through a negotiated process. That is, the group of interested stakeholders that have intervened in the case negotiate a value they all agree is appropriate, given the level of uncer-tainty and the difficulty in obtaining valid data. The consensus group in Massachusetts agreed on an adder of 50 per cent of the value of avoided energy costs to reflect the extra value of providing energy conservation and education services to poor people.[2]

Other customer sectors

Utility customers are usually divided into sectors such as domestic, industrial, large and small business, and government, for purposes of setting prices and designing energy conservation programs. While everyone might agree that conserving energy is a noble goal, some domestic and many large industrial customers have not been eager to pay more for electricity or natural gas in order to cover the costs of conservation programs through their utility prices. In some cases, the customers did not understand the value to themselves and society from energy conservation or, in the case of large industrial customers, they did not want to subsidize their competitors by making them more energy-efficient. By working together through negotiations, all customer sector needs can be taken into account when designing an energy conservation program to be funded by utility customers.

At the same time, several utilities have discovered that energy conservation is a very effective tool for industrial customer retention. An example of an electric utility using its energy conservation program to successfully retain an industrial customer took place in Massachusetts, where an ice cream factory was about to go out of business or relocate to another, less expensive area of the country. The local electric utility subsidized an energy conservation retrofit of the ice cream plant, saving the plant thousands of dollars a year in electric bills and saving the community hundreds of jobs. At the same time, the plant remained a large customer of the electric utility. This plant is now a showcase of the benefits that can be achieved through a well-designed and implemented energy conservation program.

Labor benefits

Many input–output studies have shown that energy conservation programs provide many more jobs than would the alternative – generating electricity or supplying natural gas.[3] These jobs are created through direct employment by the energy conservation industry, including energy service companies, evaluation, research and development firms, and firms manufacturing the conservation equipment; by retaining businesses in the community and the jobs they provide; and through the multiplier effect of electricity and gas bill savings described above. A study done in 1997 showed that 20,000 jobs had been created in New England in the energy conservation business since electric and gas utilities began implementing widespread conservation programs in the late 1980s.[4]

Funding

The funding of energy conservation programs has been a contentious issue ever since electric and gas utilities began implementing programs and incorporating the costs into their prices in the 1980s. Among the funding issues to be decided are whether some customer classes should cross-subsidize others; what level of funding is appropriate (there is an inherent trade-off between societal cost-effectiveness and the impact on non-participant bills); how much participants should pay as their share of the cost of efficiency improvements; whether utilities should be compensated for revenues lost due to lower sales engendered by conservation; and whether utilities should earn an incentive, or reward, for achievement of savings that surpasses projections.

Results of negotiations

As utilities and the interest groups that customarily intervened in energy conservation cases began to understand each others' positions on the issues before them, trust began to slowly develop. Strengthening this trust is the utilities' knowledge that the advocates will be monitoring their conduct to ensure compliance with settlement agreements and that the advocates will support the utilities before the regulators as long as this trust is well founded.

In addition to increased trust, negotiated settlements have led to better results than litigation. As described above, when the regulator makes the decisions, everyone loses something, and parties have no control over what they lose. In the negotiation process, each party freely chooses which among many points it is willing to lose in order to gain something else. Although this may sound like a distinction without a difference, in fact, the trade-offs arrived at voluntarily are much more stable and effective. Negotiated settlements are actually more democratic because all parties participate in the decision. As a result, the terms are more likely to be implemented with enthusiasm and effectiveness than if they had been imposed from above by a regulator. Furthermore, in an atmosphere of trust and negotiation, more information is freely shared, with the result that more comprehensive solutions can be developed.

All of the issues discussed in this chapter can be – and have been – litigated. Besides energy conservation cases, other types of cases have been

---

Western Massachusetts Electric Company
One effective compromise involved a battle between Western Massachusetts Electric Company, which wanted to lower its prices by lowering its costs (including energy conservation costs), and a large group of non-utility parties, who insisted that the utility provide expanded energy conservation programs. A solution was hammered out through settlement negotiations: a lower conservation budget but more effective measures that saved more energy in total although they cost less per measure.[5]

successfully negotiated and settled, including the guiding principles of electricity industry restructuring in Rhode Island and Massachusetts, price-setting cases in New York and elsewhere, and cases in which the regulator was reviewing the operating performance of generating plants owned by an electric utility. Any case about which stakeholders are concerned that their interests be protected (and in which they feel they can come to better solutions than the regulator might deliver) is ripe for negotiation.

As may be clear from the long list of issues that may be negotiated in any particular case, settlements are not necessarily a faster way than litigation to handle utility regulation – just better in many cases. Sometimes, negotiations take months before agreement is finally reached and a settlement is submitted to the regulator for approval. But, when a varied and representative group of stakeholders has agreed on an issue and has provided good supporting documentation, the regulator will (in most cases) approve the settlement.

Only if there are public interest concerns that have not been taken into account by the negotiators, or if new information becomes available and known to the regulator that would substantially or significantly affect the outcome of a settlement, should regulators reject a settlement in favor of making the decision themselves after litigation. Of course, sometimes political considerations will intervene in spite of the best efforts of all concerned, and a settlement is rejected. This fact should not discourage people from negotiating, because the knowledge shared and the trust engendered through the process are valuable in themselves and will continue to provide benefits long after the rejection is history.

9   Be There: A Guide to Public Participation

Modern US utility regulation is pretty much the invention of American Telephone & Telegraph Company (AT&T) and the National Electric Light Association (NELA) – the investor-owned telephone and electric industries at the turn of twentieth century. They saw regulation as protection against Populist and Progressive movements that, since the economic panic of 1873 and later economic disruptions, had galvanized anti-corporate farmer and labor organizations. By the turn of the twentieth century, these movements had developed considerable political support for governmental ownership of utilities. The political deal AT&T and NELA cut was successful at saving private ownership of utilities, but the cost utilities paid was to extend democracy into their businesses. Most of the democratic innovations described in this book were in the statute books by 1914, although it was several decades more before actual regulation developed much beyond utility–regulator negotiations. Stock manipulations that collapsed in the Great Depression of the 1930s spawned, among other things, institutionalization of the democratic participation in regulation that is taken for granted today.[1]

However, constantly increasing economies of scale and technological development meant that utility price regulation involved little more than the supervision of sharp rate cuts until the 1970s. Then, due mostly to oil price shocks and the spiraling costs of nuclear power, electricity prices skyrocketed and the current wave of domestic consumer advocacy – of which the authors have been a part – was born.

This advocacy has been extraordinarily successful. Domestic electricity prices declined relative to industrials during the 1970s, although all rates rose; between 1970 and 1982, domestic prices tripled, but industrial prices quintupled.

Since 1982, industrials have retaken some ground, but only because it was possible to keep domestic prices from rising very much in real (inflation-adjusted) terms. Further, benefits for poor people were enormously expanded. In addition, increased environmental awareness brought some substantial energy conservation programs, mandated invest-

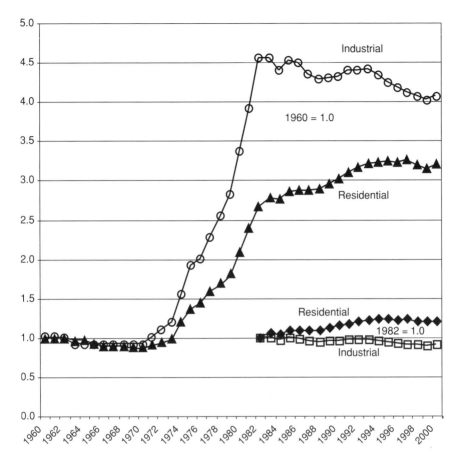

Figure 9   US Electricity Prices, 1960–2001 (Source: US Energy Information Administration)

ments in renewable energy and the end of the nuclear power construction industry in the US. Lately, industrial prices have declined in absolute (as well as real) terms, while domestic prices have been more-or-less flat in absolute terms, declining modestly in real terms.

As shown below, natural gas prices track a similar path, except that after wholesale prices were deregulated in 1986, industrial prices fell slightly while residential prices continued to climb.

Thus US utility prices and policies, from the 1970s through the 1990s, reflect the views of domestic consumers, industrial customers, labor, environmentalists and low-income advocates; for these have been the interests most commonly represented in the proceedings described in this book. The process we have described has been a controlled, non-violent battle of interests.

As discussed in earlier chapters, US utility industry restructuring movements have been driven by industrial customer demands for additional price concessions and the most benefit from new generating technologies. But, as described earlier, participation by other customers in the regulatory and legislative process has resulted in rules that will require a sharing of any benefits of new technologies just as industrial advocacy reversed earlier price gains by domestic consumer interests. Price directions are uncertain under the new regulatory regimes that are still evolving. However, what is certain is that struggles among customers and other interests will continue to be the basis for utility pricing and policy.

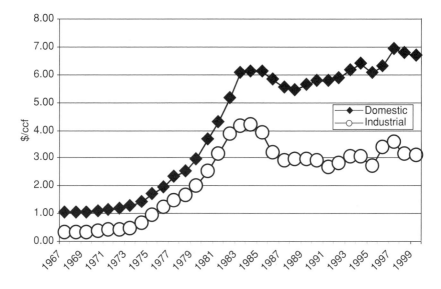

Figure 10   US Natural Gas Prices

This participation in the regulatory process has been costly and messy. But it would have been far more costly to most customers if that participation had not occurred.

Regulators operate somewhat as referees among the various interests and parties who participate in a utility case. They rely on the public record that is developed through the discovery and hearing processes described above. Those involved in the process – the ones who "show up" to ask questions and develop the record – are those whose concerns are taken into account when the regulators debate the issues and make their decisions. In a major difference from the way the process works in the UK, US regulators recognize that they need all the help they can get. Thus, participation by

---

Woody Allen Wisdom

Question: If it is the regulators' job to balance all interests and render fair and equitable decisions on rates, energy conservation and all other utility matters that come before them, why does anyone need to participate?

Answer: The Woody Allen principle: "Ninety per cent of life is showing up."

---

all parties upon whom the decisions will have an impact is usually welcomed by the regulators; it makes their job easier.

Participation through negotiation, as in the Scottish Power and other cases discussed here, can provide an even better outcome.

How do parties make democratic regulation work? Democratic regulation does not work, unless there are strong advocates on all sides – labor, industry, government, domestic consumers, environmentalists and NGOs. Some simple directives for effective advocacy follow:

- Aim high.
- Become informed.
- Participate.
- Forge alliances.
- Persist.

Aim high

Advocates are most effective when they focus on three (or fewer) simple themes that people care about. This way, they do not dilute their message by taking on too many issues at once. However, it is important to ask for enough, because one rarely receives what one does not ask for. Demand transparency. Demand the right to participate.

An example of how asking for one thing achieved something even better: public information about electricity demand and the system's capacity to meet that demand made it clear there was plenty of power in New England to get through the summer of 1987. Yet several brownouts (voltage reductions) occurred and blackouts were narrowly averted. With this information, one of the authors (representing consumers) assumed that utilities were "blinking the lights" to gain regulators' approval to complete construction of Seabrook Station, a controversial nuclear plant. In litigation, it was discovered that the utilities had scheduled three of their largest plants to be off-line for routine maintenance at the time of peak demand.

The plant was completed. But the regulator did change the rules for maintenance and planning and require investments in conservation to reduce demand. Some price increases based on investments in the plant were denied. And there have been almost no brownouts in New England since.

Become informed

One of the first steps in successful advocacy before a regulator is to be informed about the process and about particular proceedings that affect a constituency. Parties need to get in on the ground floor in order to participate fully in the debate.

Before attempting to participate directly, though, it is important that parties learn as much as possible about the issues. This can be accomplished by attending conferences on the issues, reading newsletters, reading materials put out by people and organizations that have been involved in these issues before and becoming familiar with the process. If possible, develop a relationship with the regulators and their staffs. Ask that you be kept informed about upcoming proceedings.

It is important to read the public record very carefully – the trade press, whatever the utility publishes, stock analyst reports and government reports. Many utilities in Europe and elsewhere are partly owned by companies regulated in the US, where information disclosure rules are relatively strict. Information about international holdings may be available in regulatory proceedings. Collaboration with US allies may be productive.

The best information often comes from non-public sources that can be uncovered with persistent investigation. Some of these sources will provide information to visible advocates. Parties should look for natural allies: journalists, unions (better service quality usually also translates into jobs), utility workers and government officials.

An example of how information proved critical: honest telephone workers, disgruntled with executive cheating they saw, came to us and to the newspapers with information they had obtained on the job. When brought to the attention of the regulator, the regulator forced the utility to return to customers millions of dollars that it had overcharged by having the regulated company buy supplies at inflated prices from a sister subsidiary that was not price-regulated.

Demand participation

In the US, once a petition for a price increase or other proposal is filed by a utility and a public notice is published, there is usually a period of time in which persons can intervene. This is a crucial step in the process. Parties that do not intervene at the outset forfeit their right to participate fully in the process. Some non-price cases are less formal. They may be structured as a "notice of inquiry" or as a non-contested case in which interested persons can submit comments, answer questions in informal hearings, and/or participate in technical sessions. They may be negotiated settlements, as discussed above.

In any case, whether a formal proceeding with intervention and hearings, a less formal proceeding with comments and technical sessions or a negotiated settlement, it is critical to become involved at the outset. In this way, parties are kept informed of the schedule; they will receive copies of any documents submitted or issued by the regulator; and most importantly, they will receive a list of all other intervenors or participants.

It is usually also critical to hire experts in the field to help build a case. In the US, much of the money for this purpose comes from government sources: government-approved fees for participating in cases, government-funded lawyers representing low-income families, government-funded public advocates. But much is also raised outside government – a necessity to preserve independence and power. Fund-raising methods include dues, publications, direct mail solicitations, foundation and large donor grants, and house-to-house soliciting.

With expert help, a party can construct a parallel set of accounts and resulting price structure for the utility's operations and force the utility to

---

Constructing a Set of Accounts

- Generation, transmission, distribution and administration capital costs are well established and published in the US. Price out the system as it exists using these costs.
- Fuel prices are published world-wide. Add local transportation costs and line losses.
- For labor and executive salaries, US costs are published, so use ratios with local norms.
- For supplies and materials, start with US costs and use ratios to local prices.
- Compute the rate of return the utility must be earning given the prices it is charging. Compare that to local bank savings account interest, mortgage rates, profits earned by other industries.

explain where it is wrong! Using published world prices, one can figure out what typical utility service ought to cost.

In addition to presenting alternative cost accounts, or where the main issues are other than simply price increases, parties can also conduct surveys to gather information with which to challenge the utility. Surveys can make a crucial difference. In one case, led by one of the authors, a group of consumer advocates rounded up complaints about coin-operated telephones taking money without providing service, charging for services the law required be free, and charging 2–5 times the going rate for services they did render. The advocates also physically surveyed and tested the phones. Based on this evidence, the regulator adopted customer protection rules and, in the most extreme case of overcharging (of truly captive customers, as it happened: prisoners), revoked the operator's license.

Forge coalitions

With a list of all the participants in a proceeding – whether an energy conservation proceeding, a price-setting review or any other matter before the regulator that the public becomes involved with – one can learn the identities and affiliations of others who might be interested in forming a coalition. One may think that he is the only one in the case who cares about the environment, labor, businesses or poor people and how the outcome of this particular case might affect them. And he may be right – at first. Often, people with a narrow focus on one issue fail to see the opportunities that lie within their power if they form strategic coalitions. Others whose interests may not mirror their own – and, in fact, may seem to be diametrically opposed – may become close allies. How can this be true?

A coalition that seems to make sense yet is rarely made is that of environmentalists with low-income advocates. In whose neighborhoods are the majority of the polluting plants and industries located? In whose neighborhoods are the instances of asthma and other respiratory illnesses the highest? Thus, in whose best interest is it to see that these issues are addressed along with increases and volatility in prices? Forming a strategic coalition with environmental advocates is the best way for low-income advocates to gain some control over where plants are located and whether old, dirty plants are closed or cleaned up.

Similarly, interests of domestic consumers, low-income customers, industrialists and labor merge with respect to service quality. In the California service quality case discussed above, labor unions and consumer advocates together convinced the regulator that service quality was being compromised by utility company layoffs. A decision favoring the unions and other employees benefits consumers and industrialists, as well, since service quality and system reliability depend on maintaining a strong workforce.

Domestic consumers may also share interests with businesses that provide economical telephone service or energy conservation services. For example, in a Massachusetts case reviewing the structure of the natural gas industry, a coalition pulled together by one of the authors, consisting of labor, low-income, consumer and environmental interest groups, demanded that protections be built into the new structure. These protections included maintenance of service quality, low-income discounts and energy efficiency programs. In a series of cases that are still ongoing as this is written, the regulator has already adopted some of these protections.

Why are these coalitions so important to the process and to a party's impact on the process? Regulators can only make findings and set policies based on the record in each proceeding. They therefore must rely on input from those involved in the case. If an individual or group takes a position on an issue but receives no support from anyone else, a regulator may be less likely to give it the weight it may actually deserve. However, if a regulator sees that a broad coalition of parties supports certain issues, it is more apt to be persuaded that these positions should be incorporated into regulatory policy. These positions can then become the basis for new rules by which the utilities must operate.

Where intervention is not yet a standard part of regulatory proceedings, there are other methods that a coalition of advocates can use effectively. Advocates need the reality (and others' perception of) a real power base. Fortunately, there are many potential sources of power. Information is power, as discussed earlier. People are power, as can be seen in demonstrations, bill boycotts, crowds at hearings, letters, and strategically placed calls. Press attention can be powerful. Regulators can be influenced by these demonstrations of power against utility abuses or for improvements

---

Power of the press

Teaming up with a major metropolitan daily newspaper, one of the authors surveyed check-cashing agencies' prices and policies, including prices that varied by the race of the people in the surrounding neighborhood. This resulted in a week-long newspaper series highlighting the practice, and ultimately, a new law regulating price.

in service quality or lower prices. However, usually, results are better if one does not attack the regulator making the decision.

Persist

The victories and balancing of interests described throughout this book did not come quickly or easily. The current wave of democratic confrontations began in the 1970s and is still going on. Even as laws are changed to provide better consumer protection, more competition, energy conservation, environmental protection or lower utility prices, proceedings implementing the rules and setting prices for regulated utilities will continue. Advocates cannot become complacent just because a law or regulation seems to provide the protections and benefits they fought so hard for. The devil is in the details – that is, the tariffs and terms and conditions under which the utilities will operate. Old coalitions may hold; new ones should be forged. Once a party has earned a place at the table, it should not be relinquished or all the hard work can be undermined by poor follow-through. Participation is the crucial component of the mix; without it, the regulator cannot take all views into account when making decisions.

Although democratic regulation is expensive, complex, litigious – and often chaotic – the alternative is worse. This is a fight all participants can win.

10 A History of Democratic Utility Regulation in the US

The early years

US democratic regulation of utility companies grew out of the nation's history of rebelling against unfettered monopoly ownership of essential goods and services. This aversion to monopolies can be linked to our colonial period when a sole company chartered by the Crown could control the availability and price of a cup of tea. Whatever the case may be, democratic regulation of public utilities in the US began more than 130 years ago with the railroads.

In the latter half of the nineteenth century, railroads were the lifeblood of the American economy – just as electricity would become in the twentieth. Because railroads were an essential service, no cost was too high to pay for their development, and the railroad robber barons exploited that fact to the fullest. Capital requirements for railroads far surpassed those for all other industries until the twentieth century, when they were exceeded by the capital demands of the electricity industry.[1] Because of the nature of railroads, once the up-front capital investments were made, the incremental cost to carry one more passenger or one more unit of freight was minimal. Capital requirements and economies of scale were so great that railroads came to be seen as "natural monopolies" – i.e., it made economic sense for only one railroad corporation to serve a particular route. A regulator at the time stated it this way: "competition and the cheapest possible transportation are wholly incompatible."[2] Much the same was said of electricity a few decades later.

Recognizing the importance of railroads to their economies during the 1830s and 1840s, state governments awarded special charters to privately owned railroads along with the power of eminent domain; that is, the railroads could take private property for the public purpose of railroad use by paying fair market value to the owner. In the 1860s, in order to develop the American West, the US government granted millions of acres of free land to two railroad companies, the Union Pacific and the Southern Pacific, to connect a rail line across the entire North American continent. Predating Enron by decades, Union Pacific created a fake construction company, Credit Mobilier, which then charged Union Pacific – its own parent company – twice as much to build the railroad as it cost: $100 million.[3] Union Pacific passed on this fake cost to its passengers. Excess profits went to Credit Mobilier's stockholder, Union Pacific.

While state legislatures wrote strong principles and controls into the charters they awarded to railroad companies and into other railroad legislation, these controls were generally ignored by the railroads and were not enforced by the government.[4] Railroad company owners were already "watering" their stocks (i.e., printing more and more shares of stock without physical assets to back them up) to circumvent legislated limits on profits.[5]

Into this early example of cowboy capitalism came Charles Francis Adams, a descendant of John Adams and John Quincy Adams, the second and sixth presidents of the United States. Adams recognized that railroads were natural monopolies controlled by greedy and corrupt powerful financiers. But he argued against public ownership of railroads even though Belgium, Prussia and France were successfully running state-owned railroads. For Adams, both decentralization in the American system of government and the corrupt politics of the time raised "difficult questions" about government's ability to successfully manage such a complex enterprise as a railroad company.[6] His proposed remedy, of which he convinced the Massachusetts legislature in 1869, was the first American democratic regulation of a private utility: a state commission to oversee and regulate monopoly railroads. Adam's argument about the inability of governments to manage railroads foreshadowed today's World Bank stance against public ownership of utilities (see Chapter 14), but his design evolved into the most democratic supervision of essential utilities ever devised.

The law establishing the Massachusetts Board of Railroad Commissioners was brief but powerful. It gave the Board broad investigative powers, requiring that the railroad corporations release information to the Board "at all times, on demand." This principle was called the "sunshine" approach to regulation because it emphasized information, publicity and written reports, not enforcement through coercion. In fact, the Board was given no true enforcement powers (although by 1887 the Interstate Commerce Commission exerted comprehensive supervision over US railroads).[7] Its power lay in transparency – exposure for the first time of the hitherto secret affairs of private business corporations – in order to protect the "public good." The Massachusetts Board of Railroad Commissioners became the model for all state regulatory commissions in the US. It standardized safety rules, accounting policies and reporting formats for regulated companies, and issued detailed opinions and decisions that set precedents for succeeding commissions. And it did all of this through negotiation, influencing of public opinion and persuasion, with the threat of legal action in the background to act as a stimulus to compliance by the railroads.

1880–1907

Direct current

The electricity industry began on a smaller scale than the railroads. When electric technology was in its infancy toward the end of the nineteenth century, it did not require large capital outlays or large tracts of public land. The industry grew out of the gas commercial and street lighting systems begun in 1816 and the carbon-arc electric lights of the 1870s.[8] It was September 4, 1882 when Thomas Edison opened the first central electricity generation station at Pearl Street in New York City. This station featured four key elements of the modern electricity system: reliable generation, efficient distribution, a successful end use (the incandescent light bulb, invented in 1879) and a competitive price.[9] The Pearl Street station delivered direct current electricity to 59 customers for 24 cents per kilowatt-hour (kWh). By the end of the 1880s, small central stations could be found in many American cities, each limited to a customer base of a few blocks, due to the nature of direct current.[10]

In the 1890s, hundreds of small private power companies offered electric service in cities and towns across America – sometimes as many as 30 or more in a single city.[11] At the same time, city-owned utilities primarily supplied street lighting and power to trolleys, reaching their peak share of electricity production – about 8 per cent – by 1900.[12] Meanwhile, other firms, such as electric railroads, were selling electricity that was surplus to their own needs, or in times of slack demand by their own businesses. In addition, self-contained generators called "isolated systems" were installed in factories or apartment buildings and often attached to central heating systems. These early co-generation systems made up 50 per cent of all electricity distributed in the US in 1889.[13] Most of them were based on direct current and distributed at low voltages (around 110 volts), which limited customers to within a one-mile radius of the generating plant.[14]

Alternating current

However, in 1888, Nikola Tesla designed a new, multiple-phase generator, which produced alternating currents that could transmit electricity over long distances – a technology that would soon have an enormous impact on the industry.[15] George Westinghouse was contracted to develop a hydroelectric station at Niagara Falls using this technology to transmit massive amounts of power over 20 miles to Buffalo, New York, in 1896. This station was the first large system to supply electricity to power multiple end uses (including a railway, lighting, and motor power).[16] Electric utilities spread rapidly, and technological developments and competition led to lower prices (down to about 17 cents per kWh) by the end of the century.[17]

As electric power firms took advantage of the advances in technology and the growing demand for electricity for many different end uses, they began to consolidate and take on the features of a natural monopoly. Richard T. Ely, an economist writing in 1903, wrote that electric companies, like other public utilities such as water and railroads, were "monopolies because, we know from experience, we cannot have in their case effective and permanent competition."[18] Small, private companies, as well as municipal lighting and railway or power companies, merged with or were taken over by ever-growing, more efficient large, private electric companies.[19] Yet public power systems were still being formed at the rate of 60–120 per year every year between 1897 and 1907,[20] and municipalities as well as labor unions were calling for more city-owned systems.

Public versus private ownership

Investor-owned private utilities (IOUs) saw publicly owned power companies as a serious threat to their own dominance. Once again foreshadowing today's international debate about private gains versus social goals, IOUs saw public power companies treating electric pricing and availability as public resources and vehicles to promote social goals, rather than as commodities.[21] Municipal ownership was seen as a way to derive the benefits of a natural monopoly – economies of scale, efficiency, diversity of demand and low prices – without the abuses associated with monopolies. Yet it was still not clear which model of ownership, public or private, would predominate.

One way the private companies eliminated competition from the municipals was to buy them out. When that did not work in a particular area, the private company would offer power to the municipal at low prices to undermine the ability of the municipal to build or maintain its own generators. Private companies used economies of scale and strong financial backing (and eventually regulatory protection) to increase the size of their generators and to extend their distribution systems. More and more municipals began buying most or all of their power from private utilities, such that the figure rose from less than 7 per cent of municipals that did so in 1909 to over one-third in 1923.[22] Thus, by 1922, there were 2,500 municipally owned systems in the US, but they produced less than 4 per cent of the total energy.[23]

By 1904, British-born Samuel Insull, former administrative secretary and key manager for Thomas Edison, was president of Chicago Edison in Illinois, as well as president of the National Electric Light Association (NELA) and the Association of Edison Illuminating Companies (AEIC), the two major electric industry trade associations in the US at the time. Insull had a powerful circle of associates in the industry, most of whom had worked with him for Thomas Edison.[24] The two trade organizations promoted privately owned, central station electric service in place of public power and isolated stations. They offered economies of scale through new, more efficient technologies; territorial expansion; combining loads that demanded power at different times of day (called "diversity"); and rate reductions.

As America was industrializing in the 1880s and 1890s, Populist movements developed in reaction (particularly in the South and Middle West) to represent workers and family farmers against growing concentrations of wealth and power in corporations and on Wall Street. Labor was beginning to organize to improve low wages and wretched working conditions, while farmers organized for credit, insurance and other farm needs. Populist objectives included progressive taxation, organization of labor, and cooperative and public ownership of key parts of the economy, such as utilities, banks, insurers, warehouses and commodity exchanges. Though ultimately absorbed into the two-party system, the Populist reaction to early industrialization represented a real threat to private ownership of vital public services.[25] Indeed, much of the Populist platform remains mainstream American practice, such as the right of labor to organize, public lending and loan guarantees, some forms of public insurance, and regulated commodity exchanges. But, for the most part, not public ownership of utilities.

Samuel Insull believed that state regulation of private utilities could eliminate (or minimize) the threat from the Populists to turn them into public power companies.[26] As early as 1898, Insull had spoken at a major power industry convention in Alabama where he told fellow energy leaders that competition in the electric industry was "economically wrong" and that electricity was a "natural monopoly."[27] He persuaded fellow private owners that state regulation would legitimize the monopoly status of utilities, differentiate them from the "evil" big oil and railroad companies in the public's mind, and allow them to raise money more easily because regulators would help guarantee their financial integrity for investors.[28]

In 1905, the National Civic Federation (NCF), an organization that had been formed in 1900 to develop "a systematic businessman's solution to . . . government intervention into business," formed the Committee on Public Ownership and Operation (CPOO) to undertake a study of the electric power industry.[29] Participants in the CPOO included members of NELA and AEIC, bankers, railroaders, labor unions, public power owners and professionals from other industries. While purporting to be objective, the CPOO undertook to compare only the US and British systems of electricity production and distribution, and to ignore questions of federal regulation of electric equipment and practices, or the effectiveness of nonprofit electricity systems in 500 cities and towns. They excluded a study of other types of utilities and utilities in countries besides the US and the UK,[30] but they did include consideration of exclusive franchises for utility companies (thereby framing the study to include evaluation of state regulation). According to NCF leaders who admitted it later, they did this because they recognized that "private property, properly regulated . . . [was the] preferable [outcome]."[31] It was the best way to prevail against the growing tendency to public ownership of electric companies.

1907–1929

Regulation of IOUs

The NCF published its report in 1907: the "Municipal and Private Operation of Public Utilities: Report to the National Civic Federation" (Report). The Report took no position on the benefits of private versus public ownership per se (although they did find a preference for not-for-profit utilities in Britain). However, the study was funded and promoted by the investor-owned utilities, so it is not surprising that the IOUs' position on state regulation of privately owned utilities prevailed in the end.[32]

One unanimous finding in the NCF Report – lost to today's debate over electricity deregulation – was that "free competition had proven a total and catastrophic failure."[33] Despite having almost no data on privately owned and operated systems (because the IOUs claimed these data were proprietary and would not provide them), 19 of the 21 members of the CPOO also agreed that "public utilities whether in public or private hands are best conducted under a system of legalized and regulated monopoly" and that "private companies should be subject to public regulation"[34] open to examination through a uniform system of transparent accounting and record keeping.[35] The Report called for:

1. state regulation by commission;
2. guaranteed returns on capital invested to prevent confiscation of property;
3. long-term franchises;
4. recognition of natural monopolies; and
5. equal value of all stocks in the electric company (rather than having several classes of stock, each with a different value).

These principles coincided with those of Insull and became the basis of future industry development and state regulatory practices.[36]

Many of the leaders of IOUs actively supported regulation by the states patterned after that proposed by the NCF Report. For example, Baltimore Electric Light and Power even bought ads, printed circulars and provided speakers to promote the NCF model in Maryland.[37] The system of state regulation that began in 1907 encouraged investment in privately owned companies by guaranteeing returns. With the backing of most of the central station IOUs, by the end of World War I in 1918, any potential dominance by public power was decisively defeated.[38]

The first state to establish a regulatory commission based on the principles enunciated in the NCF report was Wisconsin, in 1907, although the Adams-style Massachusetts Board of Gas Commissioners had been created in 1885 and was extended to include Electric Lights in 1887. Wisconsin was quickly followed by New York, and before the end of the decade by Vermont, New Jersey and Maryland. Massachusetts merged the railroad and utility commissions into the Department of Public Utilities in 1919. By 1921, all of the states except Delaware had established commissions with the power to regulate public utilities.[39] The main purpose of these commissions was to protect the interests of both electric companies and consumers through a process of transparent information-gathering and informal negotiations, guided by a standard of what was "just and reasonable." However, when an electric company disagreed with a commission decision on rates, the company could take the case to court, delaying action and effectively crippling the commission's authority.[40] The regulatory situation remained this way for electric companies throughout the 1920s.

Development of holding companies

In the meantime, by 1907, Samuel Insull had acquired more utility companies and changed his firm's name to Commonwealth Edison. He had successfully argued that to build multiple transmission and distribution systems in one area would be inefficient and too expensive; thus, one vertically integrated company should serve each franchised territory as a natural monopoly.[41] Other utility companies were expanding in this way in other parts of the country. During the first two decades after state regulation of the industry began, electrical output from utility companies soared from 5.9 million kWh in 1907 to 75.4 million kWh in 1927, while the real price of electricity dropped 55 per cent.[42]

Insull and others in the industry began to restructure their companies and form multi-state holding companies that controlled operating utilities. While holding companies can be useful in consolidating the operations of several smaller companies and providing services to these operating companies more efficiently than could be done by each one acting alone, the holding companies being formed at this time in the US were primarily designed to maximize profits for holding company investors.[43] The holding companies would charge affiliated utilities exorbitant prices for services such as billing, fuel procurement and construction of plant.[44] Each new holding company would buy a controlling interest in the holding company below it, such that sometimes a holding company was ten times removed from the operating companies actually producing the power. In 1912, Insull created a new parent company, Middle West Utilities, and sold his operating companies to Middle West at ten times their value. He then released more stocks and bonds and charged higher prices to the operating companies' customers to cover the inflated cost.[45] The practice became known as "stock watering" because stock investments greatly exceeded the tangible assets behind them. And each layer in the "pyramid" of holding companies demanded its profits.

This type of pyramid scheme ran rampant during the "roaring twenties" – the administration of President Calvin Coolidge. His administration instituted policies that fueled speculation and fostered the growth of huge holding companies that financed the takeover of smaller companies by issuing paper stock. During this time period, one-third of all corporate financing in America was issued by the power companies. By the end of the 1920s, holding companies had consolidated so much that only ten utility systems controlled 75 per cent of the electric power business in the US.[46] Five public utility holding company systems were controlled in 1931 by holders of stock worth less than 1 per cent of the entire system's assets.[47] And because these holding companies operated across multiple state borders, they were not subject to state regulatory jurisdiction.

The Federal government had not been completely idle all of this time, however. Between 1901 and 1920, the electric power industry had been recognized as a natural monopoly in interstate commerce, subject to Federal regulation; the Federal government owned most of the nation's hydroelectric resources (including Niagara Falls); and Federal economic development programs, including electricity generation, had increased. In 1920, the Federal Water Power Act codified Federal powers and established the Federal Power Commission to issue licenses to build and operate hydropower plants.[48]

In 1928, the Federal Trade Commission (FTC) began a six-year investigation into market manipulation by the holding companies. In 1929, the stock market crashed, breaking the speculative bubble of the holding companies and creating a clamor for more effective regulation of companies whose mandate was to serve the public good and to operate in the public interest.

1930–1970

Collapse of Insull's empire

By the time of the market crash in October 1929, Samuel Insull, along with his family and partners, had parlayed Commonwealth Edison Company into a business conglomerate that operated in 39 of the 48 states in America. It included, among others, one giant investment company in which a trusting public had invested over $100,000,000.[49] It was the third largest utility group in the country, producing about 10 per cent of the nation's total electrical power.[50] Foreshadowing Enron in many ways, its affiliates included utilities, construction companies and electrical equipment manufacturers, all of which sold stocks to other Insull affiliates. "There was tremendous pyramiding and preferential treatment of affiliated companies," according to economist Alfred Kahn.[51]

But the pyramid collapsed over the following three years. Losses to security holders would total nearly $800,000,000. Up to 600,000 shareholders, 500,000 bondholders, and Insull himself were wiped out.[52] An investigation into Insull's companies by the US Department of Justice began in September 1932.[53] By 1934, the failure of Insull's empire was being discussed on the floor of the US Senate, in order to determine where the laws and regulations had failed. One Senator, George Norris, a Republican from Nebraska, summed it up thusly: "Mr. Insull, for one, 'was careful to regulate the regulator.'"[54]

Federal action

Meanwhile, by the 1930s across the US, privately owned, large, central-ized generating stations were supplying 94 per cent of the nation's electricity,[55] and stock watering had reached its peak. Franklin Delano Roosevelt campaigned for President partly on a platform of reforming the public utility companies. In a speech he gave in Portland, Oregon, on September 21, 1932, Roosevelt decried the abuses by the utilities and the ineffectiveness of the state regulatory commissions:

> It is an undoubted and undeniable fact that in our modern American practice the public service commissions of many States have often failed to live up to the very high purpose for which they were created. In many instances their selection has been obtained by the public utility cor-porations themselves.[56]

If he were to be elected, Roosevelt promised drastic new curbs on cor-porations, and he specifically supported legislation that would bring to the light of day the nature of securities abuses and manipulation of the stock exchanges by the holding companies.[57]

President Roosevelt also supported measures to electrify the rural areas of the country. Investor-owned utilities had concentrated development of electric systems in the more densely populated areas, figuring that there was greater profit to be earned there. They had neglected rural areas to the point where only 10 per cent of American farms had electricity in 1930.[58] Congress passed the Tennessee Valley Authority Act in 1933 to electrify the southeast; the Bonneville Project Act in 1937, creating the Bonneville Power Administration (BPA), to electrify the northwest; and the Rural Electrification Act in 1936, to finance rural distribution systems. These laws provided for the building of huge dams and other power plants, exemption from regulation, loans to organizations that would distribute electricity to rural areas, and reasonably priced electricity for millions of people.[59] By 1945, almost 45 per cent of American farms were wired for electricity,[60] and prices had fallen in the Northwest from several dollars per kWh at the turn of the century to a wholesale price of 0.2 cents per kWh after the BPA was formed. The average American family earned about $100 per month in the 1930s, and this rate let them pay about $7.50 a month for lights, appliances and electric heat. Low prices charged by the Federal public power authorities forced IOUs to lower their rates as well, benefiting everyone.[61]

In 1934, Roosevelt proposed and Congress enacted the Securities Exchange Act. This Act established the Securities and Exchange

Commission (SEC) to license stock exchanges, issue regulations governing stock market operations and prohibit stock price manipulation. Then, in 1935, Roosevelt introduced the Public Utility Holding Company Act (PUHCA) to Congress, asserting Federal jurisdiction over multi-state utilities.

Public Utility Holding Company Act

Contrary to IOU support for state regulation back in 1907, investor-owned utilities and their financiers fought passage of PUHCA with at least $1.5 million and intensive lobbying. But the six-year FTC investigation into market manipulation had exposed the abusive practices of holding companies, concluding that the holding company structure was unsound and "frequently a menace to the investor or the consumer or both."[62] The FTC Report listed 19 general categories of abuse, which included the following:

1. The issuance of securities to the public that were based on unsound asset values or on paper profits from inter-company transactions. Excessive debt-to-equity ratios contributed to the bankruptcy of 53 holding companies during 1929 through 1936. Twenty-three additional holding companies with publicly held securities exceeding $530 million defaulted on interest payments. In addition, 36 utilities with outstanding publicly held securities of $345 million went into bankruptcy or receivership during that same time period. And public investors with utility preferred stock worth almost $1.5 billion at the end of 1938 also suffered great losses.[63]

2. The mismanagement and exploitation of operating subsidiaries of holding companies through excessive service charges, excessive common stock dividends and upstream loans. The combined capital assets of the 151 firms studied by the FTC were written up by $1.4 billion to inflate earnings and justify dividends. Some holding companies had provided services at such inflated prices that they exacted profits ranging from 50 per cent to over 300 per cent of the actual cost of the services. The appearance of even larger profits was created by unsound accounting methods such as inadequate depreciation of physical assets and counting as income the sale of properties to controlled subsidiaries at amounts higher than their market value.[64]

3. The use of the holding company to evade state regulation. Because 16 major holding companies produced 76 per cent of the electricity generated by privately owned plants, and just three systems produced

45 per cent of the output, operations were spread across many state boundaries.[65] Since state commissions by law could regulate only companies that were wholly within state borders, these multi-state holding companies were subject to no system of regulation before 1935.

By the middle of 1935, PUHCA was passed by both Houses of Congress and signed into law by President Roosevelt. PUHCA outlawed the pyramidal structure of interstate utility holding companies, determining that they could be no more than twice removed from their operating subsidiaries. It required holding companies that owned 10 per cent or more of a public utility to register with the SEC and to provide detailed accounts of their financial transactions and holdings – in other words, PUHCA required transparency of information. (Holding companies that operated within a single state were state-regulated and exempt from PUHCA.)

Federal Power Act

Several gaps were left in the regulatory system after passage of PUHCA. Distribution utilities, as well as integrated utilities offering generation, transmission and distribution within a state, were state regulated. But stand-alone generation or high-voltage transmission utilities could sell their monopoly services at whatever price they could get, so Federal regulation was further extended by the Federal Power Act of 1935. This Act gave the Federal Power Commission (FPC) (that had been established in 1920) regulatory power over both wholesale transactions (purchases of generation by distribution utilities) and transmission of electric power, and mandated that the FPC ensure that electricity rates are "reasonable, nondiscriminatory and just to the consumer."[66] This now meant that all electricity prices – generation, transmission, and distribution, state or federally regulated – had to be based on cost, not on whatever the market would bear.[67]

The effect of this legislation was dramatic: between 1938 and 1958, the number of holding companies declined from 216 to 18; operating companies were again regulated by the states; and this structure of the electric utility industry lasted until near the end of the twentieth century[68] (although PUHCA still faces utility opposition, and the SEC favors its repeal).[69]

Economies of scale and growth rates of approximately 8 per cent per year between 1932 and 1973 brought a steady period of declining electricity rates. Until the northeast blackout of 1965 and the energy crises of the 1970s, when growth rates collapsed and prices soared, most electric utility regulation entailed supervision of non-controversial rate cuts.[70]

However, beginning in the 1980s, the pattern seen in the 1920s and 1930s began to emerge again. After mergers and formation of new holding companies, 26 now control 40 per cent of IOU assets, 40 per cent of IOU revenues, and 50 per cent of all electricity customers in the US.[71] But this, too, is changing yet again.

1980–2002

Emerging deregulation

Responding to the oil embargo and subsequent oil price hikes in 1973, then US President Jimmy Carter proposed a comprehensive National Energy Plan that would encourage energy conservation, heavily tax fossil fuel use, change the way utility prices were set, and encourage co-generation and renewable electricity generation. By the time the US Congress was through with the Plan, not much was left. However, one important piece of legislation that survived was the Public Utility Regulatory Policies Act, or PURPA, passed in September 1978. PURPA brought an entirely new set of players into the electric industry. This law required that utilities buy power from independent power producers at prices that would cover all of the capital and operating costs of co-generators (plants that produced both heat and electricity) and small plants that generated electricity from biomass, waste or renewable resources. These so-called "qualifying facilities" were exempt from PUHCA and also from state price-regulation.[72] Thus began the erosion of the monopoly power in generation enjoyed by incumbent utilities. The stage was set for the restructuring of the entire utility industry.

After the passage of PURPA, during the mid-1980s, the federal government deregulated the natural gas industry. By the late 1980s, State public utility commissions (PUCs) began to loosen even more the regulatory bonds for electricity generation, while those pertaining to transmission and distribution were strengthened. PUCs in some states required utilities to do long-term planning by taking into account all possible resources that might be enlisted to serve electricity demand and provide reserves for reliability. This exercise, called "integrated resource planning" or "IRP," encouraged utilities to look to energy conservation and to contracts with other power suppliers to meet future need, instead of building power plants themselves. A competitive independent power supply market grew to meet this demand.

At the same time, the UK was beginning forays into deregulation of its utilities, and the US followed suit. As we described earlier, US deregulation efforts were led by large industrial customers and supported by economic theorists and scholars like Paul Joskow and Richard Schmalensee at the Massachusetts Institute of Technology.[73] However, these economists recognized that a workable deregulation scheme would require that some segments of the industry, such as retail pricing and access to the distribution system, continue to be regulated.[74] Nevertheless, energy marketers like Enron saw an opportunity to reap obscene profits from utility industry deregulation, and they took full advantage of it. We describe some of the worst abuses in Chapter 13.

We cannot tell you what will happen next, of course. But we can tell you that the future history of US utility regulation will be written by public participation in regulators' hearings rooms as well as in legislative lobbies.

11 Regulating the Multinational Utility

Until the last two decades, foreign ownership of domestic monopoly utility services in electricity, water, natural gas and telephone was rare. Now ownership of public services by international firms is quickly becoming dominant, mostly as the result of a near-universal program of privatization.[1] How foreign operators are to be regulated usually comes as an afterthought in the rush to sell state assets. In the case of Brazil, for example, the regulatory regime was not even established until *after* the privatization of properties. We have to recognize that maximizing privatization sale prices will necessarily conflict with establishing a fair and reasonable regulatory regime. Promising an uncontrolled monopoly market and unlimited profits lures buyers, but at a price. As the World Bank's former Chief Economist stated: "High prices after privatisation of infrastructure are a hidden tax paid by the public which is an unconscionable burden on developing economies."[2]

The question here is not whether privatization is wise or foolish – we leave that debate to others. We seek to answer the forgotten question: once privatized and sold to foreigners, how should these utilities be regulated? Again, we call on the US experience for guidance through the example of the purchase of a US electricity company by Scottish Power of the United Kingdom. The case is not an example of regulatory perfection. Rather it is a review of how in practice a nation successfully exercises democratic and sovereign rights over a foreign-based owner to protect local interests.

By contrasting the US practice with cases from Brazil and Bolivia, we can extract a simple rule: the more democratic the process, the better the result for society. This may seem obvious, even simplistic, but unfortunately, except in the US, the debate ends with formulas presented by experts, consultants and international agencies. There is virtually no place given to democratic participation.

United States

In 1999, Scottish Power UK sought to purchase PacifiCorp, one of America's largest vertically integrated utilities and the principal generator, transmitter and distributor of electricity in the states of Oregon and Utah. Because Scottish Power merely purchased the stock of PacifiCorp, the UK firm assumed it had little or no obligations to its US customers beyond the pricing and supply rules which applied to the company it bought.

But US consumer, labor and business organizations challenged the purchase before the Oregon Public Utilities Commission and the Utah Public Service Commission. To the surprise of the British operator, the purchase of the US company was delayed for about one year while the regulators held public hearings. The Scottish executives then found that, quite unlike the closed system in Britain, they had to open their financial records, projections of costs, employment plans, environmental programs and all manner of internal information to public review. In fact, the US regulators required Scottish Power to sign a legal waiver allowing US regulators to see documents of the company's entire international and Scottish operations, which are not available to the public or government in Scotland itself.

Most extraordinary, from the point of view of the executives from Scotland, is that they were subject to questioning, under oath and in public, by dozens of consumer advocates as well as industrial customers, lawyers for low-income organizations and even some of the company's future competitors such as Enron Corporation and the government-owned Bonneville Power Administration.

Nearly anyone could ask the foreign executives questions about their planned operations and past history – and dozens did so over several months. Faced with the possible rejection of their proposed takeover, Scottish Power initiated negotiations with customer groups. Unlike the process in other nations, the negotiations were not limited to meetings with government. Scottish Power had to reach compromises with many customer organizations before regulators would authorize their purchase of the utilities.

In Oregon, the company ultimately signed a list of 24 concessions, including price decreases, a promise to maintain open financial records and an extraordinary commitment not to use international law to set aside a decision of local US regulators. The list was detailed, including very specific levels of funding for conservation and alternative energy projects and a specific year-by-year plan for investments in system reliability. Scottish Power must double the amount of PacifiCorp's investments in energy efficiency in Oregon, invest in 50 megawatts of renewable generating resources, increase resources devoted to low-income consumers, adhere to service quality standards (with penalties for violations), and reduce prices by about $10 million annually.[3]

Two of the authors of this book advised organizations of poor people in Utah. Among the concessions obtained were first-in-the-state low-income discounts and utility-funded efficiency programs. For Americans, the Scottish Power merger was simply an application of existing practices to control multi-jurisdictional (cross-border) utilities.

In the US, utilities often operate in more than one state. Utilities that operate in more than one state jurisdiction may play a shell game to keep any of the jurisdictions from knowing exactly how much they really spend in each state. For decades until it was broken up in 1984, the old American Telephone and Telegraph Company (AT&T) charged each of its state affiliates a "license fee" equal to a flat per centage of revenues, purportedly in exchange for unspecified services of its headquarters (General) Department. However, once state regulators began to audit the General Department to determine how much was actually spent to benefit their particular states, the amount of the license fee dropped. States also found that expenditures that were not allowed as part of rates at all – such as legislative lobbying – had found their way onto the General Department's books.[4]

Similarly, many electric utilities are owned by holding companies that also own a Service Company that renders the same services to all sister subsidiaries.[5] The charges for these services can then be allocated according to how willing a particular state is to foot the bill (or how lax its regulators), rather than in accordance with the amount actually spent to benefit the ratepayers of each state. Thus a multi-jurisdictional holding company may try to obtain for itself, for each item of expense, the most favorable treatment of any jurisdiction it serves. Increasingly, US electric utilities are owned by non-US utility holding companies.[6] But it is crystal clear that the US operations remain subject to US rules about disclosure, social equity, and everything else.[7] In addition, each retail utility is subject to the rules of the state in which it operates.

Mergers and acquisitions across jurisdictional lines must be approved by multiple jurisdictions, each of which can attach conditions, e.g., conservation, social rates, renewables, merger savings to ratepayers, service quality guarantees, labor force guarantees. Thus recent mergers have resulted in new utility obligations with respect to low-income discount rates, investments in conservation, investments in renewables, and pollution controls.[8]

Brazil

The experience of Brazil was quite different. In the 1990s, with the country in need of foreign exchange reserves, there was a push to maximize gains from the sale of state-owned electricity, telephone and natural gas distribution companies. The World Bank helped by paying for consultants such as the American law firm Hunton & Williams, which represents several large US utilities hoping to bid for Brazil's utility properties. Brazil's government also hired Coopers & Lybrand, the consulting firm (now PriceWaterhouseCoopers) which also advises bidding firms. With their close knowledge of bidders' desires, the firms designed plans which would meet their needs and thereby maximize prices paid for the utilities.[9]

Unfortunately, this process substantially excluded those who would ultimately have to purchase the electricity and phone services from the new foreign owners. It also excluded the employees who would have to work for the new owners. However, this is not to say the establishment of the regulatory regime excluded any democratic element. Consumer groups and unions were given an opportunity to comment on the proposed new regulatory regime.

"Comment" is no substitute for participation – and we are unaware of any change in the proposals as a result of the consumers' and workers' intervention. The guaranteed rates of return on investment, and the state-guaranteed protections against competition for one or more decades, were unchanged by public comment. Nor was the public able to obtain any guarantee against job losses, expansion of the system or a schedule of reliability improvements. In effect, the bidders wrote their own rules, and opportunity for public comment appeared little more than a pretense of democratic process.

There is a basis for some hope for democratic regulation in Brazil. The bids and the regulatory plans were made public – and publication itself puts a practical political limit on the terms that can be granted foreigners in a nation where the public has the right to vote. Consumer groups and trade unions also had the right to challenge the bids in court, which they did with some success.[10]

The federal regulation program holds out the hope of greater democratization of the process, through a provision to turn over regulation of the utilities to the states. However, in practice, the federal government has so far resisted handing authority to the state of Rio Grande do Sul, the first state prepared to take over this function.[11]

Bolivia

Bolivia's privatization and regulation of its water system provides an example of regulation totally lacking in democratic control of foreign owners.[12]

In 1999 and 2000, the key technical utility issue of conflict in Bolivia was one that had been in contention in the US one and two decades earlier: the accounting for and charging of interest on construction work in progress. As we have stated previously, the US Uniform System of Accounts prevents water and electricity companies from charging current customers for the cost of new construction and system expansion until the work is completed. Then, construction costs (including interest) must be "capitalized;" that is, paid up-front by the company's shareholders and then charged back to consumers pro rata over the life of the project.

In the 1970s and 1980s, US electricity companies sought exemptions from the rule, asking to charge current customers for the interest on multi-billion-dollar nuclear plants under construction. The matter was dealt with as are all other utility matters: long hearings; fierce litigation; detailed public analysis of projects; loud debate in newspapers and in government hearing rooms. Regulators in each of the 50 states came to different conclusions, but in the main, the results were those unhappy but workable compromises that come from democratic processes: utilities were denied most construction surcharges but consumers had to pay a portion.

In Bolivia, the matter was settled without public hearings or public examination of the projects at stake. The results were tragic.

In 1999, a British Corporation, International Water (controlled by American construction firm Bechtel), purchased the water company serving Bolivia's second largest city, Cochabamba.[13] The newly privatized water company, Aguas de Tunari, raised prices by 35 per cent (says the company) or by 100 per cent (say consumers). The company said it raised prices because the regulator had authorized it to charge for construction work in progress on two projects: the expansion of the local water system and the building of the Misicuni Dam.

The procedure suffered from several democratic deficits. First, no one could confirm how much the new company was actually charging new customers, nor whether they used the collections for the purpose claimed as there was no system of accounts which the public could view. Nor could experts acting on behalf of the public determine whether the new private company in fact paid any sum for water company construction.

As to the violation of the basic accounting rule that future projects may not be charged to current customers, neither the water company nor the government explained or permitted debate over the matter. Furthermore, there were no public hearings to review the detailed costs and benefits of the dam project. Nor were there public hearings over the means of expanding Cochabamba's water system (where 30 per cent of the public lacked piped water). Indeed, World Bank experts issued a summary of their study concluding that the Misicuni project cost 500 per cent more than alternative water sources.[14] The new British–American company's plan to charge for water expansion, requiring large water price increases, was inferior to a proposal for expanding the system through creation of local cooperatives. The cooperative plan did not require increasing water prices because new customers would pay the new costs as the system expanded.

Cochabamba's public was given no opportunity to analyze the alternatives or argue against the proposals and water charges. While government refused to consult those affected, there was pressure from above. The World Bank's President insisted, in comments delivered on April 27, 2000, in Washington, that Cochabamba water customers pay the higher charge. Bank President James Wolfensohn took this position on the policy ground that rising water prices worldwide, in general, would provide for better allocation of the resource. Somehow this is part of the World Bank's Poverty Reduction Strategy Plan for Bolivia, which determines the nation's programs for capital spending and privatization schedule.[15]

Excluded from any real participation in the setting of the water prices and the decisions about ownership and investment, Cochabamba citizens took to the streets in April 2000. Leaders of the water protest, during a meeting with the government, were arrested (although all were released later). In the ensuing public demonstrations, two people were killed by government forces. Ultimately, the price increases were rescinded.

It is true that the US system of determining construction-work-in-progress charges was complex, difficult and litigious. But the Bolivian alternative seemed to be regulation by riot, certainly not a model to be followed. Ironically, while the secretive decision-making process appeared to be an attempt to protect foreign owners from local citizen opposition, the result was the opposite. The water bills were uncollectible and the government, to quell public unrest, terminated International Water's franchise to operate in Cochabamba. Now those investors are suing the government for reparations.

One positive result of the tragedy of Cochabamba is that international agencies, such as the World Bank, are stepping up opportunities for public dialogue on their policies. Just as the international funding agencies – the World Bank, the International Monetary Fund (IMF), and the Inter-American Development Bank – played a strong part in promoting privatisation, they will have a key role in the regulation of these companies. In Bolivia, the World Bank initiated its "Diálogo Nacional," bringing together members of what the bank calls "civil society" – various public organizations and government – to discuss the terms and implementation of the Poverty Reduction Strategy Paper which will effectively guide economic activity in the nation.[16]

Whether the Diálogo becomes a sham forum for pretend consultation or a true platform for the creation of democratic methods for regulating public services will depend not only on the World Bank and the government but also on the demand for democratic governance by the participants. The World Bank and IMF have offered forums for social dialogue which could be transformed into a powerful engine for democratizing regulatory systems.

Democracy: a value in itself

There is a value to bringing democracy to utility regulation beyond the practical value of preventing riots, reducing prices, saving jobs and making industry efficient. Bringing democracy to utility regulation is a way to reinforce the value of social dialogue, rather than conflict, to resolve basic issues of economic efficiency, employment, quality of life and fairness in the provision of public services.

What may seem arcane matters of utility accounting – such as "capitalizing construction work in progress" – become life and death issues, and the source of devastating conflicts, in nations where social dialogue breaks down. The core issue then is not markets versus regulation, nor government ownership versus private, nor foreign control versus domestic. The key issue is democratic decision-making in society versus secrecy and coercion. The latter lead to upheaval, even violence. The US system may be "adversarial," and the arguments of opposing parties in American regulatory hearings fierce, loud and often less than polite. Yet, providing this open forum for opposing beliefs and interests keeps US civil society civil. Once society concedes that the public has a right to participate actively and knowledgeably in the control of public services, issues can be resolved in hearing rooms, rather than in the streets.

12 Failed Experiments in the UK and the US

The idea for experimenting with deregulation and privatization began in the United Kingdom. As the experiments were failing in the land of their birth, some US policy-makers nevertheless decided to try their own – with changes so that, this time, markets would truly lower prices. In the meantime, UK policy-makers were busy creating their own corrections. None of the fixes on either side of the Atlantic worked. Each US state that subsequently followed with its own experiment was certain that, this time, it had cracked the code of lower prices with less regulation. None has.

The United Kingdom

The failure of competition and deregulation in the United Kingdom – where it all began – is described in earlier chapters. In the first eight years (during which only larger customers could choose alternative suppliers), domestic electricity generation prices declined by only about 2 per cent. In the same period, the prices of the fuels used to generate electricity dropped like a rock – 30 per cent for coal, 40 per cent for gas. Industry-wide, 46 per cent of workers lost their jobs. Where did the money go? As shown below, some of it went to price reductions for large customers. But over the first seven years, combined generation company accounts, filed with the regulator, showed a profit increase of 172 per cent, i.e., almost triple profits before privatisation. National Power, one of the two privatized generation companies created, paid dividends to stockholders in excess of the entire value of the corporation at the time of privatization.[1] A University of Cambridge study published by the World Bank concluded that power prices are 1–4 per cent higher than they would have been in the absence of privatization while the value of shares in National Power and PowerGen (the other privatized generation corporation) tripled.[2]

Similarly, in the first twelve years of privatization of the natural gas industry in the UK, wholesale gas prices fell 33 per cent in real terms (about flat nominally) and 61 per cent of workers have been discharged. Domestic gas prices declined in real terms, but only by 25 per cent.[3]

In the two years before privatization was implemented in 1990, the UK government raised electricity prices in order to make the industry more attractive to investors.[4] (Ironically, however, share prices shot up 40 per cent in the first week of trading alone, indicating the sale price was set too low by £963 million just for National Power and PowerGen.[5] The sale price may have accurately reflected the utilities' value at regulated prices; the increase in share price thus graphically quantifies the loss to consumers from deregulating prices.) Therefore the proper starting point for an analysis of the price impact of privatisation in the UK is 1988, from which domestic prices rose 40 per cent by 1995 and have since leveled off to an increase of 22 per cent at the year 2000. By contrast, industrial prices rose (not as much) but have now fallen to about their 1988 level.[6]

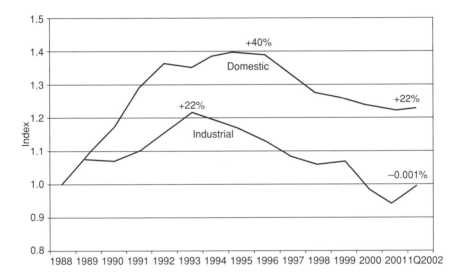

Figure 11   UK Electricity Price Gap (Source: UK DTI (2002))

On average, competition provides UK domestic consumers a 13 per cent savings from the highest price offered by electricity suppliers to the lowest,[7] or the chance to roughly break even with the price in 1988. So far, this has induced only about a third of UK domestic consumers to switch suppliers.[8] In real (inflation-adjusted) terms, between 1985 and 1999, all prices in the US as well as the UK have declined for reasons having nothing to do with regulation or privatisation, such as fuel price declines. But *regulated* prices in the US declined further, particularly for domestic customers. In the UK, industrial customers received a much larger decrease than domestic customers, 38 per cent versus 24 per cent. The regulated US domestic consumer fared better than his UK cousin, receiving a 30 per cent decrease.[9]

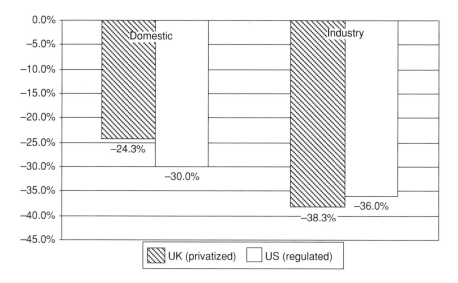

Figure 12   Real Electricity Price Decreases, US versus UK, 1985–99 (Sources: UK DTI Quarterly Energy Prices (December 2001), Boston Pacific Co. study for EPSA (US))

Domestic consumers have been able to choose generation providers since 1998 in the UK,[10] but it is not generation price reductions that have brought prices down from their 1995 peaks. An MIT study found that "Contrary to the predictions of the standard models used in this [generation] market, prices and mark-ups [from 1995 to 2000] appear not to have fallen since the early 1990s;[11] indeed, the UK regulator found in 1997 that small customers were charged 28 per cent more for generation than large consumers.[12] What kept domestic prices from going any higher were reductions in the *regulated* components of domestic customers' bills.[13]

The United States

The undemocratic ideologies of deregulation and privatisation have been as harsh to some of their inventors as to their intended victims. In something of a dance among elephants, some of the large industrial customers that lobbied hard to deregulate electricity prices in the US, in order to lower their own prices at the expense of others, have become the victims of price gouging by energy titans. While this may be poetic justice in many cases, in others the industrialists were able to re-sell entitlements to cheap electricity at unimaginable prices. These industrialists then closed shop and went home to count their profits. Thousands of jobs were lost.

The political movement for retail electricity competition in the US began with large industrial customers, who were not satisfied with the price reductions they obtained in the regulatory process over the last 20 years, after suffering substantial increases in the 1970s compared with smaller domestic (residential) increases. These customers thought they saw an opening to shift even more of the costs of the electricity system to smaller customers. The 1980s and 1990s brought a series of price drops to electricity utilities' industrial customers while domestic prices continued to climb. Industrials wanted even more cuts, without regard to what would happen to domestic prices.

To win consumers over in the debate about retail electricity competition, they were offered lower prices as part of the deregulation bargain – in

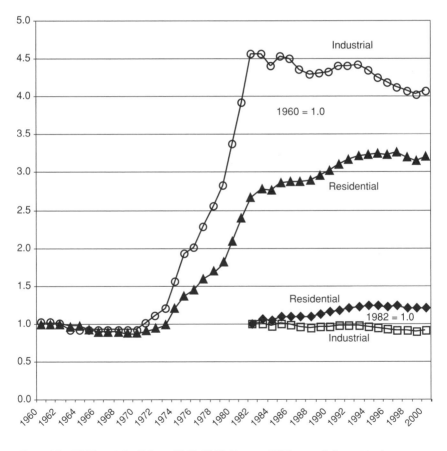

Figure 13   US Electricity Prices, 1960–2001 (Source: US Energy Information)

most cases guaranteed for a period by statute, then promised thereafter as an inevitable consequence of competition. Consumers were also offered choice, the ability to choose an electricity supplier – though not because any domestic consumer had asked for it. Indeed, after the confusion of telephone deregulation and the proliferation of telemarketed long distance offers, most consumers yearned for fewer utility choices rather than more. Furthermore, with electricity prices already among the lowest in the world and declining slowly, there was little clamor among non-low-income domestic consumers for lower prices.

As it has turned out so far, nearly all consumers – industrials included – have received neither lower prices nor choice as a result of retail competition. Nationwide only 1.2 per cent of customers, with 3.2 per cent of load, are served by competitive suppliers. Even considering only the states where there is at least some competition, only 3.2 per cent of domestic customers and 7.5 per cent of industrial customers (3.2 per cent and 13 per cent of load, respectively) are served by competition. Only 35 per cent of energy managers at medium-sized and large companies think that competition plans should be continued.[14] The experiment has been ruled a failure even by those who asked for it.

California, of course, is the most dramatic failure of retail electricity competition. Wholesale electricity prices that were as low as 2.1 cents per kilowatt-hour (kWh) in February 1999 spiked to 31.7 cents per kWh in December 2000.[15] Blackouts rolled across the state costing Silicon Valley manufacturers tens of millions of dollars.[16] Miller Beer shifted brewery production from California to Texas. Intel's CEO announced a suspension of expansion in California. Industrial plants closed all over the West, putting their employees out of work.[17] The costs of electricity deregulation in California may never be fully counted.

Nor will the profits, which include annual returns on investment over 100 per cent.[18] Reliant Energy argues this simply shows the market is working.[19]

Workers have been laid off at smelters, paper mills and mines all over the Northwest. Nineteen Montana firms planned to curtail production due to high energy prices, according to a December 2000 study of industry by the Bureau of Business and Economic Research at the University of Montana. Montana Resources closed its copper mine in Butte, displacing 325 workers. In Arizona and New Mexico, Phelps Dodge gave notice to 2,000 miners that they face layoffs due to high energy prices. Washington State predicts that "43,000 jobs could be lost over the next three years."[20] Kaiser Aluminum, at its Mead aluminum plant near Spokane, decided to sell electricity for

$400 million rather than keep production going, idling 600 workers. Georgia Pacific West shut down its paper mill in Bellingham, Washington last year, idling another 600 workers. Bellingham Cold Storage temporarily shut down half its operation and laid off 270 workers. Bonneville Power Administration asked Northwest aluminum smelters – nearly 40 per cent of US capacity – to close for two years in order to save energy.[21]

The experience of California and the West is not unique in the US. The drama of California's debacle should not divert attention from the universal failure of retail competition to date in the US:

- Volatile Massachusetts retail default price increases wiped out the 15 per cent rate cut provided by statute, as New England wholesale prices almost tripled. And there are no alternatives for domestic consumers.[22]
- High and volatile wholesale prices sent potential competitors packing.[23] Prices have eased, but only one domestic competitor has braved the new marketplace in Massachusetts.
- Consolidated Edison Co. of New York (Con Ed) domestic customers suffered a 43 per cent rate increase in June 2000. The New York Independent System Operator (ISO) predicted summer wholesale prices would rise another 46 per cent by 2005[24] until the World Trade Center calamity sharply reduced demand and, thus, cut electricity prices in half.[25] In one New York day, generation owners collected $70 million.[26]
- In the first state with retail competition, Rhode Island, competitors entered the market with price increases.[27] They later fled the state altogether.
- Instead of adopting immediate 15 per cent price reductions, as California and Massachusetts did, Pennsylvania capped prices but at higher levels than regulation would have set them. For a while this brought competition. But as wholesale prices have risen, low-priced competitors have fled every service territory except the one around Philadelphia. The power pool operator found that at least one supplier was using market power to raise the price.[28]
- According to FERC data, wholesale prices between 1997 and 2000 more than doubled in Chicago, the Upper Midwest, New York and New England; almost tripled in some parts of the South and more than tripled in other parts; and quadrupled in Texas.[29]
- Wholesale prices in the Midwest, usually around two or three cents per kWh, skyrocketed to $7.50 on June 25, 1998.[30] In one week in 1998, $500 million changed hands.[31] Then, in July 1999 the price hit $9.00 per kWh, as if a $4 gallon of gasoline sold for $1,200.[32]

Maintenance and job cutbacks

In addition to higher prices, turning electricity systems over to the marketplace has brought increased danger and more intermittent service. How? Here are explanations from two former high-flying utility leaders:

- "You must cut costs ruthlessly by 50 per cent or 60 per cent. Depopulate. Get rid of people. They gum up the works." [33]
- "We believe it is socially irresponsible to keep even one extra person employed when he or she cannot help operate the business more effectively."[34]

As they prepared for competition, many utilities slashed their maintenance budgets by laying off workers. In a recent (2001) survey of its locals, the Utility Workers Union of America (UWUA) found that staffing levels across the country are down about 35 per cent compared to 1991. A 2000 US Department of Energy (DOE) Energy Information Administration (EIA) study also found 35 per cent fewer utility workers compared to ten years before. As a result of these staff cuts:

- utilities perform inspections less frequently;
- necessary non-emergency repairs are deferred, sometimes forever;
- retiring workers are often not replaced; and
- some companies are cutting back on training programs for new employees.

At risk are system reliability, worker safety and the safety of the public.

Inspection cycles have doubled or tripled and critical equipment is often in poor condition when finally inspected. But there are not enough workers to follow up on needed repairs:

- poles are condemned but not replaced;
- load tap changers are inoperable, affecting proper voltage levels;
- uninspected transformers pose a serious risk of exploding; and
- one utility drastically reduced the ratio of in-stock to in-service transformers, from 15 per cent (1989 through 1996) to 5 per cent (1997 and 1998). Transformer and other equipment failures often occur during heat waves, when many companies will seek to purchase the same equipment at the same time. Inventory cutbacks may thus place system reliability at risk.

These widespread maintenance cutbacks culminated in the summer of 1999 with outages and disturbances, described in a special DOE report,[35] occurring in:

- New York City;
- Long Island;
- New Jersey;
- Delmarva (parts of Delaware, Maryland, and Virginia) Peninsula;
- South-Central States (Mississippi, Arkansas, Louisiana, Texas);
- Chicago;
- New England; and
- Mid-Atlantic states.

In Chicago, Commonwealth Edison's own investigation illustrates the growing national risk that deregulation has brought:

[W]hile ComEd's inspection programs seemed appropriate, there were only imperfect mechanisms in place to ensure execution [of repairs] . . . It is not clear, from a review of the records, how often inspections were actually performed, and the inspections that *were* performed may have been too passive, too cursory, to truly maintain the system.
  Additionally . . . ComEd needs to ensure better follow-up on maintenance requests. While virtually all T&D emergencies are dealt with immediately, there appear to be altogether too many deficiencies which, had they been identified and addressed sooner, would not have become critical in the first place . . . [R]outine maintenance requests . . . were rarely tracked to ensure follow-up.[36]

A similar study of the NStar system serving Metropolitan Boston found "that it saved millions of dollars by decreasing capital spending on the distribution system, allowing the Company to increase its earnings while customers paid the price with blackouts." What the study found to be growing maintenance backlogs resulted in business losses, school closings, and medical emergencies.[37]

As the DOE Report concluded after its review of the summer of 1999: "The overall effect has been that the infrastructure for reliability assurance has been considerably eroded."[38]

The California Public Utilities Commission addressed the problem head-on and "barred PGE [Pacific Gas & Electric] and SoCal Ed [Southern California Edison] from cutting costs by laying off employees involved with service and reliability . . . [The companies] are ordered to rescind any layoffs of employees that are needed to answer calls, read meters, respond to outages and connect new customers." The utilities had planned to lay off 1,400 workers.[39]

Roller-coaster prices

The most striking characteristic of the short history of retail electricity competition in the US has been the price spikes. Price volatility in New England increased 50 per cent after deregulation. In the six-plus years before the market opened, high average monthly prices averaged 1.9 times the lows, reflecting cost differentials among plants responding to various demand levels. This has increased to 3.0 times, with no apparent change in cost relationships other than fuel prices. Figure 14 shows that New England prices are thus 56 per cent more volatile than before competition.

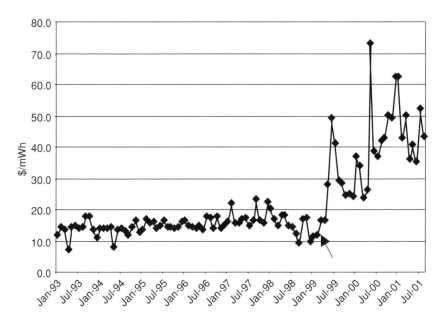

Figure 14   New England Average Monthly Wholesale Prices, 1993–2001 (Source: ISO-New England)

Gas and oil account for less than half of New England generation. At key times, spiking New England competitive wholesale electricity prices did not track gas prices.

Rising and more volatile electricity prices are thus not entirely caused by costs such as fuel costs. Furthermore, loads were stable in this period.

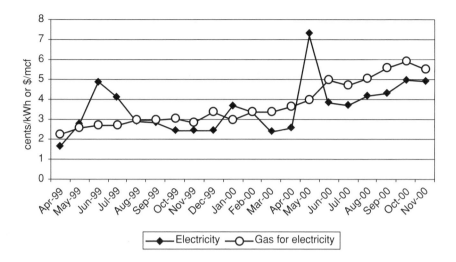

Figure 15   New England Electricity and Gas Prices, 1999–2000 (Source: ISO-New England, US Energy Information Administration)

Our findings were confirmed by a consultant hired by the Massachusetts Attorney-General, who found that New England wholesale prices were 12 per cent above a competitive benchmark (i.e., cost) over a 29-month period of 1999–2001 and that this margin skyrocketed as demand reached only 75 per cent of installed resources. The margin hit 80 per cent (of the price) when demand was still only 80 per cent of capacity, demonstrating that one cost of deregulation is the need to install additional resources in order to control prices. Furthermore, the largest price spike, to $6 per kWh, did not occur at a time of rising natural gas prices.[40]

So what caused the price spikes? Gouging. At least three studies suggest pricing has been controlled by the market players themselves. In New England, power plant operation and maintenance expenses were cut about 40 per cent and power plant outages increased 47 per cent.[41] This suggests the possibility of generation owners withholding power to create a shortage to raise prices. In New York, market power (withholding power from the market) has contributed to rising prices.[42] In California, the excess of generation prices over generation costs in two months alone totaled $565,000,000.[43] For example, Southern California Edison's Mohave Station in Laughlin, Nevada, produces power for SoCal Ed customers at about 3.5 cents per kWh but it would have sold power to Californians at about ten times that amount if AES Corp.'s effort to buy it had not been rejected by regulators on the petition of the Utility Workers Union of America.[44] According to California Public Utilities Commission President Loretta

Lynch, "withholding [of available power] was going on" to create scarcity to drive up prices,[45] echoing a finding by the California Independent System Operator.[46]

Few benefits for domestic consumers

There may nevertheless be some benefits from electricity deregulation for a small number of industrial customers. For the 7 per cent of Massachusetts large commercial and industrial customers that have found an alternative, lower prices seem to be available. But even the internet-based companies that had been marketing almost exclusively to domestic customers, Utility.com and Essential.com, abandoned Massachusetts.

After four years of open competition in Massachusetts, less than 0.05 per cent of domestic customers are served by competitive suppliers.[47] The history of Massachusetts domestic competition is displayed in Figure 16, which is drawn from Massachusetts Division of Energy Resources (DOER) data. (Note that, in order to make any change distinguishable, the top of the scale is only 1 per cent.)

This lack of competition for domestic customers is true of all states that have restructured to date, even in the so-called success story of Pennsylvania, as shown in Figure 17, which is drawn from data from the Pennsylvania Office of Consumer Advocate.[48]

Next door in Ohio, after one year, 0.2 per cent of customers have switched outside the service territory where temporary discounts were granted to competitors; in some areas, the number is zero.[49] Across other state lines, the picture is the same: in New Jersey, 0.2 per cent of *all* customers have switched;[50] 0.3 per cent of domestic customers in Maryland

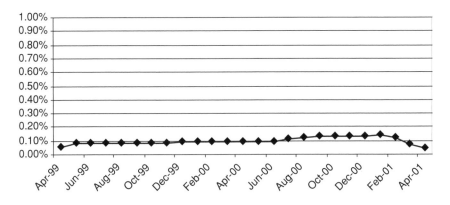

Figure 16 Massachusetts Non-Low-Income Customers Choosing Competitive Generation (Source: Mass. DOER)

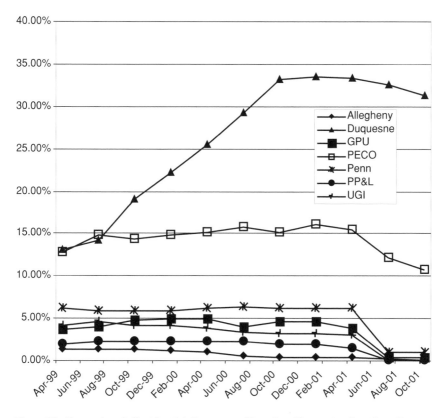

Figure 17   Pennsylvania Residential Customers Choosing Alternative Suppliers (Source: PA Office of Consumer Advocate)

have moved to a competitive electricity supplier after 18 months;[51] and only 3.7 per cent of New York homes have switched despite switching premiums in some parts of the state.[52] A survey of 58 service territories with nominal competition in 16 states found nine areas with one competitive supplier offering a price below the incumbent utility and five areas with two or three such competitors.[53]

Rhode Island reported one domestic customer subscribing to competitive supply,[54] whom we have not been able to locate.

Rising and volatile prices pose a particular burden for low-income consumers, who are already at or beyond the limit of what they can pay for energy. The average low-income consumer devotes 19 per cent of household income to energy – almost four times the burden on the median-income American family and 36 per cent more than before the recent spikes in oil and natural gas prices.[55] For the poorest of these families, most of whom are elderly or single-parent households, the burden is a quarter of their income or more. An increase in electricity bills on top of other increased energy bills is simply not manageable without cutting back on food expenditures, falling into arrears on rent or going without needed medicines. This burden is made even more difficult by dropping incomes and decreased budgeting predictability due to energy price volatility.

The most extreme recent retail utility price volatility in the US, outside California, was experienced by natural gas customers in the winter of 2000–01, when the wholesale prices passed through to customers more than quadrupled:

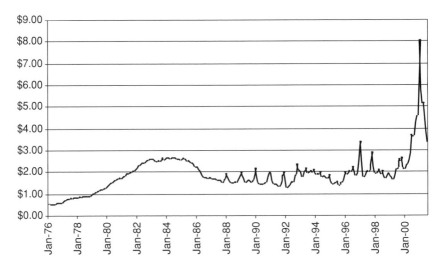

Figure 18   US Natural Gas Wellhead Price ($/mcf), 1976–2001 (Source: US DOE)

Such increasingly large price spikes have developed as a result of US wholesale deregulation of natural gas in 1984. As with electricity, harsh retail impacts are an inevitable result of establishing a competitive retail marketplace based on these short-term (spot) conditions. As Royal Dutch/Shell warned the European Commission in a talk before the Institute of Petroleum in London: "Tying gas prices purely to the mechanisms of short-run supply and demand means running the risks of tight reserves and under-investment [and consequent price increases] such as that recently seen in the US market."[56]

At the dawn of the winter of 2001–02, hundreds of thousands of families had not been able to pay their winter heating bills from the year before. In Atlanta, Georgia, 167,000 faced disconnection.[57] In Kansas, another 69,000.[58] In Arkansas, 34,000.[59]

The *Wall Street Journal* sees the current volatility caustically and recently summed up electricity competition this way:

It's a market ripe for manipulation: surging demand for an indispensable commodity, weak oversight and a chaotic new set of rules . . . The tactics include manipulating wholesale electricity auctions, taking juice from transmission systems when suppliers aren't supposed to and denying weaker competitors access to transmission lines . . . In the case of the Midwest where prices in July 1999 hit $9,000 per megawatthour [$9.00 per kWh], it was as if a $1.89 gallon of gasoline sold for $567.[60]

Academics describe such spikes as inevitable because the time-delayed nature of investment assures that there will be periods of insufficient capacity to meet demand, driving up prices: "in capital intensive industries like electricity generation, pricing at variable cost [the theoretical price of a fully competitive market] will fail to cover full costs, leading to underinvestment until scarce capacity causes prices to rise, perhaps to politically unsustainable levels."[61]

Electricity trader Catherine Flax, Vice President of Morgan Stanley, recently conceded to the Vermont Public Service Board, pointing to airline deregulation price data as an example, that introducing competition raises average prices and makes them more volatile. The advantage she points out is that a few customers can reduce the prices they pay.[62] Dynegy Chairman Chuck Watson frankly sees price volatility as a profit opportunity.[63]

Ironically, Enron itself was no foe of regulation. It just wanted to write the rules. It spent millions on political donations, apparently with the objective of installing a federal regulator who would control prices for transmission it needed and would also guarantee access to transmission lines for non-utility power such as Enron's. Enron lobbied hard to remove utilities from the generation business that it wanted to control. It lobbied for – and got – hundreds of millions of dollars in government loans and guarantees to prop up its investments abroad. And it lobbied for the California limitation on electric utility purchases to the spot market, where Enron could predict there would be little competition at the expensive end of the market where it would play.[64]

Much of the electricity debacle was predictable

Analysis and review of the experience in other industries might have led policy-makers to predict the high and volatile prices that have occurred in the electricity industry. Indeed, Utility Workers Union of America President Don Wightman did so in 1996.[65]

Nothing in the history of US deregulation suggests probable benefits for domestic customers. Competitive long distance telephone carriers incur customer acquisition (marketing) costs of $75 and more per customer. Such costs would overwhelm any potential generation efficiencies available from competition – the entire average annual domestic electricity generation bill is only about $300. In fact, in most states currently, electricity marketer margins are negative. Thus almost no competitors in any state are willing to bear the costs and risks of selling electricity to domestic consumers. Indeed, competitive supplier Duke Energy warned that retail competition would be limited by costly barriers to entry, including the need for state-of-the-art billing systems, and margins that will be "very low."[66] Enron warned the Massachusetts Department of Public Utilities[67] not to expect a lot of competition for the domestic sector: "safety net responsibility lies with the distribution company . . . it's a very difficult market." Supplier New Energy Ventures made a similar prediction of competitors steering away from certain markets, explaining: "In the competitive marketplace there's choice on both sides."[68]

Thus, once he left the presidency of the California Public Utilities Commission, where he presided over the beginning of California's debacle, Daniel Fessler expressed his opinion that it was dishonest to promise electricity price reductions from restructuring: industry has no obligation, he said, to "shield small customers from reality."[69]

The economics of the electricity industry made the current volatility easy to predict, too. Electricity cannot be stored, but supply and demand must be kept in instantaneous balance to physically protect the grid. Electricity must therefore be produced on demand from large and costly generation plants. Plant additions cannot be finely tuned to meet demand, either. Economics dictate relatively large investments. Any investor risking a large sum of capital wants some assurance of its return. Thus the incentive is to not invest until a shortage makes it almost certain that the output from a new investment will be purchased. Such a shortage also increases prices – the price signal to build new plant that some economists find hopeful about the California disaster. Eventually, enough plant is built to fill the demand, a surplus may develop and prices drop – until the next cycle of shortage and investment attracted by skyrocketing prices. In this way, especially given the lumpiness of generation investment, price volatility is an inevitable component of a market system. "[R]apid deregulation of the . . . power sectors have also reduced the incentives for specific businesses to invest in . . . excess capacity that can help smooth markets during times of disruption or unexpected volatility in demand growth."[70]

In addition, the history of other deregulated industries demonstrates the risks of market segmentation that raises prices for those with the least power in the marketplace. Cable television prices skyrocketed 36 per cent once they were deregulated in 1996 – almost triple the inflation rate.[71] Most of the benefits of natural gas deregulation in the US, for example, have gone to industrial customers. Domestic customer price increases tracked the wellhead price spikes of 2000, but earlier wellhead price decreases went to industrials:

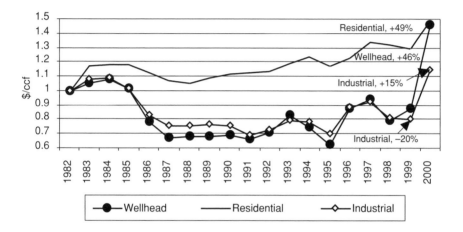

Figure 19   US Natural Gas Prices by Sector, 1982–2000 (Source: US Energy Information Administration)

Similarly, Federal Communications Commission (FCC) data show that, while deregulation brought sharply falling long distance prices for business customers – 50 per cent or more – local domestic prices rose sharply. For example, as Figures 20 and 21 illustrate, local prices in New York State jumped 46 per cent in Buffalo, nearly doubled in New York City, and more than doubled in Massena.[72]

Telephone competition also brought pre-paid local telephone service providers, who offer to re-sell a diluted version of the incumbent's local phone service for triple the price. In Ohio, for example, pre-paid providers applied to the regulator to offer service for $50 a month after a $50 installation fee; the degraded service would include no directory assistance, no operator service, no long distance, and no other service for which payment could only be collected after the service is rendered. The current telephone company in Ohio offers full service to low-income customers for $15 a month and no installation charge.[73]

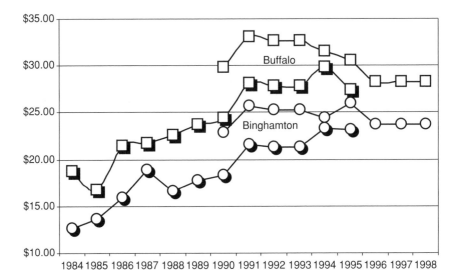

Figure 20   New York State Monthly Telephone Prices: Buffalo and Binghamton, 1984–99 (Source: Federal Communications Commission)

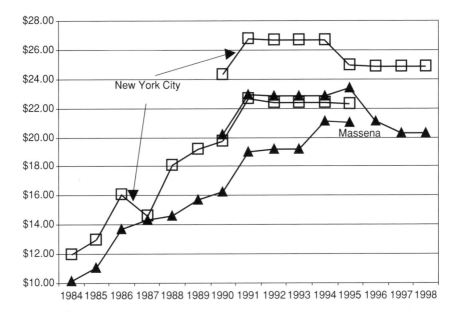

Figure 21   New York State Monthly Telephone Prices: New York City and Massena, 1984–99 (Source: Federal Communications Commission)

The democratic reaction

Thus, strong economic interests favoring electricity deregulation in order to capture benefits for a few confront overwhelming evidence that deregulation spells ruin for many. In a democratic system such as the US you would expect a reaction against deregulation. And that is exactly what is happening as this is written.

In California, not only was competition repealed, but an existing state agency (the Department of Water Resources) was empowered to purchase power for resale to distribution utilities and a new state agency (the Consumer Power and Conservation Financing Authority) was established to buy power or build power plants.[74]

In response to the growing disparity between domestic and industrial prices, which is based on power in the marketplace rather than cost differentials, Connecticut adopted a "Cap The Gap" statute (drafted by one of this book's authors) as part of its electricity restructuring statute.[75] Cap The Gap freezes the difference between domestic and industrial prices, requiring industrials to share any market benefits that may occur in the marketplace.

States have also required utilities to manage their portfolios in a manner that reduces price and price volatility, such as by hedging and long-term contracts. For example, New York State Electricity & Gas Co. (NYSEG) has hedged more than 90 per cent of its expected demand for the next two summers.[76] New York State regulatory policy requires gas utilities to take such actions:

Local [gas] distribution companies have many ways to meet their loads; they should consider all available options . . . [which] may include short and longer term fixed price purchases, spot acquisitions, the use of financial hedges . . . While we are not directing any particular mix of portfolio options, volatility of customer bills is one of the criteria, along with other factors such as cost and reliability, that LDCs should consider . . . Any utility without a diversified pricing strategy will have to meet a heavy burden to demonstrate that its approach is reasonable.[77]

In Maine, the state took over the function of electricity generation procurement, insisting on multi-year bids in order to achieve price stability. After receiving no suitable bids, the state has currently locked in three-year prices for its three largest investor-owned electricity utilities. In the case of the largest utility, Central Maine Power, the price is lower than before restructuring despite New England wholesale price volatility.[78]

Similar actions to stabilize prices have been ordered or authorized in, for example, the states of Arkansas,[79] Colorado,[80] Georgia,[81] Idaho,[82] Iowa,[83] Kentucky,[84] Michigan,[85] Oklahoma,[86] Virginia,[87] Kansas, Missouri, Mississippi and California.[88]

The most significant events with respect to retail electricity competition in the US have been the moves away from it. In addition to California, Nevada repealed its retail competition scheme altogether – the Governor signed the bill the day it was passed. Oklahoma suspended its restructuring law indefinitely. New York is considering public ownership of existing generating plants. Several other states that have enacted retail competition policies have delayed or amended them, including:[89]

- Arkansas
- Montana
- New Hampshire
- New Mexico
- Oregon
- Texas (parts of the state)
- West Virginia

Half the states never adopted retail competition policies. Those recently affirming that decision include:

- Alabama
- Colorado
- Georgia
- Louisiana
- North Carolina
- Mississippi
- Oklahoma
- Vermont

Georgia's commission chairman, after fielding 15,000 complaints in the first year of gas deregulation, vowed never to support electricity deregulation. North Carolina State Senator David Hoyle offered "to observe a moment of darkness in honor of California."

13 The Biggest Failures: California and Enron

California[1]

California is the most extreme illustration of the catastrophic potential of competition in the electricity industry. But the state is also developing a blueprint for recovery, based on democratic regulation.

California spot market prices between June and December 2000 leapt to as much as 15 times the prices of the year before; blackouts rolled across the state during six days between January and May 2001. With a promise of lower prices, old-fashioned supply-and-demand economics was used to justify the switch to competition in the California electricity industry – Enron CEO Jeffrey Skilling promised $8.9 billion a year in savings. Yet none of the conditions that classic economics relies on to explain such price leaps and supply shortages were in fact present in the latter half of 2000 or the first half of 2001. Demand was falling, which Economics 101 teaches leads to surpluses and lower prices. Supply was ample, which economics does not predict will lead to shortages and price spikes. The price of one major input factor, natural gas, did rise – but in general by a factor of 2–3

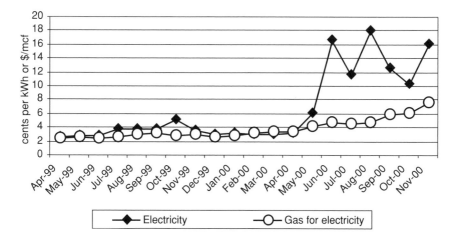

Figure 22 California Wholesale Electricity and Gas Prices, 1999–2000 (Sources: California ISO, US Energy Information Administration)

for the less-than-half-of-the-supply that requires natural gas. At most, gas prices thus explain an increase of 50 per cent,[2] not a fly-up of 15 times.

Academic study of "the extremely erratic nature of [California] electricity prices" showed "a high degree of persistence in the price level . . . where positive shocks to the price series result in larger increases in volatility than negative shocks."[3] Prices were more likely to jump up and stay up, than to decline:

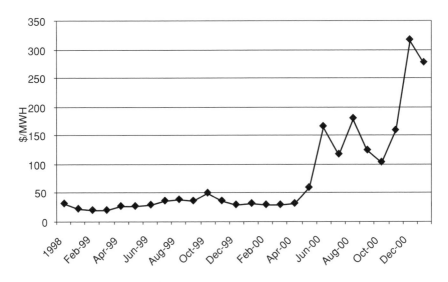

Figure 23   California Wholesale Electricity: 1998–99 averages $33, and then . . .

Although gas prices have been blamed for this volatility, only about 40 per cent of California generation is gas-fired.[4] In any event, the electricity price spike did not follow gas prices.

Prices were not pushed up by demand either, which rose a modest 1.5 per cent in the year 2000 and *fell* by 5 per cent in 2001. In four of the seven months between June and December 2000, when prices were spiking, demand was lower than the year before. When prices were at their highest, in December, demand was down 16 per cent. Blackouts rolled across the state when demand had dropped as much as 10 per cent.

Not surprisingly, Californians invested in electricity efficiency like never before. In Northern and Central California alone, in 2001, consumers bought 94,800 super-efficient refrigerators and four million super-efficient (compact fluorescent) light bulbs.[5]

Nor can the price hikes and shortages be explained by a lack of supply. Electricity capacity increased about 7 per cent in the 1990s. At the time of the blackouts, reserves were as high as 62 per cent. A mystery still under investigation, however, is the extraordinary level of unscheduled mainte-nance outages (so-called "forced outages"). Outages went from a normal 5–10 per cent in January–September 2000 to an abnormal 20–31 per cent in November 2000–May 2001. In April 2001, for example, outages were 31 per cent, 4 times the year before, and demand was 5 per cent less than the year before. Prices were nine times the level of the year before. One long-time West Coast energy consultant reviewed the performance of five major plants in 2000, finding a 50 per cent operating rate compared to an historical average of 84 per cent for comparable plants. Studies have shown that 2,600 mW to 8,000 mW of power was withheld in order to drive up prices.

So how did huge surplus supply, falling demand and record investments in efficiency bring about sustained and historic vaults in electricity prices? Economist Paul Krugman has this explanation: "widely accepted by energy economists . . . power companies found that they could make more money by shutting down some of their plants, and hence creating shortages that sent prices into the stratosphere, than they could by actually meeting demand."[6] Even the pro-competition Federal Energy Regulatory Commission agrees to some extent, ordering suppliers to disgorge a too-small portion of their ill-gotten gains.[7] In fact, early on, Perot Systems Corp., which designed the California Power Exchange computer system, showed how easy it was to "prosper in the California market structure" using public information. Perot's message: "Strategies can affect prices," such as "Bid capacity in one market and withhold in others."[8]

One of the state's distribution utilities, Pacific Gas & Electric Co. (PG&E), filed for bankruptcy protection when it could not pay the skyrocketing wholesale prices. Now it is proposing to use its bankruptcy filing as a means of evading state regulation of the power plants it still owns by spinning them off to an unregulated subsidiary.[9]

Since the price spike and PG&E's bankruptcy filing, the state has taken over the task of purchasing power for needs beyond those met by the generators retained by California's regulated distribution utilities. However, the state's post-spike contracts were based on a lingering market power that kept prices artificially high so the state has petitioned for relief. Faced with no choice but to address the offers on the table or resume blackouts, the state accepted prices that *averaged* two and a half times the 3.5 cents/kWh spot price at this writing.[10] The contracts include:

- a ten-year take-or-pay (mandatory purchase) contract with Calpine at 18.5 cents/kWh, more than five times the current (and normal) spot price at this writing;
- a short-term, two-year, take-the-money-and-run contract with Constellation Energy at 15.4 cents;
- another short-term, two-year, take-the-money-and-run contract, this time with Mirant at 14.865 cents;
- a five-year take-or-pay contract with El Paso Merchant Energy at 12.1 cents;
- a contract with Dynegy at 12.0 cents; and
- a large (up to 1,400 mW) contract with Williams Energy that guarantees Williams the price of 6.8 cents (almost double spot) but does not require Williams to sell to the state if it can do better elsewhere.

According to the state's chief contract negotiator, S. David Freeman, Enron had held out for even more and never came to terms.

As this is written, investigations continue of claims that range from pricing that violated regulatory requirements that prices be "just and reasonable" to the much more difficult-to-prove claims of criminal collusion and price-fixing. Enron and others, for example, are accused of using data about demand and available supplies obtained from their trading operations to manipulate prices by timing the withholding and

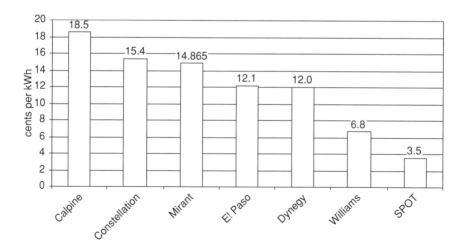

Figure 24   California Post-Spike Contracts (Source: Marcus study)

availability of power they were selling. Enron is also accused of pushing prices up by tactics such as congesting a 15 mW transmission line by bidding 2,900 mW, and trading the same power among its own subsidiaries and other traders to jack up the price before selling it into the grid.

Documents released by the Federal Energy Regulatory Commission (FERC) establish some of Enron's California schemes:

- "submitting unrealistic schedules into the California . . . market; creating, and then 'relieving,' phantom congestion on the . . . transmission grid;" this is also called "inc-ing" for the increase in scheduled load;
- " 'death star,' . . . allowing Enron to get paid 'for moving energy to relieve congestion without actually moving any energy or relieving any congestion;' " refinements of Death Star were known as Perpetual Loop, Black Widow, Red Congo, Cong Catcher, and Big Foot;
- "megawatt laundering (called 'ricocheting' in the memoranda)."[11]

Put simply, Enron would tell the California system manager that it was sending more electricity into the market than it actually intended to send. Having thus created phantom congestion, Enron would agree to reduce its phantom intended shipments and receive payment for the favor.[12] Megawatt laundering appears to be simply the practice of shipping California power out of state in order to ship it back to California free from the price caps that only applied in California.[13]

Other Enron strategies were round-tripping (buying and selling equal amounts to inflate apparent volumes and revenues), "Get Shorty" or "Fat Boy" (filing false information to inflate load projections, which would increase prices, allowing sales at the inflated prices), and "Wheel Out" (scheduling transmissions on fully constrained transmission lines, to obtain payments for relieving congestion without having to deliver since the line was full). While Enron is a convenient target, many marketers in many places across the US were apparently playing similar games. For example, Dynegy, CMS, Duke Energy and Reliant admit to round-tripping. According to the Texas Public Utilities Commission, American Electric Power, Constellation Energy, Enron, Mirant, Reliant Energy, and TXU took in millions of dollars in payments for relief of the congestion they artificially created in Texas.[14]

While investigations proceed at the California Public Utilities Commission, the state's Attorney-General, the California Senate Select Committee to Investigate Price Manipulation in the Wholesale Energy

Market (one of two legislative investigative committees), the California Electricity Oversight Board, the City of San Francisco, the Federal Energy Regulatory Commission, US Securities and Exchange Commission, US Commodities Futures Trading Commission, US Justice Department, and in at least four consumer class actions, the *best* face suppliers can put on these facts is that they engaged in lawful free market activity to hike prices and blackout California. Estimates of the statewide damage to California range to $72 billion and more, including electricity price jumps of 40 per cent and rising.

And marketers' phantom congestion games caused the January 17, 2001 blackout of Northern California, at a time when generation and transmission capacity was in fact adequate.[15]

Where did the money go? Trader profits in the first half of 2001 were 31 per cent to 212 per cent higher than the year before.

The California story is not yet over, but the seeds of a democratic Happy Ending are emerging. The state abolished the spot market that had been manipulated so badly, reversed deregulation, never gave up regulatory control over about half the state's generation, and is slowly regaining control over the balance. Ironically, this renewed control is in the hands of a new state power authority that would earlier have been anathema to privately owned utilities and power suppliers. Now the state purchases about half the state's power and has the ability to control new plant construction by either building it or contracting for it.

Deregulation proponent and MIT professor Paul Joskow agrees that suppliers withheld supply to jack up prices. "Every business exercises market power when it can, so I don't know why people are so surprised . . . I didn't see any evidence of collusion . . . It was just good business."[16] Still, he concedes, "If another California crisis emerges, the era of competition and restructuring is likely at an end . . . Maybe it was all a mistake, and it is a natural monopoly."[17]

Enron's rise and fall

The most notorious of the market manipulators was Enron. How did this company that almost no one had ever heard of before the 1990s suddenly become one of the biggest companies in the US and a household name around the world? Enron's transformation was enabled by its systematic attack on the fundamental elements of democratic regulation. Transparency was replaced by secrecy and fraud. Public oversight was removed. Enron prices were unconstrained by standards of justice, reasonableness, balance or cost. But the seeds of Enron's downfall was contained in that attack – Enron unraveled upon the reassertion of transparency, public oversight and price regulation.

The build-up

Enron began as a natural gas pipeline company – Houston Natural Gas (HNG). In 1985, after fending off a hostile takeover attempt, HNG was bought by another pipeline company, InterNorth of Nebraska, to form one of the largest natural gas pipeline companies in the US. Soon, the center of power in the merged company began to shift to Texas, and the new company was named "Enron."[18] Kenneth Lay became its CEO, and he hired Jeffrey Skilling to help him build the company. Together they changed a stodgy gas pipeline company into an internet-based energy trading, telecommunications and investment company (among other things) within 16 years.[19] By 1995, Enron controlled 20 per cent of the natural gas market and began to focus its attention on the newly deregulating electricity market.[20]

Enron participated heavily in restructuring proceedings throughout the country in order to shape the new rules to further its own goals. Enron had realized

> that it could make more money speculating on electricity contracts than it could by actually producing electricity at a power plant. Central to Enron's strategy of turning electricity into a speculative commodity was removing government oversight of its trading practices and exploiting market deficiencies to allow it to manipulate prices and supply.[21]

By 1997, one of Enron's divisions was the US's largest wholesale buyer and seller of both natural gas and electricity and, by 1999, the company was also trading in coal, paper, steel and telecommunications.[22]

On the international side, Enron was building and buying gas pipelines and power plants. In 1998, these foreign assets generated 40 per cent of Enron's total reported profits.[23] By the end of 2001, Enron listed more than 2,800 subsidiaries on financial statements filed with the SEC – many of them in off-shore tax havens like the Cayman Islands.[24] In a mere five years, from 1995 through 2000, Enron grew eleven-fold, from $9 billion in revenue to $101 billion.[25]

Creative accounting

How, then, did Enron manage this amazing growth? One, by hiring and promoting talented, smart, aggressive employees who were hungry to be cutting-edge and to make fortunes for themselves. But more importantly, by "cooking the books" and following accounting practices such as one that let Enron claim debt as equity.[26] In one such scheme, Enron simply booked as a $115 million profit what was in reality a ten-year projection from a business plan for a joint venture that actually failed. The venture barely produced revenue, let alone profits.[27]

Another diabolical scheme in which Enron disguised the extent of its debt was perfectly legal but perverse. Enron received $3.9 billion in loans from several banks, including at least $2.5 billion between 1999 and 2001 in addition to the $8 to $19 billion in long- and short-term debt that was disclosed during those years. These extra loans were recorded in the Company's financial statements as "hedging activity" or "derivatives trading" in order to conceal the extent of its debt from investors and auditors.[28]

In yet another instance, Enron booked a $370 million profit (later reversed) with respect to its New Power joint venture in retail sales of electricity, although the venture lost $497 million in the two years of 2000 and 2001. In its Investor Fact Sheet, New Power only acknowledges $383 million of the losses.[29]

The accounting part of the Enron pyramid scam began to unravel when the *Wall Street Journal* revealed Enron partnerships whose debt Enron omitted from its public books. To accomplish this hidden-ball trick, Enron had to sell a mere 3 per cent of each partnership. This in itself should be a scandal, since it allows a public corporation to lie about the amount of debt for which it is liable. Trouble was, these entities were so risky that even the super-salesmen at Enron could not pawn them off on gullible investors. Enron kept these partnerships' debt off its public books anyway, until it was caught, when it had to deduct from its public books $400 million in phony profits from the partnerships.[30]

The downfall

Because of all the complex accounting and reporting methods, Enron was able to fool lenders into thinking it was worth much more than it was, for much longer, and to obtain additional credit that would not have been available if the true story were known. But, as Fran Laserson, a vice president at Moody's Investors Services was quoted as telling the *New York Times*: "Considering that our credit rating was largely based on information now deemed by the company itself to be misleading, inaccurate, and false, it is likely that the credit rating would have been different [had we known the truth]."[31]

But there were signs of trouble before 2001. Circumstances surrounding the gas-fired power plant Enron was building in Dabhol, India, described in Chapter 14, began to unravel the empire. Meanwhile, another disaster-in-the-making was Enron's purchase of a water company in the UK, Azurix, in 1999. By August 2000, Azurix's stock had fallen from $19 per share to $5 per share, and Azurix disappeared as a company, having been folded into Enron.[32]

On October 26, 2001, the *Wall Street Journal* wrote a story about an Enron partnership called "Chewco" after a character in the *Star Wars* movie. Evidence uncovered by the *Journal* showed that Enron formed Chewco in late 1997 using loans and loan guarantees from Enron for 100 per cent of its financing (at least 3 per cent was supposed to come from outside investors, according to the accounting rules). Enron inaccurately listed Chewco as an independent company on Enron's books – thus avoiding the requirement to list Chewco's loans as Enron debt. Once the story broke, Enron admitted the improper accounting, restated earnings for the past four years and, on December 2, 2001, filed for bankruptcy protection.[33] The more information that comes out about all of Enron's myriad partnerships and accounting tricks, the more it all seems as fantastic as *Star Wars*.

After Enron imploded in the fall of 2001, an internal investigation of the company's downfall concluded that "Officers that should have been concerned with doing their fiduciary duty to shareholders instead cooked up . . . structures to circumvent already weak accounting rules."[34] The report of the investigation described a number of the phony transactions and pyramid schemes outlined above, including one where a company executive invested just $125,000 and took $12,000,000 out of the company.[35]

"Enron operated in extreme secrecy, overstating its revenues, avoiding taxes, and hiding liabilities in limited partnerships . . . Enron speculated wildly on energy futures and used the value of its stock as collateral for the spiraling loans."[36] Enron's accounting firm, Arthur Andersen, which should have been reporting these irregularities, was instead earning $27 million in one year "consulting" to Enron, in addition to taking in $25 million in the same period in "auditing fees."[37] Perhaps this explains why Andersen was, as its indictment sets forth, silent about its knowledge that Enron improperly categorized hundreds of millions of dollars in shareholder losses as if they were increases in shareholder value, why Andersen was also silent about its knowledge that Enron was telling investors that recurring costs in the third quarter of 2001 were merely one-time charges, and why

Andersen then shredded "tons" of incriminating documents to cover up the abuses. The firm was convicted of obstruction of justice in June 2002.[38]

As this is written, Enron is still writing off billions in funny money. In April 2002, Enron admitted to having overstated the value of its assets by $14 billion, and its trading portfolio by another $8–$14 billion.[39]

The money trail

Shades of Samuel Insull. But, if all the laws and regulations were still in place that were meant to prevent such abuses, how could Enron manage to build such a giant pyramid on such soft sand in so short a time? Money. Power. Money. A restructuring regulatory environment. And money. Enron gave $2.4 million and Arthur Andersen $1.4 million in political contributions in the 2000 election cycle alone.[40] In the first half of 2001, Enron spent $1.6 million on lobbying.[41]

Where did all this money go? To buy Enron protection from regulatory and legal oversight and to exempt it from its fiduciary responsibility? The numbers tell a scary story. Much of Enron's largesse seems to have bought lax oversight and freedom from providing information that would otherwise have been required by regulators to be made publicly available. In fact, as early as 1993, a ruling by the Securities and Exchange Commission exempted Enron from registering as a holding company under PUHCA. Such registration would have subjected Enron to oversight of its corporate structure and business operations.[42]

In the eight years ending in 2001, Enron gave over $700,000 to George W. Bush, current US President – more than it gave to any other politician.[43] While Bush was Governor, there was extensive correspondence between the Governor and Kenneth Lay, CEO of Enron,[44] despite President Bush's denials of knowing Lay well. After taking office, President Bush appointed a long-time Enron ally, Pat Wood, as Chairman of the Federal Energy Regulatory Commission after the incumbent Chair refused to change his views on electricity deregulation.[45] Another Bush confidant and advisor, Ralph Reed, former executive director of the Christian Coalition (a right-wing religious organization) and current Chair of the Georgia Republican Party, was hired at a hefty fee by Enron to lobby Congress using campaign contributors, talk shows and other means to help pass legislation favorable to Enron. Reed also helped Enron in the states to lobby for deregulating the electricity industry.[46]

Enron also paid a number of other well-known politicians and media types, including Lawrence B. Lindsey, an economic advisor to Bush; William Kristol, editor of the *Weekly Standard*; Paul Krugman, economist and *New*

York Times columnist; Larry Kudlow, commentator at CNBC; and Robert B. Zoellick, the US Trade Representative.[47] Enron contributed $57,499 to the (losing) Senatorial campaign of US Attorney-General, John Ashcroft, who therefore declined to participate in the criminal investigation of Enron begun by the Justice Department in the wake of Enron's bankruptcy.[48]

All told, Enron gave about $6 million in campaign contributions over twelve years. Enron also provided jobs to people who, as regulators, should have been monitoring Enron's operations. Dr. Wendy Gramm, wife of US Senator Phil Gramm, was Chair of the Commodity Futures Trading Commission (CFTC) where she exempted Enron's trading of futures contracts from government oversight. Five weeks after resigning from the CFTC, Dr. Gramm was appointed to Enron's Board of Directors, where she served on the Audit Committee responsible for verifying Enron's accounting procedures and other financial dealings. From 1993 through 2001, Enron paid Wendy Gramm somewhere between $915,000 and $1.85 million in salary, fees, stock option sales and dividends.[49] During and after the time Dr. Gramm was at the CFTC, from 1989 through 2001, Enron became the largest single corporate contributor to Senator Phil Gramm's political campaigns, giving him $101,350. Senator Gramm was a major factor in Congress's passage of a bill in December 2000 deregulating energy commodity trading. This act allowed Enron to make a killing in California. Of course, the $3.45 million Enron spent on lobbying this issue in 1999 and 2000 did not hurt the cause either.[50]

And Enron's executives themselves made out better than anyone. While blocking lower-level employees from selling their stock in the company (which made up a large fraction of their retirement accounts), top executives sold their own shares for millions of dollars just months before the share price collapsed and the company went bankrupt.

Enron's CEO, Kenneth Lay, and his family walked off with at least $100,000,000 in 2001 alone. He sold shares back to Enron in February 2001 for $4 million, when the share price was $78.79; he continued to sell throughout the year, including $20 million worth within three weeks after being warned that the company was on the verge of collapse from "a wave of accounting scandals." Thus, while Enron executives encouraged their pensioners and employees to hang on while their stock melted from $90 to 26.5 cents, the executives themselves, along with their accountants, were cashing out hundreds of millions of dollars.[51]

The aftermath

Since Enron's collapse in the fall of 2001, there has been much soul-searching and gnashing of teeth among the pundits and analysts. How could this shining star have dimmed so quickly? What went wrong? Why did no one see it coming?

Well, as it turns out, many did see it coming. Some were too intimidated to do anything with the knowledge they had. Sherron Watkins, an Enron vice president who warned Kenneth Lay that cooking the books was about to lead to Enron's collapse, was nearly fired for her audacity. Only the fear that she would go to the regulators kept Enron executives from firing or transferring her to someplace she could do no harm to them.[52]

Firms that had power contracts with Enron, such as the huge insurance corporation Kaiser Permanente, were aware of massive over-billings by Enron for at least $30 million. Enron employees were concerned that basic information management was so haphazard at Enron that the company was under-billing and over-billing and not billing clients left and right. One former Enron manager said he "found millions of dollars in billing errors. Basically, there wasn't a process in place to manage payment data."[53]

Arthur Andersen knew as long ago as early 2000 that Enron partnerships known as "Raptor" were overstating earnings and hiding losses.[54] And, an internal Andersen memo from February 2001 reveals that Andersen decided to keep Enron as a client despite the fact that "some of its accounting practices amounted to 'intelligent gambling.'"[55]

This was not the first time Arthur Andersen was caught asleep at the wheel with a utility company's crooked books, either. Back in 1989, another big utility, the Southern Company, pleaded guilty to making illegal campaign contributions to Florida politicians. This was just one impropriety that a company senior vice-president was about to report to state officials and the company's board of directors when he was blown up in an airplane explosion on his way to the appointment. A grand jury voted to charge Southern Company with criminal racketeering for manipulating its accounts and overcharging customers millions of dollars, but the Justice Department under President George H. Bush (the current President's father) stopped the prosecution. Why? In part, because the accounting had been signed off on by Arthur Andersen, the company's respected auditors.[56]

Enron's effect on electricity deregulation

Marketplace proponents assert that the Enron story ends there – a serious but containable accounting, and perhaps political, scandal. Enron's collapse has had no impact on the electricity marketplace, many claim. This is not true.

Enron was a major player in many of the state and national efforts to deregulate the electricity industry. A deregulated environment offered almost unlimited opportunities for Enron to make profits from its trading operations. But as Enron grew more powerful, its leaders became more arrogant. They thought they were immune from the normal rules of professional behavior, because almost everyone treated them as if they were. George Will, conservative columnist, puts it this way: "[T]he primary cause of Enron's collapse was not risky behavior arising from belief in a net under them. Rather, the cause was the growing arrogance of executives who became confident that no one was looking over their shoulders, watching – and understanding – what they were doing."[57]

And all of these lies and deceits were carried out despite Enron's own statement of company values: "respect; integrity; communication, and excellence." In Enron's own words: "We do not tolerate abusive or disrespectful treatment. Ruthlessness, callousness and arrogance don't belong here."[58] Yet while espousing good values, Enron's executives displayed all of those base characteristics.

Until it was stopped, Enron was able to raise millions of dollars of capital through these types of schemes, much of which it used to speculate on energy futures, create price volatility and risk where little had existed before, then sell the energy it had purchased for fat rewards – what the *Boston Globe* described as a "national casino."[59] In essence, Enron's business was extorting "protection money" by selling hedges against the price volatility it had created.

The leading hawker of the trading-will-save-you-from-the-volatility-we-created elixir, Enron, turned out to be as crooked as the snake oil salesmen of legend. To raise the huge amounts of capital with which it could influence electricity prices, Enron simply lied. Enron lied to its investors, its regulators (in the few cases where it could not avoid regulation altogether or shape it to its purposes) and even its employees and pensioners.

Enron had grown so dominant in the American West's energy markets that, at one point, it controlled more than 30 per cent of energy derivatives trading along the California–Oregon border. (Recall that such trades had been exempted from regulation by the Commodity Futures Trading Commission when Wendy Gramm was Chair.) The day after Enron declared bankruptcy and left the market, on December 3, 2001, the price of contracts on the forward markets for energy on the West coast fell 30 per cent.[60] The volume of electricity trading has declined sharply since[61] and Wall Street has punished energy companies caught emulating Enron with slashes in share prices and credit ratings.

Enron's deregulation and its deceptive accounting are two sides of the same coin. An important lesson of Enron is that deregulation made the accounting deception possible. Put another way, systematic and transparent accounting requirements – such as the Uniform System of Accounts regulated utilities must use – are the foundation for transparency that protects both investors and ratepayers.

So, did Enron's bankruptcy slow the rush to deregulate the energy industry? The jury is still out. Most witnesses at Congressional hearings on Enron's collapse thought that it did not hurt energy markets, slow energy delivery, or cause price spikes, but some Congressmen themselves said they ought to slow down and rethink electricity deregulation legislation. Representative Henry Waxman of California argued that going forward with wholesale competition in the face of Enron's failure was "a leap of faith in the ability of markets to function properly."[62]

A group of energy executives, investment bankers and accountants met in Cambridge, Massachusetts on February 16, 2002, to discuss "The New Face of Risk: Energy Strategies for the Changed World." While the title of the conference was set before the Enron collapse, the conference became about Enron and its effect on the rest of the energy industry. The consensus seemed to be that energy companies were all of a sudden "embracing the greater transparency and stronger balance sheets demanded of them by investors." The leaders recognized (unfairly, they felt) that many politicians and others blamed Enron's ability to get away with all that it had on energy deregulation. They knew they would be painted with the same brush. So many energy executives said they were going back to basics: making and selling energy that they produced through power plants, pipelines and refineries. Trading is out (or at least out of sight). Some are (not so secretly) gloating over the fall of an arrogant company that grew too big too fast.[63]

Wall Street has been quick to grasp the Enron bankruptcy lesson that the risks created by energy price volatility are not worth whatever the gains of deregulation may be – it bid down share prices of competitive generation owners and slashed their credit ratings.[64] Enron stock went from $90.38 to 26.5 cents in about 16 months. Such a 99 per cent wipe-out is hard to match, but over a period of a year or less, AES shares dropped 93 per cent, Calpine 88 per cent and Williams Energy 43 per cent.[65] Where it cannot sell long-term electricity contracts, AES Corporation is bailing out of generation altogether rather than try to capitalize on volatility by trading Enron-style.[66] MIT economist Paul Joskow worries "about financing the next cycle of power plants."[67] A managing director of RWE says two more traders are "at the verge of bankruptcy."[68] The price volatility created by deregulation is now properly regarded as a problem rather than an opportunity to make a killing.

As for Enron's effect on the future of utility regulation in the US, Enron thought it had the regulators and Congress itself in its pocket. But: "There won't be any efforts in the next five years at the state level to deregulate energy," predicts Colorado Governor Bill Owens, a Republican.[69] Enron's collapse has only strengthened the hand of those who believe in transparent information and public oversight of publicly held corporations.

14 International Democracy – Developing and Developed Countries

The soil in Johannesburg is unusually porous. Among other things, this means dumping sewage on the ground is an excellent way to spread cholera. This was demonstrated by an early 1990s, apartheid era, money-saving policy of using pit latrines in place of running water to carry off sewage. Why not use piped water now? The World Bank had earlier over-estimated the usage (and thus revenue) of the Katse Dam by 40 per cent, so there is no shortage of water. But a third of the water that reaches Johannesburg leaks into the ground. And businesses and institutions are allowed to defer payment of their water bills without being required even to put up a deposit. So the World Bank tells the poorest fifth of Johannesburgers that their response to a 55 per cent increase in water rates to pay for these financial fiascos (including the Dam's revenue shortfall) should be . . . pit latrines.

Johannesburgers were not consulted.[1]

International ideology and the real interests behind it

An ideology of marketplace economics for monopoly utility services has spread across the world, from the highly sophisticated democracies such as the US and UK, described in the last two chapters, to the developing nations of the Third World. The ideology promises economic development, efficiency and lower prices.

The promise is a lie. Most of the benefits of adopting the ideology have gone to international utility holding companies and their financiers. The benefits have been paid for by workers in lost jobs, by consumers in higher prices and reduced service, and by the poorest in the inability to afford service altogether. The ideology does not promise a democratic choice of goals or results.

Using anti-democratic principles of secrecy[2] and new-speak, the financial warriors of the developed world – led by the World Bank and the International Monetary Fund (IMF) – have, since the Thatcher–Reagan

162

revolution of the 1980s, imposed as loan conditions on the developing world the theory that economic development could lift the world's poor by selling off national infrastructure to mega-corporations. The application of this principle of trickle-down economics has boiled down to this: help poor people by raising the prices they pay for essential utilities.

The international financiers use phrases like "structural adjustment" and "floating tranche" to disguise policies of imposing loan conditions of privatization and lending money only after such conditions are met. With such secrecy, the World Bank and IMF evade democratic review, both in their sponsoring nations and in the nations on which they impose these conditions.

"Structural adjustment" is international financial new-speak for replacing state ownership and control with market forces[3] – including privatization. It is grounded in the ideological shift of the Reagan–Thatcher era and was evident by 1982.[4] By 1990–94, a third of World Bank adjustment loans[5] and about 15 per cent of all IMF loans[6] related to privatization. Nearly all IMF lending now includes structural adjustment conditions. At the World Bank, "the share of conditionalities related to private participation in infrastructure [another new-speak term for privatization] as a part of adjustment lending more than doubled between FY96 and FY99."[7]

The ideology of privatization and competition, and the will to impose it unilaterally, is claimed to be based on two foundations. One is the view that governments are bloated and corrupt. According to World Bank world water coordinator John Briscoe, for instance, the public sector is not only corrupt, but also inefficient and unaccountable.[8] But then those same governments are left to carry out privatization in a process that former World Bank chief economist Joseph Stiglitz aptly calls "briberization." Stiglitz cites cases where politicians used World Bank demands for privatization to silence critics, then sold off state-owned electricity and water utilities for a "commission" of 10 per cent that they squirreled in Swiss bank accounts.[9] Stiglitz rhetorically asks whether international bankers believed their policies would help borrowing nations or "believed they would benefit financial interests in the . . . advanced industrial world?" As for the supposed benefit, says Stiglitz, "I got to see the evidence. There was none."[10]

Indeed, it is privatized utilities that blacked out Buenos Aires for ten days in the middle of the summer (February) of 1999 and, the year before, Auckland, New Zealand, from February to May. A comprehensive international comparison of generation, transmission and distribution services found no significant difference in performance or efficiency between private and public utilities.[11] And, efficiency aside, it is not hard to figure out which institution is likely to be most responsive to costly social concerns. Faced with difficulties in places such as Brazil and Argentina, for example, the response of AES Corporation was to draw up a plan to bail out of as much as $1 billion in power plants and distribution systems.[12]

No less an authority than America's business Bible, the *Wall Street Journal*, agrees with Stiglitz's analysis: "[The IMF] is primarily a political creation, engaged in trying to alter political decisions in the countries that borrow the money rich countries . . . provide."[13] Furthermore, "IMF bailouts . . . carry the misnomer 'aid,' but those billions go to the creditors [banks], who would otherwise have to . . . take losses."[14]

The other foundation for the ideology of privatization and competition is the conclusion, arrived at without consultation with the nations in question, that government-owned public services should not lose money, and should be sold if they do, and that government operations will benefit from the revenue of such sales.[15] This ideology does not include the concept that a government social policy of service and concern for its citizens could encompass anything other than revenue and profit. Thus World Bank policy – despite its expressed concern for the poor – of "higher tariffs for previously subsidized users," because economics requires an incentive for private electricity generation.[16]

The shift in thinking demanded by this ideology was succinctly captured by Scottish Power after it was privatized:

> Firstly we focus on operating profit, seeking ways to build cash inflows by maximizing revenues . . . This focus is in marked contrast to the priorities that the company had prior to privatization . . . Our primary role was the maintenance and security of supply to our customer[s].[17]

Or, as a Merrill Lynch securities analyst put it even more bluntly: "What do investors want from a new company after privatization? . . . SUPERIOR INVESTMENT RETURN."[18] Another securities analyst makes the point this way:

> Once upon a time, long ago, private entrepreneurs established the public utilities. Then, later on, misguided socialists and nationalists took over those enterprises, turning them into unproductive state agencies. Finally, in the 1980s, people saw the light. Governments sold those utilities back to private investors. Everyone lived happily ever after.

That, truly was a fairy tale. Many utilities started as government-owned agencies that showed as much energy and acumen as their privately-owned counterparts. Some governments, in fact, socialized the utilities because of inadequacies of their private owners.

He goes on to describe the UK's establishment of an electricity transmission system that the industry failed to build; the UK's nationalization of its electricity system to create economies of scale that were lacking; Mexico's takeover of its telephone system because private capital could not expand the system; and the once widely accepted idea that society would be best off with utility rates priced at marginal cost, which no private owner could afford to do in a declining cost industry.[19] (As noted earlier, price gouging in California and elsewhere in the US has underscored the prescience of the latter point. Despite the promise of deregulation advocates that prices would fall to marginal cost, generation owners quickly figured out that marginal cost pricing would drive them to bankruptcy and instead set their prices to maximize profits.) And he might have made the further point that what looks like a financial loss to a banker may be a progressive and humane social policy to a nation.

In sum, then, the requirements of privatization and competition are based on two arguments. One argument is that government is corrupt or incompetent, which begs the question of how privatization is to be managed. The other argument is that international bankers know better what is best for a nation's people than the government to which the bankers are willing to lend.

Either way, public service consumers are better off at the hands of a weak government utility than at the mercy of a private operator that government is too weak to regulate. If international bankers really want to make a difference, they should help strengthen government operations. "Rather than impose blanket privatization, the trade unions are asking the IMF and World Bank to use their resources to help the development and modernization of public enterprises."[20]

Instead, the World Bank persuades nations that they must compete for capital investment by dropping social and regulatory policies that bankers and private utilities treat as obstacles to profit – price controls and other consumer protections, allowances for the poorest members of society, labor protections, reliability and other reasonable levels of service quality. Thus, for example, "improving collections" is the euphemism for cutting service to the poor or, as one observer puts it, "there appear to be acute conflicts between distributor profitability and affordable electricity supply to the poor."[21] Privatized utilities are encouraged to compete with each other over how many workers they can lay off.[22] Investment is attracted by transferring risks to consumers by means of prices based on high rates of return, take-or-pay contracts,[23] dollar-denominated obligations[24] and government guarantees. Government-owned utilities, like regulated utilities in the US, routinely absorb such risks as changes in demand, low-income consumer requirements and currency fluctuations as a matter of social policy. By contrast, incorporating risk buffers into private utility prices ensures that prices will rise much higher than under government ownership.

The international enforcement of the privatization-and-competition ideology is simplicity itself – no compliance, no loan. "World Bank country director Harold Wackman was quoted saying the institution would no longer fund water projects if the private sector is not involved."[25] The more delicate and bankerly phrase is "floating tranches, which are tied to fulfilling specific conditions." This is a variation of the "multitranche operation," where the continuation of lending depends on the meeting of certain conditions.[26]

New-speak terms, such as tranche and adjustment, are part of a broader aura of secrecy around privatization conditions that are profoundly antidemocratic. When more than 100 non-governmental organizations (NGOs) worldwide asked the World Bank to fully disclose adjustment-related loan documents, the response was that the World Bank's operational policy review "will not discuss development approaches in such areas as privatization."[27]

Secrecy at the IMF, observes Stiglitz, hides a multitude of failings:

- mathematical models that are out of date;
- economic models that are flawed, for example, by leaving out the potential for debtors' default or bankruptcy;
- a cookie-cutter approach so blatant that there is a story circulating of one country report being largely identical to that of another, right down to the name of the country;
- economists who know little of the country they analyze beyond its five-star hotels; and
- conclusions for which there is no evidence.

As Stiglitz concludes:

Smart people are more likely to do stupid things when they close themselves off from outside criticism and advice. If there's one thing

I've learned in government, it's that openness is most essential in those realms where expertise seems to matter most.[28]

This secrecy reflects an immense and anti-democratic international shift in power.

Internationally the balance of power has shifted further away from developing countries in favour of foreign creditors and investors, international financial organizations and industrialized countries. Everywhere the power and the reach of the state have declined. Internally, there has been a shift of power in favour of capital . . . and away from the organized working class and to some extent the middle class.[29]

So if the ideology of the marketplace for utility service does not make sense, what is the real reason international bankers are pushing it? The United States Energy Association "represents the broad interests of the U.S. energy sector"; its membership includes representatives of international electric utility investors and power plant builders, as well as government agencies and others. "[T]he promotion of U.S. energy business in international markets is one of the most important foreign and economic policy functions that the U.S. government can perform," it asserts.[30] Similar sentiments no doubt exist in boardrooms across the lands among the OECD countries that finance and thus control the World Bank and IMF.

US corporate investment in non-US utilities rose from about $2 billion to about $10 billion from 1994 to 1996, almost entirely accounted for by investment in electric utilities.[31] US corporate purchasing has continued since, including:

- Enron purchase of Sao Paulo Elektro (1998);
- AES purchase of CAESS (1998) and others (2000) in El Salvador; EDE Este in the Dominican Republic (1999); Telasi in Tblisi, Georgia (1999); and CESCO in Orissa, India (1999); and
- Public Service Electric & Gas purchase of Chilquenta in Chile (1999).[32]

At the same time, Electricité de France has invested in Brazil, Hungary, the UK, and Côte D'Ivoire. Electricité de Portugal has invested in Guatemala, Bolivia and Brazil. Suez Lyonnaise, of France, controls utilities in Togo, Senegal and Zambia. Spanish utility investments are in Brazil, Chile, Argentina, Colombia, Peru and the Netherlands (Endesa); Nicaragua,

Guatemala, Colombia, Venezuela, Dominican Republic, Panama and Moldova (Union Fenosa); and Guatemala, Bolivia and Brazil (Iberdrola). German's Eon and RWE own utility investments in the Czech Republic and Hungary.[33]

And what quietly stands behind these international utility purchases? International finance. In its last three years before bankruptcy, 1999–2001, the infamous Enron was financed by Citibank, J.P. Morgan Chase, Credit Suisse First Boston, Deutsche Bank, Merrill Lynch & Co., Banc of America Securities, and Lehman Brothers, among others. Securities underwriting fees alone in just these three years came to $214 million. And that does not count fees for lending, derivatives trading or merger advice.[34] These fees may have contributed to a certain flexibility with which these bankers treated Enron. According to one claimant's lawyer, "The banks helped and participated in transactions so that Enron could phony up its balance sheet and defraud creditors and shareholders."[35]

Facilitating these transactions was Enron's ability to obtain $7.2 billion in US and other public financing commitments, including from the World Bank, toward 38 Enron projects in 29 countries.[36]

Much of Europe's drive to privatization represents opportunity for "cash-rich and acquisition-hungry" European utilities blocked from expansion in their home markets. Since 1995, the value of European utility mergers and acquisitions is $500 billion. So far, the UK's National Grid and Scottish Power, along with Germany's E.ON and RWE, have found that US de-regulation represents opportunity as well. Close behind Europe's acquiring utilities come their financiers, the top ten in 2001 representing a list very similar to Enron's:

- Goldman Sachs
- Deutsche Bank
- Lazard
- Dresdner Kleinwort Wasserstein
- Rothschild
- Morgan Stanley
- Merrill Lynch
- Mediobanca SpA
- Credit Suisse First Boston
- Salomon Smith Barney (Citibank)[37]

As Salomon Smith Barney analyst Guy Moszkowski points out, "M&A [mergers and acquisitions] is very, very profitable. It's a big contributor to high margins and high returns on equity when it is booming."[38]

Thus the visible hand of state policy is replaced by the invisible hands of international bankers.

Developing countries

One could say that, at least, the US and other developed countries only harmed themselves when they deregulated their electricity sectors. The infliction of injury is not so voluntary in the developing world.

India

Perhaps it is not surprising that ideas cooked up half a world away are so distasteful when served in a nation that uses an entirely different recipe book. World Bank-inspired policies of privatization have drained millions of dollars from India to the pot of utilities based in the developed world.

The Indian economy is plagued by a power shortage that has been ascribed to a combination of many factors. Most of the electricity system is owned by governments, but governments have been unable to allocate enough investment capital to build plant to keep up with the pace of economic expansion. In a nation where food consumes 90 per cent of rural household incomes and more than 60 per cent of urban incomes, governments have not assigned a high priority to compensatory residential electricity prices. Rates for agriculture are kept deliberately low – about half of rural households cannot pay more. Domestic prices are also kept low – about half of urban households also cannot afford to pay more. (What are delicately called "non-technical losses" (unbilled usage often referred to as "theft") are also tolerated as a means of subsidy to the poorest of the poor.) Domestic consumption levels are barely enough for lights and fans – 58 kilowatt-hours (kWh) per month for the average rural household of eight, 75 kWh for low-income urban households.[39]

The World Bank might have considered loans and technical assistance to Indian governments to support expansion of the nation's electric infrastructure. It did not. Using both loan conditions and the persuasive powers that only a banker can have with bureaucracies and politicians, the World Bank worked behind the scenes to persuade Indian policy-makers that they should privatize the Indian electricity sector. The method *du jour*: contracting with Independent Power Producers (IPPs) – non-utility power plants owned and financed from outside the country – for new generation.

The argument was that the private sector would both eliminate corruption and relieve Indian governments of financial losses so that governments could focus on social welfare programs. The kindest thing one can say is that World Bankers are lousy policy cooks. If World Bank overseers are correct that Indian governments cannot operate an electricity system without corruption (which, to be fair, is a view also held by many Indians), is it consistent to rely on the same governments to contract for electricity without corruption?

One answer is that the Dabhol IPP, described below, is surrounded with official suspicions of bribery,[40] inflamed by an Enron employee's 1993 testimony to a US House of Representatives committee that Enron had spent $20 million "educating" certain Indians about the fine points of American capitalism.[41] Some see an Enron pattern – after the World Bank cancelled a loan to finance a costly Enron water project scheduled to be awarded without competition in Ghana, the Bank's country director there said, "I concluded that the only way they thought they could get contracts was through the back door, not through the front."[42]

A central part of the World Bank plan for India is to remove subsidies of electricity consumption in order to free up funds for social welfare programs. This totally misses the social welfare point of the subsidies. The "theft" and farm subsidies embedded in the Indian electricity system reflect political and social arrangements that Indians made and Indians must deal with. Indeed, the Bank concedes that its policies slow the expanded availability of electricity, which is contrary to Indian policy. Whether current Indian arrangements are right or wrong from an academic or ideological point of view, the question for democracy is: who should make social welfare choices in India, international bankers with no accountability to the Indian people or democratically elected Indian governments?

There is not too much doubt about the World Bank's answer to that one. In July 2000, the World Bank refused to grant a loan to the Indian state of Uttar Pradesh unless privatization of its electricity system began within three months. The Bank made its demand despite an agreement in January 2000 between the state and the Electricity Union to wait a year before privatizing in order to study the experience of other states.[43] Four months earlier, the Bank suspended a loan to Haryana because the state had democratically reached the decision to not step down the electricity restructuring path.[44]

The IPP strategy has been a general failure, producing only 3,000 megawatts (mW) of a hoped-for 40,000,[45] and resulting in continued charges of corruption, doubled prices, and government bankruptcy. Indian governments remain at the center of the electricity industry.[46] The World Bank expresses concern for the social welfare of the Indian population. But this is somehow translated to vigorous opposition to pricing adopted by the democratic Indian political system at least in part to meet social welfare objectives. Concern for the Indian population did not move the World Bank past public silence about pillaging by IPPs from outside the country.[47]

The most spectacular failure has been the Dabhol IPP. Although disfavored by the World Bank, the Dabhol project grew out of a decision nurtured by the Bank to attract foreign capital by developing IPPs. As is commonly demanded by IPPs, the investment by Enron (along with General Electric and Bechtel) in the Dabhol plant was guaranteed by the Indian state of Maharashtra,[48] prices were set in US dollars, and take-or-pay requirements called for payment of all potential output whether needed or not. When expected demand for power from the plant did not appear, and Enron raised the per-unit price of Dabhol power to cover fixed costs, the state had to raid payroll obligations to pay up.

As described in Chapter 2, power from the plant was priced at almost double the average cost in the area and more than triple the cost of the cheapest provider. The return on equity projected for the owners: about 30 per cent, compared to the 3 per cent objective of the former state Electricity Boards. State review of the proposal failed the basic test of democratic transparency and participation. Two consumer groups filed objections concerning the project's proposed tariff, capital structure and other technical details, as well as broad policy concerns. The state took exactly one day to dismiss the objections. Ironically, the World Bank had quietly advised against this particular project because it was not a least-cost source of power compared to other available alternatives and it relied on projections of demand that were well over double government growth projections (which themselves turned out to be overly optimistic). But the Bank was not very insistent about its view that, if adopted, would have displeased a major G-7 corporation. It was much more insistent about the privatization policy, which brought India to this point.[49]

The Clinton Administration in the US pressured the Indian government to accept the investment – the largest ever for India – and provided Export-Import Bank financing as well as Overseas Private Investment Corp. political risk insurance. As the deal unraveled, the Bush II Administration pressured the Indian government to salvage it, threatening to drop US support of Indian gas and oil production. As this is written, the plant is idle, the state Electricity Board faces an invoice for $240 million and counting – the claim could reach $5 billion – the project has filed a $180 million political insurance claim, and the plant is for sale in the wake of Enron's bankruptcy.[50]

Dabhol is only the most infamous of the antidemocratic power policy decisions pressed on India. As another example, starting in 1993, over the objections of experts such as those at Electricité de France, the Bank established what it hoped would be a model for electricity industry restructuring in the poor state of Orissa. The Bank-inspired "reform" process in Orissa included consultation but not democratic input. Bank consultants were told to "create a process that was irreversible"; government officials saw the consultation only as a "way of reducing tension." Bank and government officials acknowledge that open debate may have prevented the reforms they sought. So the Bank issued an ultimatum: no privatization, no loan. What were the results of this World Bank model? Government monopoly of generation and distribution was replaced by a private monopoly over three of the four new distribution zones; a private integrated monopoly controlled the fourth distribution zone and retained integrated generation. The regulator was relatively independent and transparent – it made some information publicly available, held public hearings on some issues, and refused to rubber-stamp some World Bank recommendations for price increases – but it also approved annual rate increases (76 per cent in two years) and ignored promises of social reform.[51]

When a November 1999 cyclone killed tens of thousands of people in Orissa, it also destroyed much property and parts of the electricity system AES had just purchased but failed to insure. The World Bank promotes privatization because the private sector is more efficient and less corrupt, which will therefore free government funds for social welfare. So here is the efficient corporate response to the already poor and now devastated state of Orissa: give us $60 million to rebuild the system or we will triple electricity prices. AES wound up with a loan and a 4 per cent rate increase.[52]

There may be a silver lining to the failure of World Bank-inspired policies in Orissa, Maharashtra and elsewhere. There are some indications of a decreased governmental interest in privatization, an increased interest in emphasizing social and economic development goals, and increases in democratic participation in electricity policy development.[53]

South Africa

The South African government was founded with the dedication to use the state to reach economic and social goals of equality, including constitutional guarantees of housing and basic services. But it has more recently adopted World Bank policies of privatization, increased prices and markets.

In 1994, the new Mandela government adopted a Reconstruction and Development Book that promised democratic participation in government investments to extend access to such infrastructure systems as electricity, water and telecommunications at "lifeline" rates. The World Bank's alternative demand: water rates that must reflect an average annual return to investors of 29 per cent. So privatization brought a 28 per cent increase in the price of water in Durban, South Africa, which led to shut-offs and a worsened cholera epidemic.

In electricity, South Africa's government proposes to sell about a third of the power plants owned by the state-owned Eskom, although this would raise domestic prices by 22–50 per cent. Prices already display a massive poor-supporting-the-rich approach: while large businesses pay less than 6–7 cents per kilowatt-hour, low-income families pay about quadruple the rate or more: 23–28 cents in Soweto; 48 cents in rural areas.

In an effort to ready Eskom for privatization, the utility sent workers with armed guards to remove cables serving those whom it says are behind in their bills – and their paying neighbors, whose only offense is living near families Eskom says are delinquent. Many of the bills are disputed, but Eskom nevertheless proceeded to cut off service to 60,000 families in Soweto township in the middle of winter. This is how Eskom plans to appear more profitable, in order to fetch as high a price as possible from an investor. Never mind that the winning bidder will then need to raise electricity prices in order to afford the price it pays for Eskom. The *Sunday Times* concludes that

> essential services should not be run by enterprises seeking to make money . . . This task needs to be performed by a utility with a long-term objective of improving the lives of people, rather than an outfit out to make a profit . . . The provision of electricity should not be made another playground for greedy foreign bargain hunters and unscrupulous empowerment operators who do not have the interests of poor people at heart.

South African privatization also brought a 40 per cent increase in the price of local telephone calling. The price of international calls for the already rich dropped 35 per cent.

Concludes the Congress of South African Trade Unions: "Enough. We did not fight for liberation so that we could sell everything we won to the highest bidder." Fiscal and monetary policy coordinator Neva Makgetla is even willing to compromise: "Competition is good for upper income and business, and will lead to better service. We've accepted that and we can live with that. But it should be in the context of the state providing basic service for the poor, because the private sector won't."

An academic observer suggests that the reason the World Bank may be avoiding democratic participation is that "the more participation there is in highly politicized societies such as . . . South Africa, the less likely it is that privatization will be met with consent."[54]

Brazil

In Chapters 1 and 11, we describe Rio Dark, secret rate-making and a non-participatory consultation process. Here we tell you about Brazil's choice between rolling blackouts or 20 per cent cuts in electricity use because of IMF loan conditions that prohibit state construction of needed power plants.

Flashlights were in short supply in June 2001 as the government announced mandatory 20 per cent cutbacks, enforced by 200 per cent surcharges (threatened but withdrawn) or six-day cut-offs. President Cardoso was forced to turn off the heat for his swimming pool. An 80-year-old couple hauled out their kerosene lamps from the attic. What had happened over the previous ten years to darken Brazil? The government's power plant construction fell about ten per cent below the country's sky-rocketing demand for power. To make up for the shortfall, the government drew down excess hydro storage capacity that would ordinarily cover five years of low rainfall. Since 90 per cent of Brazil's power comes from hydro, using up the hydro surplus did not leave much else.

At this point the IMF provided Brazil financing on the condition that it stop building *any* power plants, even though potential new hydro power is about triple existing capacity. Brazil's Economic Development Bank would provide the loan for a group of private companies (including AES) to buy Rio Light under a deal that allowed them to keep productivity gains for the first seven years before sharing such cost reductions with consumers. (Those "productivity gains" turned out to be a euphemism for mass firings that led to the Rio Dark described in Chapter 1.) But the IMF did not allow the country's Development Bank to finance state-owned power plant development.

The IMF thus put the likes of AES in an extraordinary bargaining position since they were now the only ones that could provide the power Brazil so desperately needed. AES's first step: announce the suspension of $2 billion in plant construction unless prices are raised for existing AES distribution operations. The government agreed to a 15 per cent price hike for privatized electricity distributors, including AES.

There is a silver lining here. In the first month of rationing in Sao Paulo, there was a 46 per cent drop in a more crude form of robbery called "lightning abductions," by which motorists were kidnapped and forced to withdraw cash from ATMs. Most of these robberies occurred after dark, when rationing had forced banks to turn off their ATMs.[55]

Other nations

India, South Africa and Brazil exemplify a worldwide swath of anti-democratic economic destruction:

- Overpriced and unaffordable privately owned power plants have been foisted off on nations, together with contracts guaranteeing payment to the private owners. Thus, 42 private power contracts at rates 33 per cent higher than the state utility's prices produced a $9 billion liability for the Philippines when predicted demand for power did not materialize.[56]
- Generators in the Dominican Republic producing about 40 per cent of the nation's power increased prices 51 per cent upon privatization. The prices are unregulated. After public protests, the government agreed to pay 42 per cent of the increase (still leaving consumers with a 30 per cent increase and taxpayers with the rest), or about $60 million a year. When the government also found the charges un-affordable, piling up arrears of more than $100 million, generators pulled the plug for up to 24 hours at a time – even at hospitals. Despite this expensive experience with privatization, the Dominican Republic announced plans to privatize its transmission system to comply with World Bank conditions.[57]
- Costa Rica could have produced electricity itself for less than its private power contracts. Costa Rica law requires that such contracts provide economic benefits for the country or consumers. According to the Comptroller General, they instead unlawfully guaranteed private profits.[58]
- Private contracts in Indonesia represent 50 per cent more electricity capacity than needed on the main islands of Bali and Java. When the government postponed construction of an Enron plant due to an economic downturn, Enron successfully invoked a $15 million political insurance policy issued by the World Bank's Multilateral Investment Guarantee Agency (MIGA), despite a pending lawsuit by

the Indonesian power utility to cancel the Enron contract on the grounds of corruption in the deposed Suharto regime. Upon MIGA's threat to deny insurance for any further projects in Indonesia, the government came up with the $15 million, for which it received exactly nothing. One piece of good news: one contract was renegotiated to nationalize the plant at an affordable price. (Similarly, Croatia tore up its contract with Enron despite US pressure.) [59]

- In order to obtain IMF funding, Korea abandoned its own two-year management evaluation that ruled out privatization.[60] However, a strike threat brought job security guarantees and a 15 per cent wage increase.[61]

- The IMF's Ecuador Interim Country Assistance Strategy for 2000 required raising the price of cooking gas by 80 per cent, and privatizing its biggest water system. A 1983 loan package had required raising electricity prices.[62]

- In Nigeria, 3,000 workers were fired from the National Electric Power Authority in order to get ready for privatization.[63]

- Argentina's privatized phone company raised prices even in a period of deflation that lowered salaries and other costs. A privatized water system raised its prices by as much as 400 per cent.[64]

- The Public Services International Research Unit database records the privatization of 45 electricity distribution systems in 21 countries between 1996 and 2001. Buyers include Enron, AES, Public Service Electric & Gas, Hydro Quebec, Electricité de France, Endesa (Spain), E.ON and RWE (Germany).[65]

- In the year 2000 alone, the IMF imposed loan conditions on twelve countries requiring privatization of water supplies or large increases in water rates. For example, the IMF requires Nicaragua to increase water and sewer rates 18 per cent a year.[66]

- As described in more detail in Chapter 11, the World Bank mandated the sale of the water system in Cochabamba, Bolivia. This was followed by the new owner's following the World Bank's policy of "full cost recovery" (sweetened by a deal under which the new owner was guaranteed a 16 per cent return after inflation). In other words, a subsidiary of Bechtel raised water prices by at least 35 per cent. In what one might think of as a bow to the will of the people, after 13 days of protests across the country, Bolivia's president cancelled both the sale and the price hikes. At least two people were killed in the government's response to the protests; 175 were injured.

- A subsidiary of UK-based Anglian Water doubled water rates in the Czech Republic between 1994 and 1997, then raised them another 40 per cent in 1998.[67]
- Privatization of water and sanitation in Tucuman, Argentina, was awarded to the bidder promising an immediate price increase of 68 per cent to finance future investments. Water quality deteriorated.[68]
- A subsidiary of UK-based Biwater raised industrial water rates in the Philippines by 400 per cent in 1998.[69]
- Since the 1995 privatization of Puerto Rico's water system operation to a subsidiary of France-based Vivendi, entire communities have been without water for as long as years, others get water only every other day, half the system's water leaks away and pollution violations are common. Vivendi's subsidiary is not even paying its telephone and power bills. As Puerto Rico Comptroller Manuel Diaz-Saldana concludes, privatization of the water system "has been a bad business deal for the people of Puerto Rico."[70]
- The World Bank insists that Ghana cannot take on further debt or deficits to pay for water or sanitation, so the services must be privatized, staff must be "rationalized" (translation: fire employees) and rates must be raised. Furthermore, claims the Bank, the private sector is more efficient. The divestiture process started out in secret, until an Enron-led group was accused of making $5 million bribes to get the deal. The World Bank drew the line at this and threatened to withdraw loans unless the sale were cancelled and re-bid. The bidding still proceeds in secrecy from the Ghanaian public, however, although this much is public: under the new rates, very poor families will be required to pay 12 per cent of their incomes just for water – 2.6 times the income fraction required of non-poor families. Not computed is the impact on the country of increased medical requirements due to water-borne illness, lowered productivity, and inability of families to obtain basic essentials.[71]

Response of the international bankers

We do not want to leave you with the impression that protests of the social destruction we have described have had no impact at all on international bankers. The IMF now says that it is responding to questions that have been raised about its "structural conditions" by reducing the number of privatization conditions it imposes.

Despite the IMF's elaborate show of worldwide consultation, this is, however, nothing more than an international game of "Who's Got the Button?" The IMF is ceding to the World Bank responsibility for such conditions as utility privatization, then imposing the requirement that its borrowers comply with World Bank conditions. According to an internal IMF memo, "Where Fund conditionality has been scaled back significantly, this often reflects greater reliance on the use of World Bank conditionality . . ."

For its part, the World Bank also makes a grand show of consultation. But its rigid position on privatization is unchanged. The Bank concedes that it is imposing privatization conditions and that it does so without much consideration for their social impact. An internal report identifies privatization as an area "where adjustment operations have not paid sufficient attention to the potentially adverse social impact of reforms." (The Bank's then chief economist Lawrence Summers put it this way in a 1992 memo: "Just between you and me, shouldn't the World Bank be encouraging more migration of the dirty industries to the LDCs [less developed countries]?") The Bank vows to do better and, indeed, its stated goals are lofty ones: cutting in half the fraction of people in developing countries living in extreme poverty and the fraction of children who are malnourished.

But let's take a close look at its plan for 2002 – privatization with price increases, preferably with no regulation:

- "The increase in private provision during the 1990s, although large by historical standards, has been smaller than might be possible."
- "To the extent possible, policymakers need to encourage competition in the provision of infrastructure services."
- "To encourage private investment, two factors need attention: political and regulatory reform, particularly in pricing, and efforts to enhance the credibility in the government's new regulatory framework. Policies that allow for full cost recovery [price increases] and that ensure the investor a reasonable rate of return . . . are the preferred alternative."
- "It is important to undertake price reform while the enterprise is still in public hands. Prices have to be increased."
- "Private sector provision has had mixed effects on tariffs and hence mixed effects on the poor . . . there are . . . examples where tariffs have risen because of the need to ensure the financial viability of service providers."
- "publicly provided infrastructure services have often delivered poor quality and inadequate coverage . . . Inefficiencies with public sector

provision of infrastructure services and fiscal constraints led governments around the world to shift to private sector provision."

- "The presence of an independent regulatory agency mitigates the risks of political interference in the privatization process and hence provides more comfort to investors."
- "Competition may substitute for regulation in protecting the economy from monopoly abuses. This is all the more important in developing countries, where the capacity for enforcing regulations is generally weak . . . competition can avoid many of the incentive, information, and enforcement problems created by regulatory regimes and, where it is effective, can substitute for regulation."
- Establishing independent, transparent regulatory agencies supervised by a strong and independent judiciary is "difficult to establish. Further, without checks and balances, bureaucratic inefficiencies may be replaced by private corruption."

The World Bank states its endorsements of transparency, accounting standards, "open disclosure of the rules of the game," and regulation that engages all stakeholders, including the poor.[72] But one of the first documents made public under the Bank's new open disclosure policy demonstrates how little substantive change there has been. Uganda must turn over management of its urban water systems (i.e., those where a private profit is possible) to private operators, "promoting efficient [higher] pricing." In rural systems, the private sector must be used for "design of small-piped systems, drilling, spring protection, public latrine construction, hand-pump, and piping supply and installation."

This is consistent with earlier requirements that the Uganda Electricity Board fire 2000 employees in 1998 and "promote private sector participation." Ultimately this policy led to World Bank financing of a hydro plant at Bujagali. In this way, an IPP owned by AES was awarded the concession for a 250 mW plant the primary use of which appears to be to export power to Kenya and Tanzania.[73]

Net change: zero. But the IMF and World Bank obviously believe they must at least appear to be responding to democratic pressures. With time, perhaps their phony responses can be turned to genuine ones.

Other developed countries

It is not only the developing world that has caught the fever of market ideology. More than two-thirds of the nearly trillion dollars in proceeds from privatization have come from OECD countries.[74] In addition to the destruction that the anti-democratic ideology of privatization has caused across the world, we turn to its anti-democratic effects on its home turf, the developed world.

In the Nordic countries, competition has been adopted by Denmark (1999 for large customers), Sweden (1996), Finland (late 1995, domestic in 1997), and Norway (1991). While NordPool generation prices dropped for a time, "the decisive element was the good availability of inexpensive hydro power."[75] But, just as in California and New England, deregulation introduced volatile prices. From July 2000 to July 2001, a period of low rainfall, prices leapt 247 per cent. But producers say prices have to climb another 3 percentage points (to about $0.225), and stay there, before they will consider building additional power plants. "The politicians aren't fully aware of what kind of monster they have created," according to Kristian May, managing director of the hard-hit Danish Steelworks.[76] Thus, under the new system, needed power plants are not built until prices skyrocket and blackouts are imposed when shortages occur because plants cannot be built in the short time between the "price signal" and the need for power. The Swedish and Norwegian energy secretaries recently agreed that "Prices in the market shall at all times balance consumption and production, which means that the prices also will reflect capacity shortage . . . The authorities responsible and system operators should also work out a set of rules and a common standard for possible power disconnection of con- sumption . . ."[77]

But even in the years of falling prices, the benefit was skewed to industrial customers. In Sweden, from 1997 through 2000, before taxes, domestic prices declined 12–16 per cent while the price for a medium-sized industrial fell 20 per cent. But after taxes: domestic prices rose 3 per cent while the industrial price fell 21 per cent. Similarly, in Finland after taxes, domestic prices declined 3–5 per cent while large industrial prices fell 11 per cent. All prices rose in Norway, for the smallest domestic customers by 15 per cent.[78] At the same time, since 1990, employment in the Nordic energy sector has been slashed by about 26 per cent.[79]

Despite strong pressure from the European Commission, Iceland thus far has been slow to embrace privatization of its electric generation, which is almost entirely hydro and geothermal. Iceland's national generation utility is regarded as very efficiently run:

The scope for reduced operating costs at the generation and transmission level in Iceland is minimal . . . we are skeptical that deregulation will

provide significant benefits from this [investment efficiency] perspective
. . . the potential for any significant downward movement in industry
costs by removing the socio-political burdens is, in our judgment, quite
modest in Iceland's case . . . there is no significant cross-subsidy between
the industrial sector and the general market in Iceland . . .[80]

The principal benefit of privatization in Iceland is projected to be the
increased ability to attract capital from outside the country[81] – which
appears to be another way of saying that international bankers require
deregulation as a condition of their loans.[82]

Indeed, the drive to privatize European electricity services may be
entirely explained by a drive by utilities (many state-owned)[83] to expand
beyond their home markets[84] and their financiers' desire for the fees that
come from the resulting mergers and acquisitions.[85] The ten largest
companies now control more than 50 per cent of the EU market, the top
three exceed 40 per cent of the market in every EU nation, and it is
projected that as few as five will ultimately dominate Europe.[86] Electricité
de France (EDF) recently purchased London Electricity, Budapest Power,
and a plant that provides 8 per cent of the UK power market. In fact, EDF
is said to have agreed to further marketization of electricity in Europe to
avoid retaliation against EDF for French restrictions on market entry.

Norway's Statkraft bought Trondheim Energiverk to become the second
largest Nordic power producer, with control of more than 50 per cent of
Norway's electricity output. The largest Nordic producer, Sweden's
Vattenfall, became the third largest supplier in Germany by purchasing
Berlin-based Bewag. Germany's E.ON is the product of a merger between
Viag and Veba. Spain's two largest electricity suppliers are merging.

European utilities have reached to the US as well, with British National
Grid Group buying New England Electric System and Niagara Mohawk
Power Corp., Scotttish Power buying PacificCorp (which also owns Utah
Power & Light), and E.ON buying Louisville Gas & Electric as part of the
UK's PowerGen.

Germany may soon illustrate the consequences of such consolidation.
Germany totally opened its electricity industry, providing choice for all
consumers in 1998 (although the European Commission only required
choice for the top 26, now 30 per cent). Wholesale prices dropped 27 per
cent by the end of 1999, 40 per cent at the end of 2000. This was not
without cost, as labor forces were cut as much as 50 per cent. Furthermore,
a London Business School analysis chalks up the price-cutting to working
off a temporary generation surplus and to unsustainable pricing designed

to force smaller generation competitors to merge with big ones. The marketplace was "transformed from a fragmented highly competitive market structure at the beginning of 1999 [about 80 regional companies and more than 800 smaller ones] to one where four dominant vertically integrated firms with a combined market share of over 90 per cent controlled the market by the beginning of 2001." The London Business School analysts predict "strategic capacity withdrawal" which "could effectively double annual average prices . . . a longer period of high prices could follow. As other countries have found, this would be much harder to reverse."[87] Small customer rates have already begun to climb.[88]

A related result of privatization and deregulation Europe is a drop in generation capacity additions, which is lowering reserve margins[89] and will ultimately lead to shortages that drive up prices.

As in the Nordic countries, New Zealand's deregulation (begun in 1993) has disfavored domestic electricity customers. In inflation-adjusted (real) terms, New Zealand generation prices declined a modest 5 per cent from 1994 to 1999, not a great success to begin with. But overall, average prices under deregulation actually rose 4 per cent, and domestic customers got the worst deal – home prices jumped 10 per cent. Deregulation and competition had caused skyrocketing retail charges (including distribution), which rose 24 per cent on average and jumped 30 per cent for domestic customers.[90]

Also like the Nordic countries, deregulation in New Zealand has brought not just higher prices but more volatile prices. Drought in this hydro-dependent system doubled spot generation prices.[91] In some months, prices reached six times the price of previous years.[92] At retail, some customers have been socked with price increases of 700 per cent and doubled prices are common.[93]

Those are the lucky ones. In the central business district of the capital city of Auckland, intermittently for five weeks, there was no electricity to be had at any price during the heat of one of New Zealand's hottest summers. The deregulated distribution utility (owned by a consumer trust) had, it concedes, allowed the four cables into the city to deteriorate to the point where they simply collapsed. A government inquiry found, and the utility admitted, that the risk of cable failure was ten times greater than the utility assumed; the utility's operational practices (maintenance) were below industry standards; and the utility even failed to react when the cables showed signs of failure. Some downtown employers had to move to Australia. A cargo ship was commandeered for its power plant (8 per cent of the needed power), but the diminished use and resulting stagnation of the water and sewer systems led to concerns about disease, lead poisoning, and explosions of sewer gas. Even criminals deserted downtown Auckland. The government's answer to blackout victims: sue the utility.[94]

We do not often quote conservative American newspaper columnists, but George Will's reaction to the euro sums up well the impact of public services privatization in the developed world:

> Who wants the euro and the superstate it implies? The EU's disparate publics do not, but . . . [o]ne [elite that does] is a commercial elite that believes the business of Europe is business – never mind freedom, democracy, justice, culture, different national characters . . .[95]

The developed world is, by virtue of its wealth, relatively more able to absorb the blackouts and high, roller-coaster prices brought by privatization. To this must be added 300,000 lost jobs in the electricity sector in Europe alone.[96] But these costs are as undemocratic, unfair to labor and devastating to the poor as anywhere else in the world.

15 Conclusion

Secrecy versus democracy

In 1990, the operator of the Wolf Creek nuclear plant in the US state of Kansas sued a lawyer, Robert Eye, for possessing documents stolen from the company's confidential files. Mr. Eye did not deny the facts. The nuclear operator, which also operates utilities in Australia and Latin America, accused the lawyer of theft and violation of commercial secrets. The court ruled that Eye could keep the stolen documents and even publish them – placing the public's right to information above the commercial interests of the plant operator. The court wrote:

> We believe the public has an overriding interest in the dissemination of information related to costs, construction and safety practices of nuclear power plants. Similar to the rationale of *United States versus Nixon,* release of the information contained within the files is one manner by which the manager of a potentially dangerous plant can be held accountable to the public.[1]

In the US, the right to information from a monopoly utility is virtually without bounds. Every nuclear plant must maintain a "public document room" which contains information about the plants, from blueprints of the piping system to the details of any radiation leaks. The key is that neither the private company nor the government may select which documents can be released for public inspection: they must all remain open. The notable exceptions are personnel files and medical reports on individual employees.

Financial records of private utilities are open as well as government's own files and reports, through the legal discovery process. Filings, inspection reports, letters, requests and other information from private companies are also accessible by any individual (from the US or any nation) by requests made through state and national Freedom of Information Acts.

America did not always have these rules for absolute transparency. The Freedom of Information Act[2] was enacted in 1966. In 1974, in *United States* v. *Nixon*, the US Supreme Court held that the President could not withhold publication of tape recordings made in the privacy of his office. Public access to nuclear files followed reaction to the Three Mile Island nuclear power plant accident in 1979. The courts and the US Congress concluded that the government often keeps secrets not to protect the public but to mislead it.

This spirit of openness in government affairs in the US also applies to private utility corporations, which must open their files, even if that harms their ability to compete. By contrast, the British electricity regulator has refused a request by the electricity workers union to divulge a report by a consultant on staffing and pay levels in the industry used to set future prices. This is regulation at its worst: there is no way for the union, the consumers, the public or even the utilities themselves to challenge the mysterious facts and opinions. Given the UK regulator's history of erroneous calculations and projections, this new secrecy is particularly troublesome, with no place in a democracy. Furthermore, a wrong judgment on staffing levels can endanger public or worker safety.[3]

Regulators in Britain have even extended "commercial secrecy" to the cost of maintaining a water meter. The effect is to bar customers from challenging the suspiciously high charges for pre-payment meters. In the case of the water companies, electricity distribution systems and local phone networks, the grounds for secrecy are especially suspect: these are monopolies which can make no serious claim that a competitor can use the information. But even where competition exists, this cannot justify concealment. "Commercial secrecy" is an oxymoron: secrecy is the enemy of free trade, information the lubricant of commerce. As the judge in the Kansas case noted: "The United States Supreme Court has stated that society has a strong interest in the free flow of commercial information."[4]

The court states that information is a right, not merely a policy.

The case against democracy

From Santiago to Tamil Nadu to Brussels, every proposed new regulatory regime begins with a stated commitment to social dialogue and transparency which is then ignored in programs and practice. Especially in those nations with newly privatized infrastructure, governments still turn to expert consultants, specialist civil servants, industry managers, international agencies, their accountants and advisors to share information and decide in secret on standards of service, price limits and terms of foreign ownership. It is a system controlled by a *nomenklatura* of specialists and functionaries. At most, unions and other public organizations are given a limited right of consultation and comment, barred from full knowledge of the bargaining and discussion taking place behind closed doors.

Peru is typical. The Comisión de Tarifas Eléctricas (CTE) is made up of three government appointees and two members of the industry it regulates. Besides the issue of the industry being asked to sit as its own judge on prices, the problem of the combination is that all information is reviewed and discussed in complete secrecy without the knowledge of consumers, labor unions or user industries. (There is a member of the commission appointed to represent the "public interest," but the member is appointed by the government and barred from revealing any of the information or deliberations of the commission to the public.) It is no surprise that Peru's system has resulted in unenviable regulatory failure and public dissent. What is surprising is that this system is the model for the European Commission's regulation of the newly freed market in international power transmissions: secretive decision-making by government and industry.[5] If democratic, open processes have produced high-quality, low-cost service in the US, why has this system been pushed aside for these closed, secretive systems? The answer is that industry has raised strong arguments against democracy. These require a response.

The first industry argument is that utility regulation is an experts' game and members of the public lack the highly technical and economic knowledge needed to make technical decisions (ignoring the embarrass-ing failures of these "experts"). But labor unions, industrial customers, competing utilities and environmental groups often have expertise well beyond the highly paid but often inexperienced consultants shaping decisions today. Once the system opens up to participation by the public, union, consumer and local government intervenors soon develop the expertise. To make democratic systems work, it is necessary to provide funding for groups to obtain expert guidance by economists, engineers and lawyers of their choosing. Finally, there is a need for values to be brought into the process, as well – not simply expertise.

The most often repeated objection to the American system is that it is litigious, adversarial, lengthy and complex. And that is true. It is the char-acteristic of democracy that it is noisy, contentious and costly to operate. It is quite easy for a government bureaucrat, a utility executive and a consultant from an international bank to reach agreement swiftly in private, undisturbed by the objections of the public. When workers, environmentalists, local government leaders, user industries and consumer groups are given an opportunity to ask questions, review the record and provide their own advice, the process necessarily becomes more cumbersome. Hearing rooms and negotiating sessions are often packed with dozens of parties, sometimes hundreds of people. A democratic process also usually produces a better result: lower prices. (We must also point out that the US system, with all its complexity, contention and involvement of legions of lawyers, produces determinations of prices, by statute, in one year or less – swifter than most ostensibly efficient expert systems.)

We have discussed democratic regulation versus regulation in secret. But to understand the advantages of open systems, we have to go to the core question: why regulate at all?

Profit motivates. The phrase is obvious, simple and repeated endlessly in economic debate over private ownership of public services. Governments and utility systems hope to enlist this powerful force, the quest for profit, to improve services and reduce prices. Oddly, while governments and neophyte regulators often invoke the profit motive, few truly believe in it; that is, few truly understand that corporations make decisions solely on the basis of seeking the highest return. The desire for profit will motivate a utility to reduce an excessive and inefficient workforce. But that same desire for profit will motivate the private operator to continue cutting the workforce until water stops flowing, lights stop glowing and gas pipes start exploding. Profit will motivate an electric company to use new technology to make more efficient use of its power lines. Profit will also motivate that company to falsely overstate the cost of the improvement to justify higher prices to a regulator. These are real, not theoretical, examples, taken from our work in the field.

As a US trade magazine recently put it: "This summer's price spikes were not only predictable, they've been envisioned over the past year and even the past decade . . . Blaming power generators is like blaming sharks for eating people."[6]

In other industries, there is a moderating influence on enterprise behavior: the market, or competition. But it is an uncomfortable truth that (despite the daydreams of some academics), distribution services in water, electricity, gas and telephone remain lock-down monopolies. One electric wire, one gas pipe, one water and sewer line, one (or two phone lines) going to a home or business mean that the ameliorative pressure of competition cannot protect the public. Even electricity generation, as the manipulation of the English Power Pool shows, is still a long way from freewheeling competition.

With the exception of water, the US has chosen the path of private ownership of public services. But, having gone down that road 100 years ahead of others, Americans have a colder, more practical view of management in the interests of stockholders. The US system simply assumes that monopoly utilities will not act in the public interest unless ordered to do so under the force of law enforced by the threat of heavy penalty. When US utility executives provide evidence of costs in a price review, they must swear an oath that makes them liable to civil and criminal charges for withholding the truth.

In 1996, when the UK sold its nuclear plants to private industry, a government spokesman said the public need not fear for its safety because British executives would never endanger their own communities. This concept of a corporate *noblesse oblige* is alien to market theory and counter to the profit motive. America's working assumption is that, unless closely scrutinized and tightly controlled, the need to maintain profits will entice a private nuclear operator to conceal dangerous system breakdowns. Britain, operating on the basis of trust, has only 162 nuclear plant inspectors. The US, with not many more nuclear plants, employs 3,000. The US system is adversarial, lacking trust in human nature, and therefore quite realistic.

In the case of one operator, the Long Island Lighting Company (described above), internal documents disclosed that the company's chief executives, to obtain price increases, hid from regulators the true costs of a nuclear plant's construction and falsified safety inspection reports to obtain an operating license.[7] The perpetrators were not evil men, merely executives overwhelmed by a construction fiasco who, to keep profits flowing, concealed the truth from regulators and the public. Only through open records, open public hearings and a swarm of inspections by government, environmental groups and industrial customers did the truth see the light of day. The company paid penalties totaling $2.1 billion; the nuclear plant was closed; and, in 1993, the company was deprivatized and electricity service for three million people was assumed by the state government.[8]

As the inexperienced regulators of Brazil and Britain learned in the case of Rio Light and Yorkshire Water, the public interest and the profit motive will, at times, conflict, with disastrous consequences for the public. This is not, by itself, a reason to bar private ownership of utilities; but it is a reason to open the system to public participation, because regulation, at heart, is the means by which democracy places public interest over private. And in order to make democratic regulation work, the rules must be strict, detailed and tightly enforced – or all the work of regulation becomes meaningless. This is not a popular view today where there is faith that market systems can replace the hard work of regulation. In the case of the Peoples Gas Company, the Illinois Commerce Commission went far beyond a general demand that the company improve its safety record. After repeated attempts at milder sanctions, these regulators ordered a very specific set of investments that the utility was forced to make: the regulator provided a detailed listing of the number of miles of 4-inch, 6-inch and 8-inch gas mains that were to be replaced year by year by the company.

The value of democratic regulation: it is democratic

We have made the case for democratic regulation on the grounds that it produces lower prices, higher quality service and secure employment. But that happy result is, ultimately, only a secondary value. Open dialogue between workers, enterprises and government; the freedom to express views; to open the secrets of monopolies and government agencies; to debate and publish facts and opinions in public; to organize as consumers, unions and enterprises for common purpose; to challenge and criticize each other's views and assertions; to force government and industry to justify their actions and seek the public's assent – i.e., democracy – is a prize far more valuable to civil society than the low prices democracy engenders. Demand democracy.

Appendix 1
The American "Rate Base" Formula for Determining Utility Prices is Identical to Britain's "RPI-X" Formula

In a typical American "rate case" (price review), regulators, in participation with utilities, consumer groups, trade unions, industrial customers and local governments, determine future prices by the following calculation:

- Calculate the utility's *NET INVESTMENT*. This is equal to the *COST OF ITS PHYSICAL PLANT LESS DEPRECIATION*. This is called the *"RATE BASE."*
- Multiply the net investment by *REASONABLE PROFIT RATE*, called a *"RATE OF RETURN."* (This target profit reflects costs of equity and debt.)
- Add in *OPERATING EXPENSES* (based on historic costs in some states, projected costs in others). These include wages, taxes and other out-of-pocket expenditures, including an allowance for DEPRECIATION.
- The sum total of these costs and the allowed return indicates the total amount of money the utility will need for the year, the *"TOTAL REVENUE REQUIREMENT."*
- Divide the Total Revenue Requirement by the projected total volume of sales. This yields the cost per unit (cents per kilowatt-hour/therms/etc.)
- Note: All the cost, volume and revenue figures are *projected* to estimate future conditions, allowing for *PRICE INFLATION* and *PRODUCTIVITY GAINS*.

The formula is written as follows:

(RATE BASE × RATE OF RETURN) + OPERATING EXPENSE = REVENUE REQUIREMENT

This is the same as:

(CAPITAL INVESTMENT × TARGET PROFIT) + OPERATING EXPENSES =
TOTAL REVENUE ALLOWED

In Britain, regulators determine price by calculating Net Investment (less depreciation) and add operating expenses to determine the Allowed Revenue which, when divided by projected sales, yields the price per unit. The calculations are based on historical data which are then adjusted for Price Inflation ("RPI") and productivity changes ("X"). Therefore, the US "rate base" formula and the UK "RPI-X" formula are arithmetically *identical*; that is, a utility company would be permitted to charge the same price per unit under either method.

Appendix 2
220 C.M.R. 12.00
Standards of Conduct for Distribution Companies and their Affiliates

Section

12.01: Purpose and Scope

(1) Purpose. 220 C.M.R. 12.00 sets forth the Standards of Conduct governing the relationship between a Distribution Company and its Affiliates transacting business in Massachusetts.

(2) Scope. 220 C.M.R. 12.00 applies to all Distribution Companies under the Department's jurisdiction. 220 C.M.R. 12.00 does not supersede existing applicable law and regulations.

12.02: Definitions

(1) Affiliate refers to any "affiliated company," as defined in G.L. c. 164, § 85, or any unit or division within a Distribution Company or its parent, or any separate legal entity either owned or subject to the common control of the Distribution Company or its parent.

(2) Antitrust Laws are federal and state statutes, including the Sherman Act,15 U.S.C. §§ 1–7, the Clayton Act, 15 U.S.C. §§ 12–27, and the Massachusetts Antitrust Act, G.L. c. 93, §§ 1–14A, and related judicial decisions.

(3) Competitive Affiliate refers to any Affiliate that is engaged in the sale or marketing of products or services on a competitive basis.

(4) Competitive Energy Affiliate refers to any Competitive Affiliate that is engaged in the sale or marketing of natural gas, electricity, or Energy-related Services on a competitive basis.

(5) Competitive Non-Energy Affiliate refers to any Competitive Affiliate that is engaged in the sale or marketing of products or service, other than natural gas, electricity, or Energy-related Services, on a competitive basis.

(5) Department refers to the Department of Telecommunications and Energy.

(6) Distribution Company refers to a natural gas local distribution company or Electric Company that provides distribution services under the Department's jurisdiction.

(7) Electric Company is defined as in G.L. c. 164, § 1.

(8) Employee refers to an officer, director, employee or agent who has specific knowledge of, or direct access to, information not otherwise available to Non-affiliated Energy Suppliers that could provide a Competitive Energy Affiliate with an undue advantage.

(9) Energy-related Services are those services the costs of which have been recovered by Distribution Companies through rates approved by the Department.

(10) Non-affiliated Energy Supplier refers to any entity, including aggregators, engaged in marketing, brokering or selling natural gas, electricity, or energy-related services to retail customers where such product or service is also provided by a Competitive Energy Affiliate.

(11) Non-affiliated Supplier refers to any entity engaged in selling or marketing products or services where such product or service is also provided by a Competitive Affiliate.

12.03: General Standards of Conduct

(1) A Distribution Company shall apply tariff provisions in the same manner to the same or similarly situated entities if there is discretion in the application of the provision.

(2) A Distribution Company shall strictly enforce tariff provisions for which there is no discretion in the application of the provision.

(3) A Distribution Company shall not, through a tariff provision or otherwise, give its Competitive Affiliate or customers of its Competitive Affiliate preference over Non-affiliated Suppliers or their customers in matters relating to any product or service that is subject to a tariff on file with the Department.

(4) If a Distribution Company provides its Competitive Energy Affiliate, or a customer of its Competitive Energy Affiliate, any product or service other than general and administrative support services, it shall make the same products or services available to all Non-affiliated Energy Suppliers or their customers on a non-discriminatory basis.

(5) A Distribution Company shall not offer or sell electricity or natural gas commodity or capacity to its Competitive Affiliate without simultaneously posting the offering electronically on a source generally available to the market or otherwise making a sufficient offering to the market.

(6) (a) If a Distribution Company offers its Competitive Energy Affiliate, or a customer of its Competitive Energy Affiliate, a discount, rebate or fee waiver for any product or service, it shall make the same available on a non-discriminatory basis to all Non-affiliated Energy Suppliers or customers.(b) If a Distribution Company offers a Competitive Affiliate, or a customer of a Competitive Affiliate, a discount, rebate or fee waiver for any product or service that is subject to a tariff on file with the Department, it shall make the same available to all Non-affiliated Suppliers and their customers simultaneously, to the extent technically possible, on a comparable basis.

(7) A Distribution Company shall process all same or similar requests for any product, service, or information in the same manner and within the same period of time, consistent with the rules set forth in paragraph (6) above.

(8) A Distribution Company shall not condition or tie the provision of any product, service, or rate agreement by the Distribution Company to the provision of any product or service by its Competitive Affiliate.

(9) A Distribution Company shall not release any proprietary customer information to an Affiliate without the prior written authorization of the customer.

(10) To the extent that a Distribution Company provides a Competitive Affiliate with information not readily available or generally known to any Non-affiliated Supplier, which information was obtained by the Distribution Company in the course of providing distribution service to its customers, the Distribution Company shall make that information available on a non-discriminatory basis to all Non-affiliated Suppliers transacting business in its service territory. This provision does not apply to customer-specific information obtained with proper authorization, information necessary to fulfill the provisions of a contract, or information relating to the provision of general and administrative support services.

(11) A Distribution Company shall refrain from giving any appearance of speaking on behalf of its Competitive Affiliate in any and all contacts or communications with customers or potential customers. The Distribution Company shall not represent that any advantage accrues to customers or others in the use of the Distribution Company's services as a result of that customer or others dealing with the Competitive Affiliate.

(12) The Distribution Company shall not engage in joint advertising or marketing programs of any sort with its Competitive Energy Affiliate, nor shall the Distribution Company directly promote or market any product or service offered by any Competitive Affiliate.

(13) Subject to paragraph (12), a Distribution Company may allow an Affiliate, including a Competitive Energy Affiliate, to identify itself, through the use of a name, logo, or both, as an Affiliate of the Distribution Company, provided that such use by a Competitive Energy Affiliate shall be accompanied by a disclaimer that shall state that no advantage accrues to customers or others in the use of the Distribution Company's services as a result of that customer or others dealing with the Competitive Energy Affiliate, and that the customer or others need not purchase any product or service from any Competitive Energy Affiliate in order to obtain services from the Distribution Company on a non-discriminatory basis. The disclaimer shall be written or spoken, or both, as may be appropriate given the context of the use of the name or logo.

(14) If a customer requests information about Energy Suppliers, the Distribution Company shall provide a current list of all Energy Suppliers operating on the system or registered with the Department, including its Energy-related Competitive Affiliate, but shall not promote its affiliate. The list of Energy Suppliers shall be in random sequence, and not in alphabetical order. The list shall be updated every sixty (60) days to allow for a change in the random sequence.

(15) Employees of a Distribution Company shall not be shared with a Competitive Energy Affiliate, and shall be physically separated from those of the Competitive Energy Affiliate. The Distribution Company shall fully and transparently allocate costs for any shared facilities or general and administrative support services provided to any Competitive Affiliate.

(16) A Distribution Company and its Competitive Affiliate shall keep separate books of accounts and records which shall be subject to review by the Department in accordance with the provisions of G.L. c. 164, § 85.

(17) The Department may approve an exemption from the separation requirements of 220 C.M.R. 12.03(15) upon a showing by the Distribution Company that shared employees or facilities would be in the best interests of the ratepayers and have minimal anticompetitive effect, and that the costs can be fully and accurately allocated between the Distribution Company and its Competitive Energy Affiliate. Such exemption shall be valid until such time that the Department determines that modification or removal of the exemption is necessary.

(18) A Distribution Company shall establish and file with the Department a dispute resolution procedure to address complaints alleging violations of 220 C.M.R. 12.00. Such procedure shall designate a neutral person to conduct an investigation of the complaint; require that said person communicate the results of the investigation to the claimant in writing within 30 days after the complaint is received; and require that such communication describe any action taken and notify the complainant of his or her right to complain to the Department if not satisfied with the results of the investigation.

(19) A Distribution Company shall maintain a log of all new, resolved, and pending complaints alleging violations of 220 C.M.R. 12.00. The log shall be subject to review by the Department and shall include the date each complaint was received; the complainant's name, address, and telephone number; a written description of the complaint; and the resolution of the complaint, or the reason why the complaint is still pending.

(20) Notwithstanding any other provisions in 220 C.M.R. 12.00, in emergency circumstances, a Distribution Company shall take any actions necessary to ensure public safety and system reliability. A Distribution Company shall maintain a log of all such actions, subject to review by the Department.

12.04: Pricing of Transactions between Distribution Companies and Affiliates

(1) A Distribution Company may sell, lease, or otherwise transfer to an Affiliate, including a Competitive Affiliate, an asset, the cost of which has been reflected in the Distribution Company's rates for regulated service, provided that the price charged the Affiliate is the higher of the net book value or market value of the asset. The Department shall determine the market value of any such asset sold, leased, or otherwise transferred, based on the highest price that the asset could have reasonably realized after an open and competitive sale.

(2) A Distribution Company may sell, lease, or otherwise transfer to an affiliate, including a Competitive Affiliate, assets other than those subject to paragraph (1), and may also provide services to an affiliate, including a Competitive Affiliate, provided that the price charged for such asset or service is equal to or greater than the Distribution Company's fully allocated cost to provide the asset or service.

(3) An Affiliated Company may sell, lease, or otherwise transfer an asset to a Distribution Company, and may also provide services to a Distribution

Company, provided that the price charged to the Distribution Company is no greater than the market value of the asset or service provided.

(4) A Distribution Company must maintain a log of all transactions with Affiliated Companies made pursuant to paragraphs (1) through (3). The log shall include the date of the transaction, the nature and quantity of the asset or service provided, the price charged, and an explanation of how the price was derived for purposes of compliance with this section. All log entries must be dated and made contemporaneously with relevant transactions. The log shall be kept up to date. The Distribution Company shall file a copy of the log with the Department no later than January 15 of each year, covering the previous year.

12.05: Penalties

(1) Any Distribution Company or Affiliate that violates any provision of this section shall be subject to a civil penalty not to exceed $25,000 for each violation for each day that the violation persists; provided, however, that the maximum civil penalty shall not exceed $1,000,000 for any related series of violations. Any such penalty shall be determined by the Department after a public hearing.

(2) In determining the amount of any penalty assessed pursuant to paragraph (1), the Department will consider the following: the appropriateness of the penalty to the size of the business of the Distribution Company or Affiliate charged; the gravity of the violation; the good faith of the Distribution Company or Affiliate in attempting to achieve compliance after notification of a violation; and any other criteria deemed appropriate by the Department under the circumstances.

(3) Nothing in 220 C.M.R. 12.00 shall be construed to confer immunity from state and federal Antitrust Laws. A penalty assessed pursuant to this subsection does not affect or preempt antitrust liability but rather is in addition to any antitrust liability that may apply to the activity.

REGULATORY AUTHORITY 220 C.M.R. 12.00: G.L. c. 164, §§ 1, 1C, 1F, 76A, 76C, 85, 85A, 94A, 94B, 94C

Notes

Introduction

1. Telephone prices cited at 1997; electricity and natural gas prices at 1999. Centre for the Study of Regulated Industries (UK); Edison Electric Institute; Office of Gas Supply Regulation (UK); American Gas Association; Consumers International; OECD; Instituto Brasileiro de Defesa do Consumidor; US Department of Energy (DOE) Energy Information Administration (EIA).
2. US Bureau of Labor Statistics.
3. US Securities and Exchange Commission (SEC) Proposed Rule: Foreign Utility Companies, 17 CFR Parts 250 and 259; SEC 2000 Annual Report, Item 9: Wholesale Generators and Foreign Utility Companies (January 31, 2001).

Chapter 1

1. Energy Association, OECD, Federal Communications Commission. (Lower prices can be found in a few nations, notably Mexico, Canada and New Zealand, where services are provided by state-owned corporations, not a subject of this study.)
2. See Appendix 1. The identity of US Rate Base and UK Rate Cap formula.
3. *Houston Power & Light* (Texas PUC 1995).
4. Ministry of Mines and Energy; Secretariat of Energy Electrobras, "Project of Reestructuring [sic] of the Brazilian Electric Sector, Executive Summary Stage VII" (1998); Matt Moffett, "Utility Privatization Leaves Many in Rio Cursing the Dark," *Wall Street Journal* (April 27, 1998); Ashley Brown (Harvard Electricity Policy Group Executive Director), "The Privatization of Brazil's Electricity Industry: Sector Reform or Restatement of the Government's Balance Sheet?" (for Inter-American Development Bank, January 2002).
5. Ministry of Mines and Energy, Secretariat of Energy, Electrobrás, *Project of Restructuring of the Brazilian Electric Sector*, Executive Summary, Stage 7 (1998) p. 42.
6. US Energy Information Administration, US Bureau of Labor Statistics.
7. Office of Water Services (Ofwat) – "Draft Determinations, Future Water and Sewerage Charges 2000–05 (July 1999).
8. Centre for Regulated Industries Statistical Series, The UK Water Industry 1995/96; Office of Water Services, *Price Review* (1995); David Hall, *Unison Plan for Water* (1996).
9. Offer, Quality of Supply Submissions 1996/97. See also "Watchdog Castigates RECS for Underspend," *Utility Week* (December 12, 1997).
10. Based on 75 million shares at 290p/share = £217.5 million for 25.7 per cent of the company = £846 million for 100 per cent. "Energis Shares Rise 2p on Debut," Financial Times (December 10, 1997); Offer, *The Transmission Price Control Review of the National Grid Company: Proposals* (1996).
11. Director General Dr. Stephen Littlechild, interview with author.

Chapter 2

1. K. Bayliss and D. Hall, "Independent Power Producers: A Review of the Issues," for Public Services International (November 2000); S. Dixit, G. Sant and S. Wagle,

"Regulation in the WB-Orissa Model: Cure Worse Than Disease," 33 *Economic and Political Weekly* no. 17 (April 25, 1998).

2. Dixit et al., "Regulation in the WB-Orissa Model;" see also "India State Pays Bills to Enron, But Electricity Crunch Persists," *International Herald Tribune* (February 16, 2001).

3. See Hunton and Williams, "Utility Privatization: The Creation of a Regulatory Structure," presented to the World Bank Seminar on Privatization of Infrastructure, April 26, 1993; Coopers & Lybrand, *Electricity Sector Restructuring Project* (1997).

4. David Hall, Unison, *Plan for Water* (1996).

5. Office of Water Services, *Ian Byatt Expands the Prospect for Future Water Prices* (October 8, 1997).

6. Before the Illinois Commerce Commission, Re: Peoples Gas Light and Coke Company, *Investigation Docket 82–0613* (1988).

7. Coopers & Lybrand, *Electricity Sector Restructuring Project* (1997); Ministry for Mines and Energy, Secretariat of Energy, Electrobrás, *Project of Restructuring of the Brazilian Electric Sector* (1998).

8. Ministry of Mines, *Project of Restructuring of the Brazilian Energy Sector* (1998) paragraphs 57 and 104.

9. "Transcriptions of Taped Conversations between CI [confidential informant] 58–8804 and Hinson, Givens," US Internal Revenue Service (1988); W.R. Hinson, Georgia Power Company, "Interoffice Correspondence, Status of Power Generation Materials October 23, 1987" (Attachment to affidavit of IRS Agent McGovern, 1988).

Chapter 3

1. Offer, *Pool Price: A Consultation by OFFER* (February 1999).

2. J. Kahn, "Economic View: Utility Deregulation: Square Peg, Round Hole?" *New York Times* (March 4, 2001).

3. Ibid.

4. Mergers and Monopolies Commission (1996).

5. *Pool Price: A Consultation by Offer*, Office of Electricity Regulation (Offer) (February 1999).

6. Dr. Littlechild, interview with author at Offer, Birmingham, England (January 25, 1996).

7. California Public Utilities Commission, Report to Governor Gray Davis (August 2, 2000) p. 26.

8. Governor Gray Davis, State of the State Address, (January 8, 2001); R. Smith, "California Puts Rate Surcharge on Power Bills," *Wall Street Journal* (4 January 2001) p. A3.

9. California Independent System Operator Market Issues/ADR Committee, "Market Analysis Report" (December 1, 1999) p. 6.

10. R. Cavanagh, "Revisiting 'the Genius of the Marketplace': Cures for the Western Electricity and Natural Gas Crises" (March 6, 2001 draft for *The Electricity Journal*).

11. In Massachusetts, the restructuring legislation mandates that the regulator set service quality standards that include employee staffing levels. By statute, these levels cannot be reduced unless as part of a collective bargaining agreement between the utility and its employees' trade union. *Massachusetts General Laws, chapter 164, section 1E(b).*

12. The price caps on SDG & E were removed in the second year of the experiment, so that company was able to pass through the price hikes to its customers, resulting in the tripling of retail prices described above.

13. "Wholesale Prices Increase Substantially," California PUC Report to Hon. Governor Gray Davis (August 2, 2000) pp. 26 et seq.; P.H. King, "Wuz We Robbed?," *Los*

Angeles Times (March 4, 2001) (relying in part on public filings to the US Securities and Exchange Commission by corporations owning generators serving California).

14. State of the State address (January 8, 2001).
15. Order Pursuant to Section 202(c) of the Federal Power Act (December 14, 2000), and subsequent orders.
16. While this book focuses on utility regulation by state governments, there is a role for the FERC in the regulation of wholesale utility markets, which we briefly discuss in Chapter 4.
17. *San Diego Gas & Elec. Co.* v. *Sellers, et al.*, Dockets Nos. EL-00–95–000 et al., *Order Directing Remedies for California Wholesale Markets*, 93 FERC 61,294 (December 15, 2000).

Chapter 4

1. *Electric Industry Restructuring*, D.P.U. 95–30 (Mass., 1995).
2. *Promoting Wholesale Competition Through Open Access Non-Discriminatory Transmission Services by Public Utilities; Recovery of Stranded Costs by Public Utilities and Transmitting Utilities*, Order 888 (FERC, 1996).
3. For example, *Southern California Edison Co.*, Emergency Motion and Petition for a Writ of Mandamus Against the Federal Energy Regulatory Commission (D.C. Cir., December 26, 2000). See also, e.g., *New England Power Pool; Proposed Revisions to Market Rule 17*, FERC Docket Nos. ER-01–368 et al.
4. For example, see Department of Market Analysis "Report on Real Time Supply Costs Above Single Price Auction Threshold: December 8, 2000–January 31, 2001" California Independent System Operator (February 28, 2001) (showing average wholesale prices rising from 3.3 cents per kilowatt-hour in 1998 and 1999 to 11.4 cents in 2000, including 31.7 cents in December 2000 and 27.8 cents in January 2001, and calling for refunds of $565 million with respect to December 2000 and January 2001).
5. US Energy Information Administration. *Accord*, Testimony of Joel F. Eisenberg before the House Subcommittee on Early Childhood, Youth and Families, Committee on Education and the Workforce, on Electric Restructuring (Oak Ridge National Laboratory, April 8, 1997) p. 9. This varies by state. Roger Colton, "Natural Gas Prices by Customer Class: Pre- and Post-Deregulation" (Fisher, Sheehan & Colton, 1998).
6. For example, R. Crandall and J. Ellig, "Electric Restructuring and Consumer Interests: Lessons from Other Industries," *The Electricity Journal* (January 1998) pp. 12, 14.
7. Robert Kuttner, *Everything for Sale* (Knopf, 1997) pp. 258, 263–4. The fraction of flights using jets has also decreased at small and medium-sized airports, as well as at some large airports. US Government Accounting Office, "Airline Deregulation: Changes in Airfares, Service, and Safety at Small, Medium-Sized and Large Communities" (GAO-RCED-96–79) (1996) pp. 47–9. Non-stop and one-stop service at some large airports is down sharply (e.g., Washington National: number of non-stop destinations down 18 per cent, one-stops down 42 per cent; Kennedy: non-stops down 24 per cent, one-stops down 63 per cent). Ibid., pp. 74–5.
8. Other large cities with net price increases since deregulation include Atlanta (+6 per cent), Dallas-Ft. Worth (+10 per cent), Detroit (+5 per cent), Minneapolis (+17 per cent), Chicago (O'Hare, +1 per cent), and Philadelphia (+1 per cent). US Government Accounting Office, "Airline Deregulation: Changes in Airfares, Service, and Safety at Small, Medium-Sized and Large Communities" (GAO-RCED-96–79) (1996) pp. 29–30, 60–3. Fares are 41 per cent higher at airports where there is no competition, 54 per cent for short flights – 57 per cent at Pittsburgh and Cincinnati. Office of the Assistant Secretary for Aviation and International Affairs, "Dominated Hub Fares" (US Department of Transportation, January 2001).

9. In 1996, business fares increased about 25 per cent while leisure ticket prices declined slightly. S. McCartney, "Business Fares Increase Even as Leisure Travel Keeps Getting Cheaper," *Wall Street Journal* (November 3, 1997) p. A1. Four months later, the *Journal* reported business fares up 21 per cent over the previous year, leisure fares up 16 per cent. "Trends in Travel Costs," *Wall Street Journal*, p. B9 (March 6, 1996). Kuttner describes "Astronomical and Capricious Fares" as another result of deregulation. Kuttner, *Everything for Sale*, p. 265.

10. P.G. Gosselin, "Companies Find More Money in Fewer Customers," *Boston Globe* (March 9, 1998) p. A1.

11. "Electricity Savings Compared," OFFER survey published in *Utility Week* (June 11, 1999) p. 22.

12. "Electricity Shake up Leaves Consumers Confused," press release of Consumers' Association, <www.which.net/whatsnew/pr/may99/general/confused.html (May 24, 1999)>.

13. Steve Thomas, "The British Model: A Decade of Experience," presentation to Congresso Brasileiro de Energia, Rio de Janeiro (December 1999); personal communication (March 2001).

14. "Electricity Shake-up Leaves Consumers Confused," press release of Consumers' Association (www.which.net/whatsnew/pr/may99/general/confused.html) (May 24, 1999).

15. US Bureau of Labor Statistics, Consumer Price Index (local residential telephone component) (1984–96); AT&T prices for ten-minute cross-country call (as filed with and compiled by Federal Communications Commission) in Waldon and Lande, *Reference Book of Rates, Price Indices and Household Expenditures for Telephone Service* (FCC, 1997). Long distance operators say the overall long-distance decreases are much larger than 50 per cent. T. Price (CEO, MCI), letter to the editor, *Washington Post* (January 31, 1997) p. 20 (70 per cent).

16. *NYNEX*, DPU 97–18 (Mass. 1997); *NYNEX*, Order 22,562 in DS 97–028 (NY PUC 1997).

17. M. Cooper and G. Kimmelman, "The Digital Divide Confronts the Telecommunications Act of 1996" (Consumer Federation of American and Consumers Union 1999) p. 51.

18. James McConnaughey et al., *Falling Through the Net II* (US Department of Commerce 1999) charts 4–5.

19. "Exploring the Digital Divide," *Consumer Reports* (February 2001) p. 6; see James McConnaughey et al., *Falling Through the Net II* (US Department of Commerce 1999) chart 1.

20. NOW Communications et al., Case Nos. 98–1466-TP-ACE et al. (PUC of Ohio 2000) (rejecting Phone Shark application).

21. Frank P. Darr, "Prepaid Telephone Service Companies: New Players and the Regulatory Mission" (1999) p. 10.

22. Affidavit attached to Plaintiff's Motion of July 1998, *Pedro* v. *Murphy et al.*, C.A. No. 94–3724-C (Mass. Suffolk Superior Ct., comparing FCC tariffs of T-Netix and AT & T).

23. B. DeMello and T. Wilson, "State and National Action Plan [SNAP] Activities" (report to NARUC Committee on Consumer Affairs 1999).

24. Personal communication with Walter Bolter, formerly staff, Florida PSC (October 7, 1999).

25. B. DeMello and T. Wilson, "State and National Action Plan [SNAP] Activities" (report to NARUC Committee on Consumer Affairs 1999).

26. Maine Public Advocate, *Ratewatchers Phone Guide* (July 2000). "Residential Long Distance Comparison Chart," *Tele Tips* (Telecommunications Research and Action Center April 1999) pp. 2–3.

27. For example, National Consumer Law Center, *Unfair and Deceptive Acts and Practices* (4th edition 1997 and Supp. 1998).

28. 47 U.S.C. §253(b), inserted by the Telecommunications Act of 1966.

Chapter 5

1. The terms "price," "rate" and "tariff" are used interchangeably in this book.
2. For example, R. Rudolph and S. Ridley, *Power Struggle* (Harper & Row, 1986), pp. 189–90 (falsely claiming a report had been destroyed punished by fines and forced resignations).
3. *New England Tel. & Tel. Co.* DPU 89–300 (Mass. 1990).
4. *New England Tel. & Tel. Co.,* DPU 92–100 (Mass. 1993).
5. For example, *NOW Communications et al.,* Case Nos. 98–1466-TP-ACE et al. (PUC of Ohio 2000).
6. *Boston Edison Co. et al. reliable service,* DPU 87–169-A (Mass. 1988).
7. For example, *Public Service Co. of New Hampshire,* Bankruptcy Court Case No. 88–00043 (D.N.H.).
8. For example, Rudolph and Ridley, *Power Struggle,* p. 190.
9. For example, *New York Tel. Co. et al.,* FCC 90–57 (1990), *New York Tel. Co.,* Case No. 90-C-0191 (NYPSC 1990).
10. *New York Tel. Co.,* Case No. 90-C-0191 (NYPSC 1990).
11. For example, *Boston Edison Co.,* DPU 85–266-A/271-A (Mass. 1986).
12. *Rochester Gas & Elec. Co. – Ginna,* Case No. 28116 (NYPSC 1984).
13. *Fitchburg Gas & Elec. Co. v. DPU,* 375 Mass. 571, 380 NE2d 1304, 1308 (1988); e.g., *Boston Edison Co.,* DPU 85–266-A/271-A (Mass. 1986).
14. *Western Mass. Elec. Co.,* D.P.U. 85–270 (Mass. 1986).
15. See *NYNEX,* DPU 97–18 (Mass. 1997); *NYNEX,* Order 22,562 in DS 97–028 (NH PUC 1997).
16. Rudolph and Ridley, *Power Struggle,* pp. 189, 185.
17. *Medina et al. v. Illinois Bell Tel. Co.,* Docket No. 59700 (Ill.CC 1977).
18. *Boston Edison Co. – Edgar,* EFSB 90–12/12A (1992).
19. For example, *Greater Media, Inc. et al. v. DPU,* SJC-6150 (Mass. 1993).
20. For example, *Duquesne Light Co. v. Barasch,* 488 U.S. 299, 315–16 (1989).
21. For example, *West Ohio Gas Co. v. PUC,* 294 US 63 (1935) (presumption of prudence); *Bluefield Water Works & Improvement Co. v. PSC,* 262 US 679 (1923) (utility due process right to return on public service investment commensurate with risk); *FPC v. Hope Natural Gas Co.,* 320 US 591 (1944) ("end result" or balancing due process test).
22. For example, *People ex rel. Hartigan v. Illinois Commerce Commission,* 117 Ill.2d 120 (1987); *Business and Professional People for the Public Interest v. Illinois Commerce Commission,* 136 Ill.2d 192 (1988); *Business and Professional People for the Public Interest v. Illinois Commerce Commission,* 146 Ill.2d 175 (1991); *People ex rel. Hartigan v. Illinois Commerce Commission,* 148 Ill.2d 348 (1992); *Alliance for Affordable Energy v. New Orleans City Council,* 578 So.2d 949 (La.App.4 Cir. 1991).
23. See generally J.C. Bonbright, *Principles of Public Utility Rates* (Columbia University Press, 1961).
24. For example, Mass. G.L. c. 30A.
25. For example, U.S. Const., Am. V, XIV.
26. For example, D.C. Code sec. 43–402; New York Public Service Law, secs. 65 (1), 66; Ohio R.C. sec. 4927.02.
27. 42 U.S.C. §254(f). See, e.g., Ohio R.C. sec. 4927.04(A).
28. For example, *Midwestern Gas Transmission Co.,* 36 FPC 61 (1966), *aff'd., Midwestern Gas Transmission Co.v. FPC,* 388 F.2d 444 (7th Cir.), *cert. den.,* 392 US 928 (1968).
29. *Western Mass. Elec Co.,* DPU 85–270 (1986); *Western Mass. Elec. Co.,* DTE 97–120 (1999); *Penna. PUC v. Phil Elec Co.* (1997); *NEP v. FERC,* 668 F.2d 1327 (D.C. Cir. 1981), *cert. den.* 457 US 1117 (1982) (used and useful principle). See also re disallowance of other imprudent investments and expenses, *Florida Power Corp.,* 413 So.2d 1189; *Carolina Power & Light,* 49 PUR 4th 188 (NCUC 1982); *Consumers Power Co.,* 14 PUR 4th 1 (Mich. PSC 1976). The "used and useful" principle endures after

at least a century. *Smyth* v. *Ames*, 168 US 466 (1898); *Natural Gas Pipeline* v. *FERC*, 765 F.2d 55 (1985), *cert. den.*, 474 US 1056 (1986).

30. "Proceeding on the Motion of the Commission to Investigate the Cost of Construction of the Shoreham Nuclear Generating Facility – Phase II" (Order and Opinion, NY PSC December 16, 1985).

31. P.S. Cross, "Return on Equity," *Public Utilities Fortnightly* 44 (December 2000) (Survey October 1999–September 2000).

32. *Bluefield Water Works & Improvement Co.* v. *PSC*, 262 US 679 (1923) (utility due process right to return on public service investment commensurate with risk); *FPC* v. *Hope Natural Gas Co.*, 320 US 591 (1944) ("end result" or balancing due process test).

33. *Public Service Co. of New Hampshire*, Bankruptcy Court Case No. 88–00043 (D.N.H.). As noted, due process is not an absolute protection against losses. *Market St. Ry. Co.* v. *RR Comis. of Calif.*, 324 US 548 (1945).

34. See *FPC* v. *Hope Natural Gas Co.*, 320 US 591 (1944).

35. For example, *Office of Consumers' Counsel* v. *Ohio PUC*, 67 OhioSt.2d 372, 424 NE2d 300 (1981). See generally, Bonbright, *Principles of Public Utility Rates*; A.E. Kahn, *The Economics of Regulation* (John Wiley & Sons, vol. I 1970; vol. 2 1971).

36. Prices charged by most municipal and other government-owned utilities are not regulated by public service commissions. Many other books, monographs and articles have been written with a wide range of viewpoints about these entities, so we will not discuss them further here.

37. US DOE EIA, American Water Works Association.

Chapter 6

1. *ICC* v. *B & ORR* 145 US 263 (1892) (reduced rate commuter tickets to reduce urban congestion); see M. Keller, *Regulating a New Economy* (Harvard University Press, 1990) p. 63.

2. J. Oppenheim and T. MacGregor, *Low Income Utility Issues: A National Perspective* (October 2000).

3. For example, W. Baker, *Gas and Electricity Competition . . . Who Benefits?* (National Right to Fuel Campaign, Centre for Sustainable Energy, September 1999).

4. See generally, National Consumer Law Center, *Access to Utility Service* (1996 and 1998 Supp.) chapters 3–6, 14, 19.

5. Oppenheim and MacGregor, *Low Income Utility Issues.*

6. J.S. Peters, S.A. Baggett and K. Seiden, *Process and Impact Evaluation of New England Power Service Company's Appliance Management Program* (Research Into Action, 1999), US Energy Information Administration (1997 consumption).

7. L.G. Berry, M.A. Brown and L.F. Kinney, *Progress Report of the National Weatherization Assistance Program* (Oak Ridge National Laboratory, 1997).

8. *Order Continuing and Expanding the System Benefits Charge for Public Benefit Programs* in Case 94-E-0952, *Competitive Opportunities* (January 26, 2001).

9. "Energy and the Poor – The Forgotten Crisis" (National Consumer Law Center, 1989).

10. Meg Power, "The Winter Energy Outlook for the Poor" (Economic Opportunity Studies, December 20, 2000).

11. "Energy and the Poor – The Forgotten Crisis."

12. Lester W. Baxter, "Low-Income Energy Policy in a Restructuring Electricity Industry: An Assessment of Federal Options" (Oak Ridge National Laboratory, ORNL/CON_443, July 1997).

13. Many of these reports are summarized in J. Howat and J. Oppenheim, "Analysis of Low-Income Benefits in Determining Cost-Effectiveness of Energy Efficiency Programs" (National Consumer Law Center, 1999).

Chapter 7

1. B. Biewald et al., *Performance-Based Regulation in a Restructured Industry* (National Association of Regulatory Utility Commissioners 1997), chapter 5.
2. Docket 82–0163, Illinois Commerce Commission (1988).
3. *Levy et al.* v. *Peoples Gas Light Co.* (Ill.C.C. 1979).
4. *Western Mass. Elec. Co.*, 165 PUR 4th 70 (Mass. DPU 1995).
5. Docket 78–0078 (Ill.C.C.).
6. *New England Tel. & Tel. Co. – Service Quality*, DPU 89–300-Q (Mass. 1990).
7. For example, Mass. G.L. c. 164, sec. 1E. Service standards have also been made a condition of mergers. For example, *Scottish Power plc and PacifiCorp*, Docket UM 918 (Oregon, 1999).
8. Draft Decision of J. Wong, Administrative Law Judge, *Opinion Regarding the Emergency Motion Seeking to Prevent the Utilities from Implementing Layoffs* in A00–11–038 et al. (February 23, 2001, approved by California PUC March 15, 2001) pp. 1–2.
9. Ibid., pp. 28–9.
10. Ibid., pp. 43–4.
11. US Department of Energy, Energy Information Administration (US DOE EIA).
12. Opinion and Order Approving Settlement Agreement (NY PSC No. 18, 1988).
13. For example, Communications Act of 1934, sec. 1; see A. von Auw, *Heritage and Destiny* (Praeger, 1983) pp. 48–50, 97 et seq.

Chapter 8

1. Action, Inc. et al., Joint Motion for Approval of Proposed Guidelines Regarding Cost Effectiveness, Monitoring and Evaluation Issues and Shareholder Incentives, filed in Mass. DTE Docket No. 98–100 (April 14, 1999).
2. In recent filings with the regulators, the Massachusetts electric utilities have estimated that the benefits of providing energy efficiency services to their low-income customers outweigh the costs by a ratio between 2 and 3-to-1 (2:1 and 3:1). *NStar Companies*, DTE 00–63; *National Grid Co.*, DTE 00–65; *Western Mass. Elec. Co.*, DTE 00–79.
3. S. Laitner et al., "Employment and Other Macroeconomic Benefits of an Innovation-Led Climate Strategy for the United States," 26 *Energy Policy* 425 (1998).
4. Northeast Energy Efficiency Council, Comments in Mass. DPU 96–100 (February 20, 1998).
5. *Western Mass. Elec. Co.*, DPU 92–88 (1993).

Chapter 9

1. For example, J. R. T. Hughes, *The Governmental Habit* (Basic Books, 1977) pp. 97 et seq.; Illinois Office of Consumer Services, *A Consumer's Guide to the Economics of Electric Utility Ratemaking* (US Department of Energy 1980) pp. 4 et seq., 13, 72 et seq., 113 et seq.; M. Keller, *Regulating a New Economy* (Harvard University Press 1990) pp. 60 et seq.; J. O. Robertson, *America's Business* (Hill and Wang, 1985) at 174 et seq.; R. Rudolph and S. Ridley, *Power Struggle* (Harper & Row, 1986) pp. 38 et seq.; H. Zinn, *A People's History of the United States* (HarperCollins 1980) pp. 282 et seq.

Chapter 10

1. Thomas K. McCraw, *Prophets of Regulation* (Cambridge, Mass.: Harvard University Press, 1984) p. 9.
2. Ibid., quoting Charles Francis Adams in "Railroad Commissions," *Journal of Social Science*, 2 (1870), p. 234, emphasis in original.
3. Peter Carlson, "High and Mighty Crooked: Enron is Merely the Latest Chapter in the History of American Scams," *Washington Post* (February 10, 2002) p. F1.
4. McCraw, *Prophets of Regulation*, p. 11.
5. Ibid., p. 13.
6. Ibid., p. 11.
7. Ibid., pp. 19, 58, 81–93.
8. Alexander Lurkis, *The Power Brink* (New York: The Icare Press, 1982) pp. 11–12; *The Changing Structure of the Electricity Industry, Appendix A: History of the U.S. Electric Power Industry, 1882–1991*, p. 1; *Appendix B: Historical Chronology*, US DOE EIA (1996).
9. *The Changing Structure of the Electricity Industry, Appendix A: History of the U.S. Electric Power Industry, 1882–1991*, p. 1.
10. Ibid.
11. "Roll on Columbia: Woody Guthrie and the Bonneville Power Administration" Study Guide Part 4, Public vs. Private Control of Electric Utilities.
12. *The Changing Structure of the Electricity Industry, Appendix A: History of the U.S. Electric Power Industry, 1882–1991*, p. 1.
13. Patrick McGuire and Mark Granovetter, "Business and Bias in Public Policy Formation: The National Civic Federation and Social Construction of Electric utility Regulation, 1905–1907" (1998) p. 6, *Public Power Now Magazine* (2001).
14. Richard Hirsh, "Emergence of Electrical Utilities in America," p. 1, in Richard Hirsh, ed., *Powering the Past: A Look Back* (Smithsonian Institution, 1998) (http://americanhistory.si.edu/csr/powering/thepast.htm).
15. Bernard Finn, "Origin of Electrical Power," p. 6, in Hirsh, ed., *Powering the Past* (http://americanhistory.si.edu/csr/powering/thepast.htm).
16. *The Changing Structure of the Electricity Industry, Appendix A: History of the U.S. Electric Power Industry, 1882–1991*, p. 1.
17. Ibid.
18. Hirsh, "Emergence of Electrical Utilities in America," p. 4.
19. *The Changing Structure of the Electricity Industry, Appendix A: History of the U.S. Electric Power Industry, 1882–1991*, p. 2.
20. Richard Rudolph and Scott Ridley, *Power Struggle: The Hundred Year War over Electricity* (New York: Harper & Row, 1986) p. 38.
21. Patrick McGuire and Mark Granovetter, "Business and Bias in Public Policy Formation: The National Civic Federation and Social Construction of Electric utility Regulation, 1905–1907," *Public Power Now Magazine* (2001) pp. 2–3 (1998).
22. Rudolph and Ridley, *Power Struggle*, p. 44.
23. Hirsh, "Emergence of Electrical Utilities in America."
24. McGuire and Granovetter, "Business and Bias in Public Policy Formation: The National Civic Federation and Social Construction of Electric utility Regulation, 1905–1907," p. 5.
25. For example, H. Zinn, *A People's History of the United States* (Harper, rev. edn 1995) pp. 279 et seq.
26. Ibid.
27. Rudolph and Ridley, *Power Struggle*, pp. 38–9.
28. Hirsh, "Emergence of Electrical Utilities in America," p. 4.
29. McGuire and Granovetter, "Business and Bias in Public Policy Formation: The National Civic Federation and Social Construction of Electric Utility Regulation, 1905–1907," pp. 6, 8.

30. The CPOO rejected offers by a French association to evaluate their utilities, and of a US expert to review German utilities. Ibid., p. 8.
31. Ibid., pp. 7 and 9.
32. McGuire and Granovetter, "Business and Bias in Public Policy Formation: The National Civic Federation and Social Construction of Electric Utility Regulation, 1905–1907," pp. 11–13.
33. Ibid., pp. 11–12.
34. Ibid., p. 11.
35. Rudolph and Ridley, *Power Struggle*, p. 39.
36. McGuire and Granovetter, "Business and Bias in Public Policy Formation: The National Civic Federation and Social Construction of Electric Utility Regulation, 1905–1907," pp. 13–14.
37. Ibid., p. 16; *Public Power Now!!! Internet Magazine.*
38. Granovetter and McGuire Proposal part 3: "Evolution of the Electricity Industry in the United States," p. 5 (www.Stanford.edu/class/soc315a/nsf96.pdf). In this period (until 1913) AT&T similarly consolidated its nationwide, nearly universal monopoly by controlling long-distance connections. John Brooks, *Telephone* (New York: Harper & Row, 1976) pp. 135–6.
39. Rudolph and Ridley, *Power Struggle*, p. 40; Thomas McGraw, *Prophets of Regulation* (Cambridge, Mass.: The Belknap Press, 1984).
40. Rudolph and Ridley, *Power Struggle*.
41. "Public vs. Private Power: from FDR to Today," PBS – Frontline (www.pbs.org/wgbh/blackout/regulation/timeline.html); Thomas Hughes, *Networks of Power* (Baltimore: Johns Hopkins University Press 1983) pp. 204–26.
42. Hirsh, "Emergence of Electrical Utilities in America," p. 7 (http://americanhistory.si.edu/csr/powering/thepast.htm).
43. "Public vs. Private Power: from FDR to Today."
44. Amy Abel, "RS20015: Electricity Restructuring Background: Public Utility Holding Company Act of 1935 (PUHCA)," Congressional Research Service, Report for Congress (January 7, 1999).
45. Rudolph and Ridley, *Power Struggle*, p. 42.
46. "Public vs. Private Power: from FDR to Today."
47. Federal Trade Commission, Report on Utility Corporations, S. Doc. No. 92, 70th Congress, 1st Sess. (1928–1935) (hereinafter referred to as "FTC Report"), pt. 72-A, pp. 154–66.
48. Ibid.
49. Francis X. Busch, *Guilty or Not Guilty? An Account of the Trials of the Samuel Insull Case, et al.* (New York: The Bobbs-Merrill Company, 1952) pp. 128, 132.
50. Joel Seligman, *The Transformation of Wall Street: a History of the Securities and Exchange Commission* (Boston: Houghton Mifflin, 1982) p. 21.
51. Quoted by Rebecca Smith in "Enron's Rise and Fall Gives Some Scholars a Sense of Déjà Vu," *Wall Street Journal* (February 4, 2002) p. A6.
52. Ralph F. Be Bedts, *The New Deal's SEC: the Formative Years* (New York: Columbia University Press, 1965) p. 22.
53. Despite charges for three different crimes and three trials, Samuel Insull, his family members and associates were cleared of all criminal charges by 1935. Insull continued to be hounded by civil litigation until shortly before his death in 1938. Busch, *Guilty or Not Guilty?*, pp. 131, 192–4.
54. Quoted by Smith in "Enron's Rise and Fall Gives Some Scholars A Sense of Déjà Vu."
55. *The Changing Structure of the Electricity Industry, Appendix A: History of the U.S. Electric Power Industry, 1882–1991*, p. 2.
56. FDR's 1932 Speech on Public Power, reprinted in *The Public Papers and Addresses of Franklin D. Roosevelt, Vol. 1, 1928–32* (New York: Random House, 1938) p. 727.
57. Busch, *Guilty or Not Guilty?*, p. 131.

58. Hirsh, "Emergence of Electrical Utilities in America," p. 9.
59. *The Changing Structure of the Electricity Industry, Appendix A: History of the U.S. Electric Power Industry, 1882–1991*, p. 3.
60. Hirsh, "Emergence of Electrical Utilities in America," p. 9.
61. "Roll on Columbia: Woody Guthrie and the Bonneville Power Administration," Study Guide Part 4, Public vs. Private Control of Electric Utilities.
62. Amy Abel, "RS20015: Electricity Restructuring Background: Public Utility Holding Company Act of 1935 (PUHCA)," Congressional Research Service, Report for Congress (January 7, 1999) p. 2.
63. "The Regulation of Public Utility Holding Companies," SEC Division of Investment Management (June 1995).
64. Ibid.
65. FTC Report, pt. 72-A, p. 37.
66. "Public vs. Private Power: from FDR to Today."
67. Carl Wood, "CPUC Commissioner Gives a Short History of Utilities and Deregulation in California," *Public Power Now Internet Magazine* (http://ppn.hurstdog.org).
68. "Public vs. Private Power: from FDR to Today."
69. The SEC has advocated for repeal of PUHCA since the early 1990s and has been ignoring some of its provisions. An SEC approval in 2000 of a merger between two non-contiguous utility companies to form one of the largest utilities in the US was vacated by the District of Columbia US Court of Appeals, which found that the SEC had "overreached in its interpretation" of PUHCA. If this ruling is upheld, it will have major implications for the current spate of consolidations in the electric and natural gas industries. Bryan Lee, "Decision Overturning AEP Acquisition Could Threaten Utility Consolidation," www.WSJ.com, January 18, 2001.
70. "Public vs. Private Power: from FDR to Today"; Scott Fenn, *America's Electric Utilities* (New York: Praeger, 1984) pp. 6–7, 25–7; *The Changing Structure of the Electricity Industry, Appendix A: History of the U.S. Electric Power Industry, 1882–1991*, p. 3.
71. SEC Commissioner Isaac C. Hunt, Jr., "Testimony Concerning The Public Utility Holding Company Act of 1935 and the Current Energy Situation in California," n. 3, before the Committee on Financial Services of the US House of representatives (June 20, 2001).
72. Hirsh, *Power Loss*, pp. 73–4, 86–7.
73. Paul L. Joskow and Richard Schmalensee, *Markets for Power: An Analysis of Electric Utility Deregulation* (Cambridge, Mass.: The MIT Press, 1985).
74. Ibid., pp. 212–13.

Chapter 11

1. Securities and Exchange Commission Proposed Rule: Foreign Utility Companies Release No. 35–27342; File no. S7–05-RIN 3235-AF78 and AF79 (January 31, 2001).
2. Dr. Joseph Stiglitz, interview with author, January 23, 2001.
3. Scottish Power plc and PacifiCorp in Docket UM 918; see *NW Coalition Energy Report* (Northwest Energy Coalition, November 1999) p. 5.
4. N.R. Danielian, *AT&T* (Vanguard Press, 1939) pp. 170 et seq., 355 et seq., 396 (summary of FCC Telephone Investigation and reports to Congress of 1935–39).
5. Ibid., p. 394; Western Mass. Elec. Co., DPU 91–290 (Mass. 1992). Favoritism in the other direction is equally unlawful, such as sale at favorable prices of utility service to an unregulated affiliate. *Portland General Electric*, 51 FERC, par. 61,108 (1990). See Codes of Conduct in Appendix 2.

208 Democracy and Regulation

6. For example, National Grid acquired the New England Electric System and Niagara Mohawk Power Corp., and Scottish Power acquired PacifiCorp and Utah Power & Light Co.

7. For example, Scottish Power in Oregon acknowledges it purchased PacifiCorp subject to the jurisdiction and approval of the Oregon Public Utility Commission pursuant to Oregon R.S. sec. 757.511. Application of Scottish Power plc and PacifiCorp in Docket UM 918.

8. For example, *Puget Sound Power & Light*, 176 PUR 4th 238 (1997) (service standards and penalties).

9. Hunton and Williams, "Utility Privatization: The Creation of A Regulatory Structure," presented to The World Bank Seminar on Privatization of Infrastructure, April 26, 1993; Coopers & Lybrand, *Electricity Sector Restructuring Project (1997)*; Ministry of Mines and Energy, Secretariat of Energy, Electrobrás, *Project of Restructuring of the Brazilian Electric Sector*, Executive Summary, Stage 7 (1998).

10. IDEC counsel Maria Inez Dolci, personal communication (January 2000).

11. Rio Grande do Sul Gov. Olivio Dutra, personal communication (January 2000).

12. See generally G. Palast, "New British Empire of the Damned," *The Observer* (April 23, 2000).

13. World Bank, "Bolivia: Public Expenditure Review" (June 14, 1999).

14. Ibid., p. xxix; World Bank, "Memorandum of the President of the International Development Association and the International Finance Corp. to the Executive Directors on a Country Assistance Strategy of the World Bank Group for the Republic of Bolivia" (May 21, 1998).

15. Transcript of comments by World Bank Director James Wolfensohn, Washington, DC (April 12, 2000).

16. Jose Maria Vera, Report of the Monitoring Visit to Bolivia to Support PRSP (Oxfam, 21 July 2000).

Chapter 12

1. Steve Thomas, "Has Privatisation Reduced the Price of Power in Britain?" (UNISON, 1999); UNISON, "Privatisation and Liberalisation of the Energy Market" (1998).

2. David Newbery and Michael Pollitt, "The Restructuring and Privatisation of the U.K. Electricity Supply – Was It Worth It?" (World Bank Group, Public Policy for the Private Sector Note No. 124, September 1997). *Accord*, David Newberry, *Privatisation, Restructuring, and Regulation of Network Utilities* (The MIT Press, 2001) pp. 235 et seq.

3. Thomas, "Has Privatisation Reduced the Price of Power in Britain?"; UNISON, "Privatisation and Liberalisation of the Energy Market" (1998).

4. Thomas, "Has Privatisation Reduced the Price of Power in Britain?".

5. Dexter Whitefield, *Public Service or Corporate Welfare* (Pluto Press, 2001) p. 168.

6. UK Department of Trade & Industry (2002).

7. Energywatch (December 2001).

8. Less than a fifth in part of Scotland (www.ofgem.gov.uk/prices/switching.htm) (January 2001).

9. UK DTI Quarterly Energy Prices (December 2001); Boston Pacific Co., for EPSA.

10. Thomas, "Has Privatisation Reduced the Price of Power in Britain?"

11. Andrew Sweeting, "The Effect of Falling Market Concentration on Prices, Generator Behaviour and Productive Efficiency in the England and Wales Electricity Market" (MIT Economics Department, May 2001).

12. Steve Thomas, "Theory and Practice of Governance of the British Electricity Industry," 1 *International Journal of Regulation and Governance* 1, 15 (June 2001) Table 2.

13. Ibid., Table 1, p. 9; Thomas, "Has Privatisation Reduced the Price of Power in Britain?".

14. RKS Research and Consulting, press release (February 28, 2002; November 2001 survey) in "Businesses Find Few Benefits with Deregulation, Study Finds," US Department of Energy Electricity Restructuring Update (March 4, 2002).

15. California Independent System Operator, Department of Market Analysis, "Report on Real Time Supply Costs above Single Price Auction Threshold: December 8, 2000–January 31, 2001," Appendix C (February 28, 2001).

16. For example, Lynda Gorce, "Another Day in the Dark for Californians," *Boston Globe* (January 19, 2001) p. A3; Rebecca Smith et al., "California Power Crisis: Blackouts and Lawsuits and No End in Sight," *Wall Street Journal* (January 19, 2001) p. A1.

17. For example, Robert Gavin, "Power Crunch Roils Other Western States," *Wall Street Journal* (January 24, 2001) p. A2; Bloomberg News, "Phelps Dodge Says Energy Costs May Force Layoffs," *New York Times* (January 26, 2001) p. C3.

18. Mark Cooper, "Electricity Deregulation and Consumers: Lessons from a Hot Spring and a Cool Summer" (Consumer Federation of America 2001) p. 22.

19. *Myths Debunked: The Real Story of Wholesale Power Costs in California* (July 6, 2001) in Cooper, "Electricity Deregulation and Consumers: Lessons from a Hot Spring and a Cool Summer," p. 23.

20. *Wall Street Journal* (March 13, 2001).

21. John McKinnon, "Agency Request to Shut Smelters Revives Conflict Issue for O'Neill," *Wall Street Journal* (April 20, 2001) p. A16.

22. For example, Peter Howe, "Mass. Electric to Hike Rates up to 69%," *Boston Globe* (April 3, 2001] p. C1; Peter Howe, "Few in Mass. switch electric suppliers," *Boston Globe* (January 11, 2001) p. E9; Massachusetts Division of Energy Resources (www.state.ma.us/pub_info/migrate.htm).

23. Bruce Mohl, "Utility.com Stops Taking Customers," *Boston Globe* (December 29, 2000) p. C1.

24. A. Sullivan and N. Hegedus, "Con Ed Customers Get Tough Lesson on Deregulation," *Wall Street Journal* (August 23, 2000) p. B6; J. Covert, "Mismanagement of NY Power Market Costs Millions – Utilities," *Dow Jones Newswire* (October 5, 2000); A. Caffrey, "New York Energy Prices May Rise Sharply by '05," *Wall Street Journal* (April 18, 2001) p. A10.

25. Energy prices in the New York City zone fell from 8.5 cents on the Friday before September 11, 2001 (i.e., September 7) to 4.1 cents the following Friday.

26. Mark Cooper, "Electricity Deregulation and Consumers: Lessons from a Hot Spring and a Cool Summer" (Consumer Federation of America 2001) p. 18.

27. Bob Wyss, "New Utilities Charge More, not Less, for Power," *Providence Journal-Bulletin* (June 29, 1997) p. A-1. At least one supplier, New Energy Ventures, declined to provide power there. Jeffrey Krasner, "For Real Competition in Energy Market, the Price Isn't Right," *Wall Street Journal* (December 31, 1997) p. NE3.

28. Ken Rose, "Wholesale and Retail Market Overview," presentation to National Association of Regulatory Utility Commissioners Committee on Electricity (National Regulatory Research Institute February 11, 2002); Kathleen Davis, "California, Pennsylvania Deregulation Falls into Legal Limbo," *Electric Light & Power Magazine* (February 22, 2002); Christian Berg, "Only Discount Power Supplier for Much of State Pulls out," *Lehigh Valley Morning Call* (January 23, 2001) p. A1.

29. R. Smith and J. Fialka, "Electricity Firms Play Many Power Games That Jolt Consumers," *Wall Street Journal* (August 4, 2000) p. A1.

30. Staff Report to the Federal Energy Regulatory Commission on the Causes of Wholesale Electricity Pricing Abnormalities in the Midwest During June 1998 (September 22, 1998) Figures 3–5.

31. Mark Cooper, "Electricity Deregulation and Consumers: Lessons from a Hot Spring and a Cool Summer" (Consumer Federation of America 2001) p. 18.

32. R. Smith et al., "Electricity Firms Play Many Power Games That Jolt Consumers," *Wall Street Journal* (August 4, 2000) p. A1.
33. Enron's former CEO Jeff Skilling, quoted in *Journal of Commerce* (April 7, 1997).
34. Dennis Bakke, now CEO of AES, in ibid.
35. DOE Power Outage Study Team (POST), "Interim Report: Findings from the Reliability Events of Summer 1999" (January 2000).
36. *A Blueprint for Change: Executive Summary for the Investigative Report By Commonwealth Edison* (September 15, 1999) p. A-11.
37. Joint Comments of Massachusetts Attorney General and Division of Energy Resources in DTE 99–19, 01–65 and 01–71A, describing a report by ABB Consulting (January 24, 2002).
38. p. S-1.
39. Draft Decision of Administrative Law Judge Wong, *Opinion Regarding the Emergency Motion Seeking to Prevent the Utilities from Implementing Layoffs* in A00–11–038 et al. (February 23, 2001, approved by California PUC March 15, 2001) pp. 1–2.
40. James Bushnell and Celeste Saravia, "An Empirical Assessment of the Competitiveness of the New England Electricity Market" (February 2002) pp. 9, 12–13, 18–19, Figures 1 and 7. The analysis focused on the plants that are neither hydro nor nuclear, which must run for operational reasons; these thermal plants can vary their output to meet strategic objectives. Thus the margins analyzed are demand not satisfied by non-thermal supplies vs. installed thermal supplies. In the mid-Atlantic states of the Pennsylvania–New Jersey–Maryland (PJM) pool, margins averaged 25 per cent over an eight-month study period, largely because of summertime demand against constrained capacity.
41. Synapse Energy Economics, "Generator Outage Increases: A Preliminary Analysis of Outage Trends in the New England Electricity Market" (Union of Concerned Scientists, January 2001).
42. NYDPS Pricing Team, "Interim Pricing Report on New York State's Independent System Operator" (December 2000). *Accord*, J. Stutz et al., Comments of the Public Utility Law Project on the DPS Staff Interim Pricing Report (January 2001); A. Caffrey, "New York Energy Prices May Rise Sharply by '05," *Wall Street Journal* (April 18, 2001) p. A10; Sullivan and Hegedus, "Con Ed Customers Get Tough Lesson on Deregulation," p. B6; J. Covert, "Mismanagement of NY Power Market Costs Millions – Utilities," *Dow Jones Newswire* (October 5, 2000).
43. California Independent System Operator, Department of Market Analysis, "Report on Real Time Supply Costs Above Single Price Auction Threshold: December 8, 2000–January 31, 2001" (February 28, 2001) Appendix C.
44. The purchase was rejected by the California Commission in docket 99–10–023 (December 2000).
45. At a panel of the National Association of Regulatory Utility Commissioners (NARUC) (February 11, 2002).
46. Kathleen Sharp, "Price-gouging Inquiries Target Enron," *Boston Globe* (March 3, 2002) p. A12.
47. Massachusetts Division of Energy Resources, "Customer Migration Data" (July 2001) (www.state.ma.us/doer/pub_info/migrate.htm).
48. "Pennsylvania Electric Shopping Statistics" (July 2001).
49. Robert Tongren, Ohio Consumers' Counsel, "End-of-year Report: A Review of Ohio's Electric Market in 2001" (January 9, 2002); Jon Kamp, "Ohio's Electricity-Deregulation Efforts See Early Successes, but Need Refining," *Wall Street Journal* (January 16, 2002) p. B7A; Ken Rose, "Wholesale and Retail Market Overview," presentation to National Association of Regulatory Utility Commissioners, Electricity Committee (National Regulatory Research Institute February 11, 2002) (data through September 30, 2001).

50. New Jersey Board of Public Utilities, "New Jersey Electric Statistics" (October 31, 2001); Rose, "Wholesale and Retail Market Overview."

51. "Maryland Office of People's Counsel Report on Electric Choice" (January 16, 2002). There is only one competitive supplier, serving part of the state.

52. Ken Rose, "Wholesale and Retail Market Overview," presentation to National Association of Regulatory Utility Commissioners, Electricity Committee (National Regulatory Research Institute, February 11, 2002) (data through July 2001).

53. Rose, "Wholesale and Retail Market Overview" (as of January 14, 2002; we excluded the data from the then two-week-old Texas markets).

54. Brooks Barnes, "Nothing Personal," *Wall Street Journal*, p. R12 (September 17, 2001).

55. Meg Power, "The Winter Energy Outlook for the Poor: Low-Income Consumers' Energy Bills in the Winter of 2000–2001" (Economic Opportunity Studies, December 2000).

56. Matthew Jones, "Shell Warns Liberalisation Could Hit Prices," *Financial Times* (February 18, 2002), quoting Linda Cook, chief executive of Shell's gas and power unit.

57. Atlanta *Journal-Constitution* (August 9, 2001).

58. Wichita *Eagle* (September 13, 2001).

59. Editorial, "How to Avert Disaster: *Know it when you see it coming*," *Arkansas Democrat-Gazette* (October 16, 2001) and "Train Wreck Averted: *Thank you, Public Service Commission*" (October 29, 2001); J. Tomich, "Group Opposes Gas-bill Pay Plan," *Arkansas Democrat-Gazette* (November 2, 2001).

60. R. Smith et al., "Electricity Firms Play Many Power Games that Jolt Consumers," *Wall Street Journal* (August 4, 2000) p. A1.

61. David Newberry, *Privatization, Restructuring, and Regulation of Network Utilities* (The MIT Press, 2001) p. 422.

62. Discussion of "Competitiveness of Regional Wholesale Power Market/Evolution of Competition" presentation, New England Wholesale Market Roundtable in docket 6330 (Montpelier, April 12, 2001).

63. Rebecca Smith, "Power Traders See Profits Rise on High Prices," *Wall Street Journal* (April 18, 2001) p. A3.

64. Jerry Taylor, "Enron Was No Friend to Free Markets," *Wall Street Journal* (January 21, 2002) p. A12; Robert Borosage, "Enron Conservatives," *The Nation* (February 4, 2002) p. 4. See Newbery, *Privatization, Restructuring, and Regulation of Network Utilities*, p. 263 ("the price-setting part of the [California spot] market is relatively thin, and of the 30 sellers in the market, only four were important price setters once prices exceed $75/mWh [7.5 cents per kWh], with few playing a price-setting role as the prices rose further." As noted above, prices in California *averaged* more than 7.5 cents per kWh for more than half of the year 2000.)

65. Utility Workers Union of America, "Toward A Utility Industry That Works for Everyone" (March 1996). See also J. Oppenheim, "Potential Costs of Competition: A Customer Perspective – Brownouts, Death Spirals and Alternatives," in S. Limaye, ed., *Utility Opportunities for New Generation* (Washington and Palo Alto: Edison Electric Institute and Electric Power Research Institute, 1989).

66. "Duke Energy Planning on Retail Margin that are [*sic*] Very Low," *Restructuring Today* (October 10, 1997) p. 1.

67. Now the Department of Telecommunications and Energy. Docket 96–100 (1997).

68. Ibid.

69. "Former CPUC president doubts lower prices to come from choice," *Restructuring Today* (April 7, 1997) p. 1, quoting Daniel Fessler at a conference sponsored by *The Electricity Journal*.

70. Edward Morse, Chair of Independent Task Force et al., "Strategic Energy Policy Challenges for the 21st Century" (Council on Foreign Relations, 2001). While we do not agree with CFR's overall support for retail competition, CFR makes the key

point that an unregulated market has no incentive to build adequate supply (inventory, in CFR's terms) to assure reliability and minimize price volatility. One option is a mandatory reserve margin.
71. Yochi Dreazen et al., "Why the Sudden Rise in the Urge to Merge snd Form Oligopolies?," *Wall Street Journal* (February 25, 2002) p. A1.
72. Two lines are shown for each city because the FCC changed the way it computes the cost of local residential telephone service. Prices in the period covered by the later line (1990–98) were relatively stable.
73. Unlike in many other states, the application was rejected in Ohio. NOW Communications, Inc. et al., Public Utilities Commission of Ohio docket 98–1466-TP-ACE et al. (decided November 2, 2000).
74. Dec. 01–09–060 (Calif. PUC, September 20, 2001); Assembly Bill No. 1 from the First Extraordinary Session (Ch. 4, First Extraordinary Session 2001) (AB 1X) (February 1, 2000); San Francisco *Chronicle* (August 25, 2001).
75. H.B. 5005, sec. 75; Public Act 98–28 (1998).
76. NYSEG Form 8-K (September 18, 2000) p. 2.
77. Statement of Policy Concerning Gas Purchasing Practices, pp. 4–5, Case 97-G-0600 (April 28, 1998).
78. Personal communications, Consumer Advocate Stephen Ward (October 29, 2001), consumer consultant Barbara Alexander (October 30, 2001).
79. *Arkansas Gas Utilities*, 210 PUR4th 325 (Ark. PSC 2001) 210 PUR4th 325 (Ark. PSC 2001).
80. Dec. No. C01–207 in Colo. PUC Docket No. OIR-0835 (March 27, 2001).
81. *Savannah Electric Power Co.*, 210 PUR4th 335 (Ga. PSC 2001).
82. *Intermountain Gas Co.*, Order No. 28783 in Case No. INT-G-01–3 (Ida. PUC, July 13, 2001), 210 PUR4th, No. 2, p. iv.
83. Docket No. RMU-00–6 (Iowa Utils. Bd. June 21, 2000).
84. *Western Kentucky Gas Co.*, 210 PUR4th 331 (Ky. PSC 2001).
85. *Consumers Energy Co.* (gas), 212 PUR4th 175 (Mich. PSC, 2001).
86. *Oklahoma Natural Gas Co.*, 211 PUR4th 230 (Okla. Corp. Comm. 2001).
87. *Washington Gas Light Co.*, 212PUR4th 375 (Va. St. Corp. Comm. 2001).
88. R. Linden, "Gas Price Prudence: From Hedge-and-Hope to Best Practice," *Public Utilities Fortnightly* (October 1, 2001) p. 34.
89. J.D. Oller and D.A. Murray, "Cascading Caution: California Crisis Delays Deregulation," *Public Utilities Fortnightly* (September 1, 2001) p. 52; US Department of Energy, Energy Information Administration, "Status of Electric Industry Restructuring Activity as of September 2001" (updated monthly and www.eia.doe.gov), "Deregulation put off in Vermont," *Boston Globe* (December 19, 2001); S.W. Hadley et al., "The Potential Economic Impact of Electricity Restructuring in the State of Oklahoma" (Oak Ridge National Laboratory for Oklahoma Corporation Commission October 2001) (predicts rate increase of as much as 20 per cent); Edison Electric Institute, "State Restructuring Scorecard" (October 31, 2001).

Chapter 13

1. The Foundation for Taxpayer and Consumer Rights, "Hoax: How Deregulation Let the Power Industry Steal $71 Billion from California" (January 2002); Kathleen Sharp, "Price-gouging Inquiries Target Enron," *Boston Globe* (March 3, 2002) p. A12; "California Trims Energy Usage," *Los Angeles Times* (February 27, 2002); Rebecca Smith, "PG&E is Facing Two-Pronged Attack by State," *Wall Street Journal* (January 11, 2002) p. B2; "PG&E Undeterred by Judge's Warning on Reorganization," *Wall Street Journal* (February 11, 2002) p. A4; Robert McCullough, Testimony before the

Senate Energy and Resources Committee (January 29, 2002); "Revisiting California," *Public Utilities Fortnightly* (April 1, 2002) p. 28; Paul Joskow and Edward Kahn, "A Quantitative Analysis of Pricing Behavior in California's Wholesale Electricity Market during Summer 2000: The Final Word" (Massachusetts Institute of Technology, February 4, 2000); Michael Liedtke (AP), "Regulators Say They're Close to Proving Power Manipulation," *Inland Empire Online* (January 25, 2002); "An Abuse of Power?," *Seattle Post-Intelligencer* (April 23, 2001); David Kravets (AP), "California Attorney General Says Expect More Energy Lawsuits," *San Diego Union-Tribune* (January 24, 2002); Craig Rose, "Link is Seen to California in Enron Flop," *San Diego Union-Tribune* (December 4, 2001); "Enron Was Standard for Deregulation," *San Diego Union-Tribune* (November 29, 2001); "Estimates Start at $50 billion for Deregulation Cost," *San Diego Union-Tribune* (July 8, 2001); Rich Connell, "Ratepayer Suits to Go Forward, Judge Rules," *Los Angeles Times* (August 1, 2001); Class Action Complaint, *Hendricks et al.* v. *Dynergy Power Marketing, Inc. et al.* (California Superior Court, San Diego County November 29, 2000); Tyson Slocum, "Blind Faith: How Deregulation and Enron's Influence Over Government Looted Billions from Americans," *Public Citizen* (December 2001); Nancy Dunne, "Ferc to Probe Trading Arm's Pricing Policy," *Financial Times* (February 14, 2000); Jason Leopold, "Former Employee Says Enron Manipulated California Power Market," Dow Jones Newswires (February 21, 2002); William Marcus, "A Blueprint for Renegotiating California's Worst Electricity Contracts" (Utility Consumers' Action Network et al., February 2002); Rebecca Smith, "California Regulators to Ask FERC to Void Pacts," *Wall Street Journal* (February 25, 2002) p. A6; Julie Earle, "California Will Ask Ferc to Review Power Contracts," *Financial Times* (February 25, 2002); Mitchell Benson, "California's Power Negotiations Drag On as State Politics Heat Up," *Wall Street Journal* (March 25, 2002) p. A2; Water Code, sec. 80110, AB1X Stats. 2001 (1st Extraord. Sess.), ch. 4, sec. 4, p. 10; *Suspension of Direct Access*, Calif. PUC Dec. D-02–03–055 in Rulemaking 02–01–011 (March 21, 2002); Richard Stevenson, "Enron Trading Gave Prices Artificial Lift, Panel is Told," *New York Times* (April 12, 2002).

2. If gas were the only input and tripled in price, electricity prices would increase three times. Since less than half of the electricity supply is powered by gas, a tripling of the gas price would yield no more than half the increase – 1.5 times, which is an increase of 50 per cent.

3. Christopher Knittel and Michael Roberts, "An Empirical Examination of Deregulated Electricity Prices" (Program on Workable Energy Regulation, University of California Energy Institute, October 2001).

4. U.S. General Accounting Office, "Energy Markets – Results of Studies Assessing High Electricity Prices in California" (No. GAO-01–857, June 2001) p. 4.

5. Jason Johnson, "Sales of energy-saving items set record/PG&E's program of rebates used up," *San Francisco Chronicle* (December 7, 2001) p. A-21; Mary James, "Californians Take on Energy Crisis," *Home Energy* (March/April 2002) p. 11.

6. Paul Krugman, "The Power Perplex," *New York Times* (op-ed, February 26, 2002).

7. For example, Order in EL00–95–012 (October 5, 2001).

8. Perot Systems Corp., presentation (n.d.) pp. 2, 5, 8 released by California Sen. Joseph Dunn; Elliot Spagat, "Perot Says it Tried to Sell Advice," *Wall Street Journal* (June 7, 2002) p. B6; Christopher Parkes, "Perot Systems Denies 'Economic Rape,'" *Financial Times* (June 7, 2002) p. 18.

9. At this writing, the state has opposed the move, the judge has agreed to review an alternative state plan, and the matter is pending.

10. This is about what the price of electricity was at wholesale before the so-called competitive market was opened.

11. Quotations are from e-mail letter, Donald Gelinas, Associate Director, FERC Office of Markets, Tariffs and Rates, to Sam Behrends, IV, Esq., LeBoeuf Lamb Greene & MacRae, LLP (attorneys for Enron) (May 6, 2002), describing: Stoel Rives LLP

Memorandum, Christian Yoder and Stephen Hall to Richard Sanders Re: Traders' Strategies in the California Wholesale Power Markets/ISO Sanctions (December 6, 2000), Stoel Rives LLP Memorandum, Christian Yoder and Stephen Hall to Richard Sanders Re: Traders' Strategies in the California Wholesale Power Markets/ISO Sanctions (December 8, 2000), Brobeck Attorneys draft Memorandum, Gary Fergus, Jean Frizzell (Gibbs & Bruns LLP) to Richard Sanders re: Status Report on Further Investigation and Analysis of EPMI Trading Strategies (n.d.). The latter document sets forth a more benign interpretation of the strategies, from Enron's point of view. FERC and other investigations continue as this is written. The Star refinements are described in additional documents and summarized in Memorandum, Robert McCullough to McCullough Research clients, re: Congestion Manipulation in ISO California (McCullough Research, June 5, 2002).

12. Stoel Rives LLP Memorandum, Christian Yoder and Stephen Hall to Richard Sanders Re: Traders' Strategies in the California Wholesale Power Markets/ISO Sanctions (December 6, 2000); Stoel Rives LLP Memorandum, Christian Yoder and Stephen Hall to Richard Sanders Re: Traders' Strategies in the California Wholesale Power Markets/ISO Sanctions (December 8, 2000); Memorandum, Robert McCullough to McCullough Research clients, re: Congestion Manipulation in ISO California (McCullough Research, June 5, 2002).

13. Stoel Rives LLP Memorandum, Christian Yoder and Stephen Hall to Richard Sanders Re: Traders' Strategies in the California Wholesale Power Markets/ISO Sanctions (December 6, 2000); Stoel Rives LLP Memorandum, Christian Yoder and Stephen Hall to Richard Sanders Re: Traders' Strategies in the California Wholesale Power Markets/ISO Sanctions (December 8, 2000); "Attack of the Clones: Prevented, Defeated or Coming Soon?," 4 E-Cubed no. 10 (PennFuture e-mail newsletter, May 24, 2002).

14. Stoel Rives LLP Memorandum, Christian Yoder and Stephen Hall to Richard Sanders Re: Traders' Strategies in the California Wholesale Power Markets/ISO Sanctions (December 6, 2000); Stoel Rives LLP Memorandum, Christian Yoder and Stephen Hall to Richard Sanders Re: Traders' Strategies in the California Wholesale Power Markets/ISO Sanctions (December 8, 2000); Memorandum, Robert McCullough to McCullough Research clients, re: Congestion Manipulation in ISO California (McCullough Research, June 5, 2002); "Attack of the Clones: Prevented, Defeated or Coming Soon?," 4 E-Cubed no. 10 (PennFuture e-mail newsletter, May 24, 2002); Peter Thal Larsen, "Is the Energy Trading Market Worth Saving?," *Financial Times* (May 31, 2002) p. 17; Joseph Kahn, "With Markets Flawed, Enron's Tactics May Live On," *New York Times* (May 12, 2002).

15. Memorandum, Robert McCullough to McCullough Research clients, re: Congestion Manipulation in ISO California (McCullough Research, June 5, 2002) p. 17. The ISO disputes this.

16. Michael Liedtke (AP), "An Abuse of Power?," *Seattle Post-Intelligencer* (April 23, 2001).

17. Alan Fischer, "Many States Reconsidering Electric Competition, MIT Professor Says," *Arizona Daily Star* (Tucson, February 1, 2002).

18. Mimi Swartz, "How Enron Blew It," *Texas Monthly* (November 2001) p. 138.

19. Ibid.

20. Ibid., p. 172.

21. Tyson Slocum, "Blind Faith: How Deregulation and Enron's Influence over Government Looted Billions from Americans," *Public Citizen* (December 2001) p. 3.

22. Swartz, "How Enron Blew It," pp. 172–3.

23. Ibid., p. 176.

24. "Blind Faith: How Deregulation and Enron's Influence Over Government Looted Billions from Americans," *Public Citizen* (December 2001) p. 25.

25. Financial Highlights in Enron Annual Reports to Shareholders for the years 1998 and 2000.

26. John D. McKinnon and Greg Hitt, "How Treasury Lost in Battle to Quash a Dubious Security," *Wall Street Journal* (February 4, 2002) pp. A1 and A8.

27. Paul Solman, "Accounting Alchemy," *NewsHour with Jim Lehrer* (Public Broadcasting Service, January 22, 2002); Anne E. Kornblut, "Ex-Enron chairman Cancels Testimony," *The Boston Globe* (February 4, 2002) p. A7.

28. Daniel Altman, "Enron Had More Than One Way to Disguise Rapid Rise in Debt," *The New York Times* on the Web (February 17, 2002).

29. Rebecca Smith, "How Enron's Plan to Market Electricity Nationwide Fizzled," *Wall Street Journal* (March 25, 2002) p. A1; New Power Co., "NewPower Reports 2002 Full Year and fourth Quarter Results," (press release, February 23, 2002); New Power Holdings, Inc., "Investor Fact Sheet" (n.d., on newpower.com web-site on April 2, 2002).

30. John Emshwiller, "Enron Report Suggests Officials Knew about Secretive Partnership," *Wall Street Journal* (February 19, 2002) p. A2; John Emshwiller and Rebecca Smith, "Murky Waters: A Primer on Enron Partnerships," *Wall Street Journal* (January 21, 2002) p. C1.

31. Altman, "Enron Had More Than One Way to Disguise Rapid Rise in Debt."

32. Swartz, "How Enron Blew It," p. 176.

33. Emshwiller, "Enron Report Suggests Officials Knew About Secretive Partnership," p. A2.

34. Rebecca Smith and John R. Emshwiller, "Internal Probe of Enron Finds Wide-Ranging Abuses," *Wall Street Journal* (February 4, 2002) pp. A3 and 8.

35. Ibid.

36. *Boston Sunday Globe Editorial* (January 20, 2002) p. G6.

37. Ibid.

38. Indictment, *United States of America* v. *Arthur Anderson, LLP*, CRH-02–121 (filed March 7, 2002, US District Court, Southern District of Texas); Flynn McRoberts et al., "A Final Accounting: Repeat Offender Gets Swift Justice," *Chicago Tribune* (September 4, 2002).

39. "Enron Estimates $14bn Writedown," *Financial Times* (April 23, 2002) p. 18.

40. *Boston Sunday Globe*, Editorial (January 20, 2002) p. G6.

41. "Group Finds Discrepancy in Enron's Costs," *The Boston Globe* (January 30, 2002) p. A10.

42. Michael Schroeder, "SEC Feels Heat Over Exemptions to Enron," *Wall Street Journal* (January 21, 2002) p. A8.

43. Albert R. Hunt, "A Scandal Centerpiece: Enron's Political Contributions," *Wall Street Journal* (January 17, 2002) p. A15.

44. Floyd Norris and David Barboza, "Lay Sold Shares for $100 Million," *The New York Times on the Web* (February 16, 2002).

45. Albert R. Hunt, "A Scandal Centerpiece: Enron's Political Contributions," *Wall Street Journal* (January 17, 2002) p. A15.

46. Joe Stephens, "Bush 2000 Adviser Offered to Use Clout to Help Enron," *Washington Post* (February 17, 2002) p. A1.

47. Ibid.

48. "Enron's Power Failure," *Boston Globe*, Editorial (January 20, 2002) p. G6.

49. Slocum, "Blind Faith: How Deregulation and Enron's Influence over Government Looted Billions from Americans," pp. 3, 15–16; US Senate Financial Disclosure Report, The Center for Responsive Politics (www.opensecrets.org).

50. Ibid., pp. 3–4.

51. On February 15, 2002, Enron's share price closed at 26.5 cents. Floyd Norris and David Barboza, "Lay Sold Shares for $100 Million," *The New York Times on the Web* (February 16, 2002).

52. Lou Kesten, "Lawyer Advised Enron to Appease Possible Whistle-blowers," *The Boston Globe* (February 18, 2002) p. A5.

53. Miles Moffeit, "Enron Workers Tell of Huge Overbillings," *The Boston Globe* (February 17, 2002) p. A10.
54. "Enron's Auditors Debated Partnership Losses," *Wall Street Journal* (April 3, 2002) p. C1.
55. "Andersen Boss Warned before Enron about Flawed Audits," *Financial Times* (April 12, 2002) p. 1.
56. Greg Palast, "Enron: Not the Only Bad Apple," *Guardian*, (London) Special Report (February 1, 2002).
57. George F. Will, "Arrogance of Unrestrained Executives Led to Enron's Downfall," *The Boston Globe* (January 21, 2002) p. A13.
58. Enron Annual Report 1998 – "Our Values."
59. Editorial, "Enron's Power Failure," *Boston Globe* (January 20, 2002) p. G6.
60. Jeanne Cummins, "U.S. Probes Enron's Effect on Power Prices," *Wall Street Journal* (January 30, 2002) p. A4.
61. "Enron's Collapse Leaves Reshuffle of Energy Trading," *Dallas News* (March 7, 2001).
62. Reuters (February 13, 2002); *Electric Power Daily* (February 14, 2002).
63. Neela Banerjee, "The Energy Industry Gauges the Enron Damage," *The New York Times on the Web* (February 18, 2002).
64. Mark Golden, "Power Points: Wall St. May Knock Bloom off Deregulation," Dow Jones Newswires (December 7, 2001); Rebecca Smith and Alexei Barrionuevo, "Energy Industry Looks to Shed Billions in Assets," *Wall Street Journal* (January 2, 2002) p. C1; Neela Banerjee, "The Energy Industry Gauges the Enron Damage," *New York Times* (February 18, 2002); Sheila McNulty, "Trading Ideas to Help Restore Confidence," *Financial Times* (February 19, 2002) p. 21; Martha Brannigan, "AES Shares Decline 32% Despite Plans to Eliminate Costs," *Wall Street Journal* (February 20, 2002) p. A4; and "AES Approves Restructuring Plan," (February 19, 2002) p. A4; Martha Brannigan, "AES Reviewed for Downgrade From Moody's," *Wall Street Journal* (February 21, 2002) p. A10; Martha Brannigan, "AES Seeks to Reassure Investors Worried over Dilution of Equity," *Wall Street Journal* (February 22, 2002) p. A4; "Nymex Delists Power Contracts," *Financial Times* (February 19, 2002) p. 22.
65. Rebecca Smith and John Emshwiller, "Enron Prepares To Become Easier to Read," *Wall Street Journal* (August 28, 2001) p. C1; "New York Stock Exchange Composite Transactions," *Wall Street Journal* (August 29, 2001) p. C3; and *Wall Street. Journal* (February 21, 2002) pp. C5–C7.
66. Brannigan, "AES Shares Decline 32% Despite Plans to Eliminate Costs;" and "AES Approves Restructuring Plan," p. A4.
67. Alex Berenson, "Power Giants Have Trouble Raising Cash for Plants," *New York Times* (May 16, 2002).
68. RWE Trading managing director Stefan Judisch in "Energy Traders See More Grief," *Financial Times* (February 14, 2002) p. 16.
69. Gerald Seib and John Harwood, "For Bush, Popularity May Not Translate Into Victories at Home," *Wall Street Journal* (January 25, 2002) pp. A1, A2. *Accord*, Joseph Kahn and Jeff Gerth, "Collapse of Enron May Reshape the Battlefield of Deregulation," *New York Times* (December 4, 2001); Stephen Labaton, "States Seek to Counter U.S. Deregulation," *New York Times* (January 13, 2002) p. 23; Dan Morgan, "Focus on Enron Delays Electricity Reform," *Washington Post* (February 11, 2002) p. A8.

Chapter 14

1. Petrus Mashishi (President, South Africa Municipal Workers Union, SAMWU), "Why Corporatising Water and Selling Other Services is not Necessary," *City Press Newspaper* (October 31, 1999) (www.cosatu.org.za/samwu/igmarchcityp.htm).

2. For example, Michael Phillips, "World Bank Agrees to Further Disclosure but Stops Short of Public Board Meetings," *Wall Street Journal* (September 6, 2001) p. A24.

3. Dharam Ghai (Director), "Structural Adjustment, Global Integration, and Social Democracy" (United Nations Research Institute for Social Development (UNRISD) 1992) p. 4.

4. World Bank, Operations Policy and Country Services, "Adjustment Lending Retrospective – Final Report" (2001) p. 56 n. 128; Brendan Martin, *In the Public Interest?* (Zed Books 1993) p. 73.

5. World Bank, Operations Policy and Country Services, "Adjustment Lending Retrospective – Final Report" (2001) p. 56 n. 128.

6. IMF, Policy Development and Review Dept., "Structural Conditionality in Fund-Supported Programs" (2001).

7. "Private Sector Development Strategy – Directions for the World Bank Group" (December 3, 2001) par. 64, in K. Bayliss and D. Hall, "Another PSIRU critique of another version of the World Bank private sector development strategy" (Public Services International Research Unit, January 2002) p. 11.

8. David Boys, "World Bank to PSI: Corruption is the Reason," World News No. 20 (Public Services International 2000).

9. Greg Palast, "The Globalizer Who Came in From the Cold," London *Observer* (April 29, 2001).

10. Joseph Stiglitz, "What I Learned at the World Economic Crisis," *The New Republic* (April 17, 2000) (discussing IMF loans to East Asia).

11. Michael Pollitt, *Ownership and Performance in Electrical Utilities* (Oxford University Press 1995), in K. Bayliss, "Privatization of Electricity Distribution" (Public Services International Research Unit April 2001) pp. 15–17; and K. Bayliss and D. Hall, "A PSIRU response to the World Bank's Private Sector Development Strategy: Issues and Options" (Public Services International Research Unit October 2001).

12. Neil Irwin, "AES to Dump its Weakest Plants," *Washington Post* (February 7, 2002) p. E2; Chad Terhune, "AES Corp. Posts 80% Decrease in Quarterly Net," *Wall Street Journal* (February 6, 2002) p. B13.

13. George Melloan (columnist), "Wither the IMF? A Top-Down Reform is Unlikely," *Wall Street Journal* (July 3, 2001) p. A15.

14. M. A. O'Grady (ed.), "The IMF in Argentina: Bailouts for Investors," *Wall Street Journal* (September 7, 2001) p. A15.

15. Yusuf Bangura, "Public Sector Restructuring: The Institutional and Social Effects of Fiscal, Managerial and Capacity-Building Reforms" (UNRISD 2000) pp. 5, 15.

16. Jack Glen, *Private Sector Electricity in Developing Countries* (World Bank 1992) p. 15, in Martin, *In the Public Interest?*, p. 111.

17. "Pursuit of Shareholder Value in an Emerging Industry," *Financial Times* "World Electricity" conference paper, London, 1992, in Martin, *In the Public Interest?*, p. 111.

18. Richard Toole, "What Do Investors Want from the New Company after Privatization?" in Leonard S. Hyman, *The Privatization of Public Utilities* (Public Utilities Reports, 1995) p. 177. Emphasis in original.

19. Leonard S. Hyman, *The Privatization of Public Utilities* (Public Utilities Reports 1995) pp. 3–4. Marginal cost is the cost of the last unit of output, for electricity a kilowatt-hour, and includes no capital costs. In the case of electricity, marginal costs include the fuel and variable operation and maintenance expense of the marginal (last) kilowatt-hour.

20. "IMF and World Bank: An Urgent Need for Reform," *Trade Union World* (International Confederation of Free Trade Unions, November 2001) p. 8.

21. K. Bayliss, "Privatization of Electricity Distribution" (Public Services International Research Unit April 2001) p. 27.

22. For example, regarding Greek Public Power Corp.: "Despite the company's announcement prior to the [share] float that it would reduce its 31,000-strong work

force by 20% by 2005, analysts still see Public Power as over-staffed, compared with peers such as Electricidade De Portugal SA, which has a work force of around 12,000." Paul Tugwell, "Greek Public Power Shares Open 3% Below IPO Price," *Wall Street Journal Europe* (December 13, 2001) p. 16.

23. Take-or-pay contracts guarantee payment irrespective of sales.

24. Denominating obligations in dollars removes currency risk.

25. "Water Plan for Nairobi on Course," *Daily Nation On the Web* (September 15, 2000). See generally K. Bayliss and D. Hall, "A PSIRU response to the World Bank's 'Private Sector Development Strategy: Issues and Options'" (Public Services International Research Unit October 2001) pp. 6–7; and "Another PSIRU critique of another version of the World Bank private sector development strategy" (January 2002) pp. 3, 6–7.

26. World Bank, Operations Policy and Country Services, "Adjustment Lending Retrospective – Final Report" (2001) pp. xvi, 123.

27. Globalization Challenge Initiative, "IMF Structural Adjustment Programs" (letter to World Bank); "Letter from World Bank to NGOs Regarding Consultation on Structural Adjustment Policy" (June 12, 2001); Globalization Challenge Initiative, "Update on World Bank Structural Adjustment Lending Policy – World Bank Plans to Revise Adjustment Lending Policy but without Reconsidering the Content of Structural Adjustment," all on Globalization Challenge Initiative web-site, www.challengeglobalization.org. Globalization Challenge Initiative is supported by the Ford Foundation, the Charles Stuart Mott Foundation, and the John D. and Catherine T. MacArthur Foundation.

28. Joseph Stiglitz, "What I Learned at the World Economic Crisis," *The New Republic* (April 17, 2000).

29. Dharam Ghai (Director), "Structural Adjustment, Global Integration, and Social Democracy" (United Nations Research Institute for Social Development (UNRISD) 1992) p. 23.

30. United States Energy Association, Trade and Development Committee, "Toward an International Energy Trade and Development Strategy" (October 2001) p. 6.

31. US Energy Information Administration, *Electricity Reform Abroad and US Investment* (1997) Figure ES-1.

32. K. Bayliss, "Privatization of Electricity Distribution" (Public Services International Research Unit April 2001) pp. 8–9.

33. Ibid., pp. 17–18. A more comprehensive list is contained in US Energy Information Administration, "Update of Appendix Tables from *Privatization and the Globalization of Energy Markets*" (www.eia.doe.gov/emeu/pgem/update/index.html) (2000).

34. John Emshwiller et al., "How Wall Street Greased Enron's Money Engine," *Wall Street Journal* (January 14, 2002) p. C1.

35. Mitchell Pacelle, "Enron Investors Question Roles of Big Banks," *Wall Street Journal* (April 5, 2002) p. C1.

36. Sustainable Energy & Economy Network and Institute for Policy Studies, *Enron's Pawns: How Public Instituions Bankrolled Enron's Globalization Game* (March 2002).

37. Evelina Shmukler, "Cross-Border M&A Lifts Banks," *The Wall Street Journal Europe* (December 12, 2001) p. 15.

38. Gary Silverman, "Wall Street Yearning for an M&A Revival," *Financial Times* (March 21, 2002) p. 15.

39. Ranjan Kumar Bose and Megha Shukla (Tata Energy Research Institute, New Delhi), "Electricity Tariffs in India: An Assessment of Consumers' Ability and Willingness to Pay in [the state of] Gujarat," 29 *Energy Policy* 465 (2001).

40. *Report of the (Government of Maharashtra) Energy Review Committee*, April 2001 (view of two of five members); Navroz K. Dubash and Sudhir Chella Rajan, "The Politics of Power Sector Reform in India (World Resources Institute, April 2001); Khozem

Merchant, "Bombay Power Plant Illuminates Shadowy Path to State Approval," *Financial Times* (January 12–13, 2002) p. 4.

41. Merchant, "Bombay Power Plant Illuminates Shadowy Path to State Approval," p. 4.

42. Stephen Fidler, "Enron: Over There and Overpaying," *Financial Times* (February 12, 2002) (quoting Peter Harrold) p. 19.

43. Public Services International, "India's Energy Workers Strike back at World Bank" (October 8, 2000).

44. Navroz K. Dubash and Sudhir Chella Rajan, "The Politics of Power Sector Reform in India" (World Resources Institute, April 2001).

45. Khozem Merchant, "Mirant Pulls out of Energy Project in India," *Financial Times* (December 14, 2001) p. 22. Another 2,500 mW are under construction.

46. Navroz K. Dubash and Sudhir Chella Rajan, "The Politics of Power Sector Reform in India" (World Resources Institute, April 2001); A.K. Basu (Secretary, Ministry of Power), "Power Sector Reforms" (Bank of India, Vision 2001) (www.shilpabichi-tra.com/v065.htm); Antonette D'Sa, K. V. Narasimha Murthy, and Amulya K. N. Reddy, "India's Power Sector Liberalisation: An Overview," *Economic and Political Weekly* (Mumai, India, June 5, 1999).

47. See, e.g., re World Bank's public posture, Navroz K. Dubash and Sudhir Chella Rajan, "The Politics of Power Sector Reform in India" (World Resources Institute, April 2001).

48. It was the failure to secure such a guarantee that caused Mirant to abandon construction of what would have been one of the largest power plants in India. Merchant, "Mirant Pulls out of Energy Project in India," p. 22.

49. *Report of the (Government of Maharashtra) Energy Review Committee*, April 2001; Kate Bayliss and David Hall, "Independent Power Producers: A Review of the Issues" (Public Services International Research Unit, November 2000) and "A PSIRU response to the World Bank's 'Private Sector Development Strategy: Issues and Options'" (October 2001); Navroz K. Dubash and Sudhir Chella Rajan, "The Politics of Power Sector Reform in India"; Sucheta Dalal, "The Whole World's Full of Broken IPP deals," *The Indian Express* (January 14, 2000), and "Enron: Does the Government Have the Guts?" (January 10, 2001) (www.rediff.com/money/2001/jan/10dalal.htm); John Elliott, "India State Pays Bills to Enron, But Electricity Crunch Persists," *International Herald Tribune* (February 16, 2001) p. 15; "State looks at Dabhol deal with Enron," CNN (April 24, 2001); Pratap Chaatterjee, "Enron in India: The Dabhol Disaster," *CorpWatch* (July 20, 2000); Sanjay Jog, "State to Review Dabhol Power Project Phase-II," Bombay *Indian Express* (November 26, 2000); James Luckey, "Lessons from Dabhol" *Energy Markets* (October 2000) p. 20.

50. Michael Phillips, "U.S. Fought for Company's Project in India," *Wall Street Journal* (January 21, 2002) p. A8; Albert Hunt, "Enron's One Good Return: Political Investments," *Wall Street Journal* (January 31, 2002) p. A19; Anon., "Enron Properties outside the U.S. Hit Auction Block," *Wall Street Journal* (January 22, 2002) p. B4; Khozem Merchant, "Bombay Power Plant Illuminates Shadowy Path to State Approval," p. 4; Kate Bayliss and David Hall, "A PSIRU response to the World Bank's 'Private Sector Development Strategy: Issues and Options'" (Public Services International Research Unit October 2001); Khozem Merchant, "Europeans Eye India Plant," *Financial Times* (January 22, 2002) p. 24.

51. Navroz K. Dubash and Sudhir Chella Rajan, "The Politics of Power Sector Reform in India" (World Resources Institute, April 2001); Prabir Purkayastha, "The Andhra Electricity Tariff Hikes: the Real Face of Reform (Delhi Science Forum n.d.).

52. K. Bayliss, "Privatization of Electricity Distribution" (Public Services International Research Unit April 2001) p. 17; Dilip Bisoi, "Cesco Threatens to Discontinue Power Restoration in Cyclone-hit Rural Areas," *Indian Express* (January 8, 2000); Prabir Purkayastha, "The Andhra Electricity Tariff Hikes: The Real Face of Reform (Delhi Science Forum n.d.).

53. Navroz K. Dubash and Sudhir Chella Rajan, "The Politics of Power Sector Reform in India" (World Resources Institute, April 2001).

54. Patrick Bond (Senior Lecturer in Economic Policy, University of the Witwatersrand Graduate School of Public Policy and Development Management), "Privatization, Protest and Participation, (presented to World Bank/NGO Dialogue on Privatization, Washington, DC, October 1997); Congress of South African Trade Unions (COSATU), "Why Does COSATU Oppose Privatization?" (August 16, 2001); "Stop Privatization Now!" (July 2001); "Poor People before Profit," *The Shopsteward* (June 2001); South African Municipal Workers Union (SAMWU), "Union Condemns Services Disconnections and Growing Use of Private Security Companies" (June 6, 2001); Johannesburg Anti-Privatization Forum (APF, a coalition of SAMWU, citizen groups, and others), "APF Condemns Eskom's Planned Mass Cut-offs in Soweto, Eskom Privatization" (March 30, 2001); Anna Cox, "Sowetans to Defy Eskom over Cutoffs," *The Star* (June 3, 2001), Clive Sawyer, "Huge Eskom Rate Hike Sparks Outcry," (May 11, 2001), Krisendra Bisetty, "Angry Crowd Threatens Electricity Technicians" (May 22, 2001), both published in *Daily News*, all at www.iol.co.za (Independent Online); "South Africa," Public Services International, *Research Network News* No. 36 (2000); Henri Cauvin, "Privatization Snag in South Africa," *New York Times* (November 2, 2001) p. W1.

55. Personal communication, Ildo Luis Sauer, Professor do Promgrama de Pos-Graduacao em Energia da USP, Sao Paulo (August 2001); personal communication, Dr. Stephen D. Thomas (May 2001); "Heavy-duty GTs to Help Brazil," *Power* (Platts September–October 2001) p. 7; US Energy Information Administration, "Brazil Country Analysis Brief" (June 2001); Jonathan Karp, "AES Suspends Plans in Brazil for Power Plants," *Wall Street Journal* (May 9, 2001) p. A23; Jonathan Karp and Matt Mofett, "Electricity Rationing Roils Brazil, Leaving U.S. Utility in a Spot," *Wall Street Journal* (July 30, 2001) p. A1; Larry Rohter, "Energy Crisis in Brazil Brings Dim Lights and Altered Lives," *New York Times* (national edition, June 6, 2001) p. A1; "Brazil Intervenes to Help Utilities Cover $2-Bil. Losses from Rationing," *Electric Utility Week* (McGraw Hill, November 21, 2001) p. 20; Jonathan Karp, "As Sao Paulo Darkens, Robbery News Brightens," *Wall Street Journal* (August 17, 2001) p. A7.

56. Kate Bayliss and David Hall, "Independent Power Producers: A Review of the Issues" (Public Services International Research Unit, November 2000).

57. Ibid.; Kate Bayliss, "Privatization of Electricity Distribution" (Public Services International Research Unit April 2001) pp. 12–13.

58. Bayliss and Hall, "Independent Power Producers: A Review of the Issues."

59. Ibid.; and "A PSIRU response to the World Bank's 'Private Sector Development Strategy: Issues and Options'" (October 2001) pp. 11–12; Bretton Woods Project, "Bank Private Sector Arm under Fire from NGOs and Congress" (August 2001) (www.globalpolicy.org/socecon/bwi-wto/wbank/2001/08miga.htm).

60. The Korean National Electrical Works Union, "Electric Industry Privatization Methods in the ROK" (1999).

61. Public Services International, *Research Network News* No. 37 (2000).

62. Greg Palast, "Failures of the 20th Century: See Under I.M.F.," London *Observer* (October 8, 2000).

63. Jude Owuamanam, "3,000 National Electric Power Authority Staff Get Sack Letters," Lagos *Post Express* (September 11, 2000).

64. Anthony Faiola, "Argentina Doubts Market Wisdom," *Washington Post* (August 6, 2001) p. A1; Greg Palast, "Who Shot Argentina?" London *Observer* (August 11, 2001).

65. Kate Bayliss, "Privatization of Electricity Distribution" (Public Services International Research Unit April 2001) pp. 8–9.

66. Globalization Challenge Initiative (project of Ford Foundation, Charles Stuart Mott Foundation, and John D. and Catherine T. MacArthur Foundation), "IMF and World

Bank Push Water Privatization," *News and Notices for IMF and World Bank Watchers* (Spring 2001).

67. Public Services International, "Paying for Privatization: Higher Prices, Lower Employment" (March 2000) p. 1.

68. World Bank, *World Development Report 2002: Building Institutions for Markets* (2001).

69. Public Services International, "Paying for Privatization: Higher Prices, Lower Employment," p. 1.

70. Carmelo Ruiz-Marrero, "Puerto Rico: Water Company Near Collapse," *The Black World Today* (May 28, 2001) (www.tbwt.com/content/article.asp?articleid=771); and "It's the Drinking Straw From Hell!" *Puerto Rico News* (July 8, 1997) (www.neravt.com/left/ruiz7.htm).

71. Integrated Social Development Centre (Accra North, Ghana) and Globalization Challenge Initiative (supported by Tides Center, Ford Foundation, Charles Stewart Mott Foundation, John D. and Catherine T. MacArthur Foundation), "Water Privatization in Ghana?" (May 2001 draft) (www.challengeglobalization.org).

72. International Monetary Fund and World Bank, "Strengthening IMF–World Bank Collaboration on Country Programs and Conditionality" (August 2001); Managing Director, International Monetary Fund, to Heads of Departments and Offices, "Streamlining Structural Conditionality" (September 18, 2000); International Monetary Fund, "IMF Concludes Discussions on Strengthening IMF–World Bank Collaboration on Country Programs and Conditionality" (Public Information Notice 01/92, September 4, 2001); IMF Policy Development and Review Dept., "Streamlining Structural Conditionality: Review of Initial Experience" (July 2001); "Conditionality in Fund-Supported Programs – Overview" (February 2001); World Bank, "Development Goals," (www.developmentgoals.org/findout-about.html); *World Development Report 2002: Building Institutions for Markets* (2001); World Bank Operations Policy and Country Services, "Adjustment Lending Retrospective – Final Report" (June 2001). See Bayliss and Hall, "A PSIRU Response to the World Bank's 'Private Sector Development Strategy: Issues and Options'," and "Another PSIRU critique of another version of the World Bank Private Sector Development Strategy" (January 2002) p. 11.

73. "Report and Recommendation of the President of the International Development Association to the Executive Directors on a Proposed Credit of SDR 116.2 Million (US$150 Million Equivalent) to the Republic of Uganda for a Poverty Reduction Support Credit" (World Bank Report No. P7442-UG, March 23, 2001); Letter of Intent between World Bank and Republic of Uganda (1998), *in* Vincent Lloyd and Robert Weissman, "Against the Workers," *Multinational Monitor* (affiliated with Ralph Nader, September 2001); Bujagali Hydro Project, "Bujagali Hydroelectric Project Briefing" (Washington, DC, June 27, 2000) (www.bujagali.com/bujagali_in_brief/africarehtml); Deepak Gopinath, "The Greening of the World Bank," *Infrastructure Finance* (Sustainable Energy and Economy Network (SEEN)) of the Institute for Policy Studies, Washington, DC, September 1996).

74. Dexter Whitfield, *Public Service or Corporate Welfare* (Pluto Press, 2001) p. 48.

75. Swedish National Energy Administration, *Electricity Market 2001*, p. 2; Sam Weinstein, "The Nordic Energy Market" (Public Services International Research Unit January 2002). Competition has not necessarily meant privatization, however. In Norway, 85 per cent of generation is government-owned and ultimately all is planned to be; a considerable fraction of Finnish and Swedish generation investment is from governments; and most of Denmark's distribution, transmission, and generation system is owned by governments or consumers. Some privatization is under debate. Weinstein, n. 5 and 11, secs. 4B, 5A–B, 6A.

76. F. Schwartzkopf and K. Haug, "High Nordic Prices Generate Complaints, Not Plants," Dow Jones Newswire (August 30, 2001). This was no one-month trend. On average,

January to April prices doubled from 2000 to 2001. Swedish National Energy Administration, *Electricity Market 2001*, p. 24.

77. Minutes of November 22, 2001, meeting, in Sam Weinstein, "The Nordic Energy Market" (Public Services International Research Unit January 2002) n. 13, sec. 6D.

78. Swedish National Energy Administration, *Electricity Market 2001*, pp. 24–6; Energy Market Authority (Finland), Electricity price (www.energiamarkkinavirasto.fi/eng/index.html). However some Norwegian industrial customers saved more than 50 per cent. Weinstein, "The Nordic Energy Market," sec. 2.C.

79. Ibid., sec. 9B.

80. Resource Strategies, "Electricity Deregulation: International Experience and its Relevance to the Icelandic Situation" (1998) pp. 18–21.

81. Ibid., pp. 21–3.

82. For example, investment bankers are increasingly dependent on fees generated from European mergers and acquisitions among privately owned utilities. Evelina Shmukler, "Cross-Border M&A Lifts Banks," *Wall Street Journal Europe* (December 12, 2001) p. 15.

83. James Luckey, "Fitting In" (re Electricité de France), *Energy Markets* 39 (April 2001); Nicholas George, "Vattenfall Victory Increases Debt Burden," *Financial Times* (December 11, 2001) p. 22; "Valeria Criscione, "Statkraft Buys Rival," *Financial Times* (December 17, 2001) p. 19.

84. Neal Boudette, "E.ON Leads Revival of Europe's Utilities" (also re RWE, Suez Lyonnaise des Eaux), *Wall Street Journal* (February 7, 2002) p. A 13.

85. Shmukler, "Cross-Border M&A Lifts Banks," p. 15.

86. Claude Turmes, "The Revision of the Electricity Market Directive," Working Document PE309.069 (European Parliament Committee on Industry, External Trade, Research and Energy DT\456139EN.doc December 12, 2001). While similar predictions are made in the US, and the top ten wholesalers controlled 60 per cent of the market in 2001, the top three controlled 30 per cent. Excluding Enron, the top three controlled only 19 per cent. *Power Marketer Sales Statistics* (McGraw Hill, December 2001), in Electric Power Supply Association, "Competitive Power Supply Industry Facts" (January 2002).

87. J. Bower, D.W. Bunn and C. Wattendrup, "A Model-based Analysis of Strategic Consolidation in the German Electricity Industry," 29 *Energy Policy* 987 (October 2001); Andrew Taylor, "Competition Proves Illusive," *Financial Times* (December 11, 2000).

88. Mark Hand, "The European Power Forum: New Rules, New Players," interview with Claude Turmes, Member of European Parliament (Luxembourg), *Public Utilities Fortnightly* (February 1, 2002) p. 24.

89. Michael Carter (senior energy analyst, Platts), "Western Europe: The New Hot Spot?," *Public Utilities Fortnightly* (February 1, 2002) p. 12.

90. Ministry of Economic Development, Energy Markets Policy Group, "Chronology of New Zealand Electricity Reform" (2001); Ministry of Economic Development, Inquiry into the Electricity Industry (2000).

91. Fran O'Sullivan, "Californian Dreaming is not a Reality," Power to the People, *New Zealand Herald* (September 2001) p. 7 (prices doubled in the year 2001).

92. Infratil, "Infratil Update – New Zealand electricity: Lessons from the Winter of 2001" (September 9, 2001) p. 4.

93. Paula Oliver, "Squeals of Pain over Power Rises," *New Zealand Herald* (August 23, 2001) Paula Oliver and Angela Gregory, "Huge Power Bills Force Schools to Cry 'Help,' " *New Zealand Herald* (August 22, 2001).

94. "A Kiwi World News Special: Auckland: A City in the Dark" (www.kiwiclub.org/news/specials/specbo.html) (quoting Reuters, AP and other news sources regarding February 20–March 27, 1998 blackout).

95. George Will, "A Sad Turning Point for Europe," *Boston Globe* (December 30, 2001) p. D7.
96. European Federation of Public Service Unions (EPSU), "EPSU amendments to the Directive amending Directives 96/92/EC and 98/30/EC concerning common rules for the internal markets in electricity and natural gas," submitted to European Parliament January 25, 2002.

Chapter 15

1. *Kansas Gas & Electric* v. *Eye*, 789 P.2d 1161, 1168 (Kansas 1990).
2. 5 USC 552 et seq.
3. Unison, *Energy Bulletin* (December 1999).
4. *Kansas Gas & Electric* v. *Eye*.
5. Oxera, *Guide to the Economic Regulation of Latin American Utilities*.
6. L.K. Rader, "Coulda, Woulda, Shoulda," *Energy Markets* 1 (October 2000).
7. The Racketeering and Corruptly Influenced Organizations (RICO) case is *County of Suffolk et al.* v. *Long Island Lighting Co., et al.*, 87 Civ. 646 (JBW). See, e.g., 710 F. Supp.1428 (1998); 907 F.2d 1295 (2d.Cir.1990).
8. New York Public Service Commission, Opinion and Order Determining Prudent Costs and the associated case record "Proceeding on the Motion of the Commission to Investigate the Cost of Construction of the Shoreham Nuclear Generating Facility – Phase II," established May 21, 1979; Order and Opinion, December 16, 1985 (Imprudence: penalties); New York Public Service Commission, Opinion and Order Approving Settlement Agreement, November 18, 1988 (takeover agreement, including deprivatization of electricity distribution system).

Index

Compiled by Sue Carlton

About the Authors

GREGORY PALAST over the past 25 years has provided expert advice on regulation to government, labor, consumer and industry organizations in eight nations. Palast has conducted nearly 100 price reviews of electric, gas and telephone companies for government in twelve US states. As Economist, then Executive Director, of the New York State Legislature's Commission on Science and Technology, he drafted several laws regarding public ownership of utilities, prices and taxation, including the law deprivatizing the Long Island electricity company. Palast has lectured extensively on regulation in Europe and Latin America, including at Cambridge University and the University of Sao Paulo. Palast founded the Labor Coalition on Public Utilities, an organization of public service and industrial unions concerned with consumer rights. He published widely in technical and popular press (*New Economy, Public Utilities Fortnightly, Consumer Policy Review*) and writes a column for the London *Observer*. In 1997, the *Financial Times* of London awarded him the David Thomas Prize for his writing on Secrecy and Democracy in Regulation; and in 2000, he was nominated Britain's Business Journalist of the Year. His book of investigative journalism, *The Best Democracy Money Can Buy,* was published by Pluto Press earlier this year. Palast is Investigative Reporter for BBC Television's *Newsnight*. He obtained his MBA in regulation and international finance from the University of Chicago.

JERROLD OPPENHEIM, a graduate of Harvard College and Boston College Law School (Juris Doctor), directed energy and utility litigation for the Attorneys General of New York and Massachusetts. In his 31-year career, he has played a key role in the development of regulatory policy in US states as legal counsel and advisor for state governments, consumer organizations, low-income advocates, labor unions, environmental interests, industrial customers, and utilities. Oppenheim directed consumer and utility legal assistance programs for low-income clients in New York and Chicago for the US federal government's legal assistance program. He was founding Director of Renewable Energy Technology Analysis (RETA) at Pace University Law School and, recently, directed the energy and telecommunications program at the National Consumer Law Center, a non-profit law firm based in Boston. Oppenheim led pioneering negotiations of energy conservation agreements with all electric and natural gas utilities in Massachusetts and has won precedent-setting cases on utility plant siting, low-income discounts, investment in generating plant, establishment of service quality standards, and abolition of discriminatory credit and marketing practices. He has lectured and published widely in the US and internationally on public utility and consumer law topics, including recent monographs for the National Association of Regulatory Utility Commissioners (NARUC), AARP (formerly the American Association of Retired Persons), the National Council on Competition and the Electric Industry, the European Federation of Public Service Unions (EPSU) and, with Theo MacGregor, The Bergen Conference (Norway), the Confederation of State and Municipal Employees (BSRB, Iceland), and the European Trade Union Institute (ETUI).

THEO MacGREGOR was, until 1998, director of the Electric Power Division of the Massachusetts Department of Telecommunications and Energy (DTE), the state's utility regulator. She led the agency's efforts to develop policies and procedures for guiding the restructuring of the electric industry and for evaluating electric and gas utility companies' energy efficiency programs. In her decade with the DTE, MacGregor instituted the practice of involving regulatory staff in settlement negotiations for energy conservation cases and worked closely with utility companies, consumer groups and many other stakeholders to develop consensus positions. As founder of MacGregor Energy Consultancy, specializing in electric industry and other utility issues, she has provided expert analysis on electric industry regulation, performance-based ratemaking, energy efficiency program design, social programs in the utility sector, and international regulation for regulatory commissions, government agencies, utilities, and US and international NGOs. She designed an innovative program for low-income people to obtain multiple energy and social services by one telephone call. She also created a program by which plant operators offset emissions through investments in energy efficiency. MacGregor holds an MBA from Simmons College School of Management in Boston, Massachusetts.

Updates, additional information, research documents and an opportunity for readers to speak to the authors can be found at
www.DemocracyAndRegulation.com